MW00799660

CULTURE AND ONLINE LEARNING

Additional titles in our
ONLINE LEARNING AND DISTANCE EDUCATION series
edited by Michael Grahame Moore

ONLINE, BLENDED, AND DISTANCE EDUCATION IN SCHOOLS
Building Successful Programs
Edited by Tom Clark and Michael Barbour
Publication date: Fall 2014

WEB 2.0 FOR ACTIVE LEARNERS
By Vanessa Dennen
Publication date: Spring 2015

Also available in this series:

LEADING THE E-LEARNING TRANSFORMATION OF HIGHER EDUCATION
Meeting the Challenges of Technology and Distance Education
Published in association with The Sloan Consortium
By Gary Miller, Meg Benke, Bruce Chaloux, Lawrence C. Ragan, Raymond Schroeder,
Wayne Smutz, and Karen Swan

ASSURING QUALITY IN ONLINE EDUCATION
Practices and Processes at the Teaching, Resource, and Program Levels
Edited by Kay Shattuck

CULTURE AND ONLINE LEARNING

Global Perspectives and Research

Edited by *Insung Jung and Charlotte Nirmalani Gunawardena*

Series Foreword by Michael Grahame Moore

STERLING, VIRGINIA

COPYRIGHT © 2014 BY
STYLUS PUBLISHING, LLC

Published by Stylus Publishing, LLC
22883 Quicksilver Drive
Sterling, Virginia 20166-2102

All rights reserved. No part of this book may be reprinted
or reproduced in any form or by any electronic, mechanical,
or other means, now known or hereafter invented, including
photocopying, recording, and information storage and
retrieval, without permission in writing from the publisher.

Library of Congress Cataloging-in-Publication Data
Culture and online learning : global perspectives and research / edited
by Insung Jung and Charlotte Nirmalani Gunawardena.
    pages cm. -- (Online learning and distance education series)
  Includes bibliographical references and index.
  ISBN 978-1-57922-854-5 (cloth : alk. paper)
  ISBN 978-1-57922-855-2 (pbk. : alk. paper)
  ISBN 978-1-57922-857-6 (consumer e-edition)
  ISBN 978-1-57922-856-9 (library networkable e-edition)
  1. Distance education--Computer-assisted instruction--Social aspects.
  2. Multicultural education--Computer-assisted instruction.
  3. Education and globalization.
  I. Jung, Insung, 1959- editor of compilation.
  II. Gunawardena, Charlotte Nirmalani editor of compilation.
  LC5803.C65C85 2014
  371.35'8--dc23

2014015242

Printed in the United States of America

All first editions printed on acid-free paper
that meets the American National Standards Institute
Z39-48 Standard.

Bulk Purchases

Quantity discounts are available for use in workshops and for
staff development.
Call 1-800-232-0223

First Edition, 2014

10   9   8   7   6   5   4   3   2

To the memory of my father, Young-kyu JUNG, who always believed in me.
—Insung

*To the memory of my father, C. H. Gunawardena, who taught me to value diversity;
and Deborah LaPointe, who wrote with me about culture.*
—Lani

CONTENTS

Tables

Figures

This book is about the challenges, problems, and opportunities arising when online distance education is delivered to people who study in different national or community cultures. It is the third in the Online Learning and Distance Education series published by Stylus Publishing. The first publication in the series focused on leadership (Miller, Benke, Chaloux, Ragan, Schroeder, Smutz, & Swan, 2013), and the second focused on quality assurance (Shattuck, 2014). Now in this new book, we invite readers to consider the added complexities of these and other challenges when situated in the multivaried contexts that are identified by the simple word *culture*. This is, of course, a word that is problematic itself, interpreted in many ways, with differences in meaning also being attributable to differences in the cultures of the persons defining it. Such definitional uncertainties are faced head-on by the editors of this book, the first chapter of which opens with a discussion of the many ways in which the term has been used in research and thereby introduces readers immediately to some of the most important issues that will be encountered in greater depth in subsequent chapters. This opening also points out that a source of further insights into the character of culture is found in the different interpretations and definitions by the book's contributors. For the intriguing fact is, as the editors explain, that our concepts of culture are culturally determined. Acknowledging this leads us directly to one of the core issues recurring throughout this book, which is how to articulate and analyze issues surrounding the use of online teaching and learning in non-Western societies using theoretical frameworks that have been developed in North America and Europe. The authors in this book are exceptionally well qualified to address this and similar issues, themselves coming from a variety of different countries and cultures, led by the editors, who, while having established eminent reputations in the American higher education culture, are also grounded in two contrasting non-Western cultures.

Readers might be particularly intrigued, as I was, by one resolution of the formidable task of cross-cultural communication, which is the proposition that the Internet has produced its own culture, "blurring the boundaries between the real and virtual worlds, where participants develop their own rules for what is appropriate behavior online" (p. 7, this volume). This line of thinking leads to the conclusion that "cultures travel with students and through technologies" with the result that "online learning has the great potential to motivate and engage students in participating in cross-national exchanges of cultures and the creation of new cultures" (p. 8, this volume). Such a vision raises the very idea of globalization to a higher plane than hitherto, beyond the prosaic level of mere subject teaching toward one in which the outcome might be truly better understanding among peoples of different nations and communities, a prize that would certainly count as an achievement of online distance learning that has eluded any previous educational attempt at such global understanding.

This is idealistic of course (and why not!?), but I should conclude this foreword by emphasizing that the book before us aims to be not only a discourse of ideas and a discussion of research. The editors have also paid heed to the series policy of tempering theoretical conversation with information that can be applied by teachers and other practitioners faced with developing programs in the real world—in this case, with an emphasis on the really global world. To this end we note that both the editors and many of their contributors draw on long careers as practicing distance educators, as well as draw on their research and scholarship. It is also notable that this set of contributors reflects a rich kaleidoscope of different cultural perspectives, including those of—to mention only some of the countries represented—India, Korea, China, Spain, Oman, Malaysia, and Turkey. I am grateful to Dr. Insung Jung and Dr. Charlotte Nirmalani Gunawardena for their efforts to bring together this remarkable team of authors, and I also thank those contributors for their willingness to share the fruits of their research, study, and experiences in this third book in Stylus's Online Learning and Distance Education series.

Michael Grahame Moore
Distinguished Professor of Education Emeritus,
The Pennsylvania State University

References

Miller, G., Benke, M., Chaloux, B., Ragan, L. C., Schroeder, R., Smutz, W., & Swan, K. (2013). *Leading the e-learning transformation of higher education: Meeting the challenges of technology and distance education*. Sterling, VA: Stylus.

Shattuck, K. (Ed.). (2014). *Assuring quality in online education: Practices and processes at the teaching, resource, and program levels*. Sterling, VA: Stylus.

1

PERSPECTIVES ON CULTURE AND ONLINE LEARNING

Charlotte Nirmalani Gunawardena and Insung Jung

When we began writing this book, one of our initial challenges was to come up with a definition of *culture* that would encompass the diversity of perspectives that are explored herein. A corresponding challenge was to select an appropriate definition from the array of definitions of *culture*, a definition that would describe culture and online learning. We explored a range of definitions, from Margaret Mead's (1932) early definition of *culture* as "the whole complex of traditional behavior which has been developed by the human race and is successively learned by each generation" (p. 17) to the new, emergent, rapidly growing concept of cyberspace as culture, "lived culture, made from people, machines and stories in everyday life" (Bell, 2001); *cybercultures* as "sustained attempts by diverse groups of people to make sense of multifarious activities, linguistic codes, and practices in complicated and ever-changing settings" (Wheeler, 2009, p. xi); or *cultures of flow*, meaning cultures enabled by the flow of digital information (Breslow & Mousoutzanis, 2012, p. xii). We came to the conclusion that any attempt to generate an appropriate definition of *culture* for this book was a futile task. Therefore, instead of developing yet another definition to add to the debate on defining *culture*, we proceeded with a working definition drawing from Edward T. Hall's early statement, "Culture is communication and communication is culture" (Hall, 1959, p. 186), as this observation clearly presents the link between culture and online learning. This observation accommodates the notion that culture can be negotiated online through a communication process mediated by technology interfaces that themselves are culturally produced. Culture impacts every facet of online learning, from course and interface design, to communication in a sociocultural space, and to the negotiation of meaning and social construction of knowledge; thus, a definition of *culture* that is flexible, dynamic, and negotiable is more appropriate to understand the online learning context.

Goodfellow and Hewling (2005) helped us to conceptualize culture as negotiated in online discussions, and Raffaghelli and Richieri (2012) argued that "networked learning should emphasize Bruner's idea about education as *forum* where culture is not transmitted but generated through interaction" (pp. 102–103; italics in original), leading to new learning cultures. In an online learning context, "the identities of participants become part of the knowledge constructed as well as the means of construction" (Goodfellow & Lamy, 2009, p. 176). As Reid (1995) noted, "This web of verbal and textual significances that are substitutes for and yet distinct from the networks of meaning of the wider community binds users into a common culture whose specialized meanings allow the sharing of imagined realities" (p. 183).

This chapter is not an attempt to offer one clear definition of *culture* for the online learning context. Instead it aims to expand our thinking about what we mean by *culture* by discussing some of the ways in which the term has been defined and used in studies, to help our readers better understand the subsequent chapters where the chapter authors have adopted their own approach to understanding culture in an online learning context of their interest. The chapter also explains how our book is organized to examine issues of culture and online learning in depth. We address issues of culture from (a) the diverse perspectives of our authors; (b) the emerging body of interdisciplinary research on globalization, the Internet, the sociocultural context of online learning, technology-based language learning, and virtual communities; (c) our own previous work on culture and online learning (Gunawardena, 2013, 2014; Gunawardena & LaPointe, 2007, 2008; Jung, 2012; Jung, Kudo, & Choi, 2012; Jung & Lee, 2013; Jung & Suzuki, 2014); and (d) our combined experiences conducting research studies in numerous countries including Australia, Cambodia, Canada, China, France, India, Indonesia, Japan, Korea, Malaysia, Mexico, Mongolia, Morocco, the Netherlands, Singapore, South Africa, Spain, Sri Lanka, Taiwan, Thailand, Turkey, United Kingdom, United States, and Vietnam.

In the next section, we begin discussing early "essentialist" definitions of *culture* (the notion that culture is an essential attribute of people who share the same physical and social environment [Goodfellow & Lamy, 2009]) and move to more recent thinking about culture as fluid and negotiated in online contexts by diverse participants.

Are Dimensional Constructs Adequate for Understanding Culture Online?

When distance educators became interested in examining issues of culture in the online environment, they began with two prominent "essentialist" dimensional frameworks that were developed by Hofstede (1980) and Hall (1959, 1976) to characterize and classify the similarities and differences they observed between diverse cultural groups. We examine these two dimensional frameworks next.

Given the lack of a universally applicable theory for classifying cultural differences, Hofstede's cultural dimensions framework was used by many researchers to explain cultural differences in online education (Callahan, 2005; Cronjé, 2011). On the basis of the analysis of cultural values collected from IBM employees, Hofstede (1980) derived four cultural dimensions (power distance, individualism/collectivism, masculinity/femininity, and uncertainty avoidance), which became the hallmarks of his framework. He added a fifth dimension, long-term orientation, based on his research in Hong Kong (Hofstede & Bond, 1988), and a sixth dimension, indulgence versus self-restraint, based on the data collected from the World Values Survey with people from around 100 countries (Hofstede, Hofstede, & Minkov, 2010). Even though Hofstede expanded his model, researchers have predominantly used the first four dimensions of his framework to describe cultural differences in online learning.

However, several researchers (Ess, 2009; Fougere & Moulettes, 2007; McSweeney, 2002) have pointed out the limitations of Hofstede's dimensions to explain culture, citing the following factors: (a) limitations of bipolar dimensions, (b) assumption that members of a national culture are homogeneous, (c) sample based on a single multinational organization, (d) participants predominantly middle-class males, (e) neglect of subcultures within various countries, (f) dated results as cultures are not static but change over time, and (g) the danger of stereotyping individuals of a particular culture. Ross and Faulkner (1998) pointed out that relying solely on dimensional information for understanding a particular culture can be limiting. They believed that dimensional information can serve as a useful starting point to understand culture, but they cautioned against the danger of overgeneralizing or treating it as an absolute. They advocated using Hofstede's dimensions with culture-specific approaches that will provide more contextual understanding.

One question we need to ask ourselves as online educators is whether Hofstede's dimensions will be useful for understanding the diverse cultures that constitute an online environment. For example, Gunawardena et al. (2001) used Hofstede's dimensions to examine differences in group process and development between U.S. and Mexican online learners and found that the Mexican participants (who exhibit high power distance characteristics according to Hofstede's framework) look to the online medium as a liberating medium that equalizes status differences. Therefore, their interactions online would not necessarily reflect high power distance communication. This same finding emerged in the study of Moroccan and Sri Lankan cybercafé users who engaged in anonymous chat, which is discussed further in chapter 4.

This brings up questions we need to ask ourselves, which Goodfellow and Lamy (2009) explored: Are cultural frameworks developed in the West useful for understanding culture in global e-learning environments? Because much of the e-learning research has been conducted in the West, are we imposing our ethnocentrism by the frameworks we use to define *culture*? In this vein, Miike (2004) argued that most culture and communication research deals with non-European (non-American) cultures as targets for analysis but not as resources for theory building. What is problematic is that the mental layer of European (American) cultures is frequently used to analyze the behavioral and material layers of non-European (non-American) cultures. Miike (2002) showed the limitations of using Western approaches to understanding cultural differences in communication processes and pointed out three important themes that emerge in establishing an Asian paradigm of communication—relationality, circularity, and harmony—with the underlying assumptions that (a) communication takes place in "contexts" of various relationships, (b) the communicator is both active and passive in multiple contexts, and (c) mutual adaptation is of central importance as adaptation is the key to harmonious communication and relationships. In this book we provide our readers the opportunity to explore some of these diverse perspectives on culture with our authors who represent a variety of international contexts. Chapter 7 discusses the roots of Western and Asian worldviews and how they influence social construction of knowledge online.

The next prominent dimensional framework that has been employed to understand culture online is Hall's (1959) conceptualization of high-context and low-context communication styles, and by extension indirect (high-context) and direct (low-context) styles of communication. According to Hall, in high-context cultures in countries such as China, Japan, and India and in Arab countries in the Middle East, when people communicate they tend to read both spoken and unspoken languages, pay attention to the context in which they are engaged, and focus on communicative cues such as silence and body language. In these cultures, many things are left unsaid, letting the context explain. In low-context cultures in places such as Germany, Scandinavian countries, and the United States, people communicate explicitly in text and speech.

Hall's conceptualization of high- and low-context communication has also been used to explain differences in thought patterns and rhetorical traditions (Ishii, 1982). Citing the work of Shigehiko Toyama, who observed that Anglo Americans think in "line" whereas Japanese think in "dots" and who characterized Anglo American thought patterns as a "bridge" and Japanese thought patterns as "stepping-stones," Ishii (1982) observed that this distinction in thought patterns can be supported by Hall's high-context and low-context conceptualization. The American bridge model (analogous to linear thinking) is an example of low-context communication where the speaker organizes his or her ideas and tries to send them explicitly and directly as if building a bridge from one point to another. The listener or reader is to cross the bridge by receiving the messages as they are explicitly sent. On the other hand, in the Japanese stepping-stone approach, the speaker organizes ideas and sends them implicitly and indirectly as if arranging stepping-stones in the courtyards of temples and places of worship to ensure harmony and balance. "Sometimes the arrangement itself is not clear and the listener or reader must infer or surmise the intended meaning. Haiku poems serve as good examples" (Ishii, 1982, p. 84). The stepping-stone thought pattern is symbolic of a high-context culture where the listener is responsible for "bridging the gaps" within the stones by choosing how she or he will "step from one stone to another" (Tuleja, 2005, p. 68). Tuleja added that this form of spatial logic can be quite foreign to those who want facts lined up in order.

We believe that Hall's high- and low-context conceptualization is a useful framework for understanding cultural differences in online communication, as it provides a basis for understanding differences not only in communication but also in thought patterns. Chapter 4 shows how this framework helped to analyze communication differences in both Moroccan and Sri Lankan cultures, as context is important to understanding a message and its connotations; many Moroccans and Sri Lankans adopt indirect communication styles. Therefore, Hall's conceptualization helped to analyze differences in communication styles in this study.

Even though Hofstede's and Hall's frameworks have been useful starting points for the analysis of cultural dimensions, Ess and Sudweeks (2005) called for the expansion and refinement of their models in the context of online learning as more cultural factors (approximately 22 factors) affect teaching and learning online. With the advent of globalization and cross-border communication through telecommunications technologies, individuals who identify with multiple frames of reference and cultures engage in forming new virtual communities whose culture is difficult to define. The online context also provides fertile ground for the construction of hybrid identities that transcend national identities. In this regard, Ess and Sudweeks (2005) noted that what interests researchers is how national identities, as well as other cultural identities such as ethnicity, youth culture, gender, and so on, interact with intercultural communication online; that is, already removed from the face-to-face setting. So, our next question is, What are some useful constructs for understanding culture in the online context?

From Bipolar Dimensions to Holistic Views of Culture

"Culture hides more than it reveals, and strangely enough what it hides, it hides most effectively from its own participants" (Hall, 1959, pp. 29–30). This statement clearly articulates the hidden culture in an online environment: that which is explicit, known, or observable in a culture from that which is implicit, unknown, and hidden—even to members of the culture. With the advent of MOOCs (massive open online courses) that teach to worldwide audiences, we are now faced with the challenge of developing a better understanding of both explicit and implicit aspects of culture that emerges online. We discuss next several frameworks that move us away from a bipolar dimensional view to a more holistic view of culture.

Shaw and Barrett-Power (1998) provided a detailed and precise mapping of the elements that constitute cultural differences by stressing the importance of considering the impact of both apparent and less visible aspects of cultural variability. The model differentiates between two sources of cultural differences: readily detectable attributes and underlying attributes. Readily detectable attributes are those that can be easily recognized in a person such as age, gender, or nationality/ethnic origin. Underlying attributes are divided into two categories. The first category (Underlying Attributes I) represents cultural values, perspectives, attitudes, beliefs, and conflict resolution styles, which are closely correlated with readily detectable attributes. The second group of attributes (Underlying Attributes II) includes socioeconomic and personal status, education, functional specialization, human capital assets, past work experiences, and personal expectations. These attributes are less strongly connected to nationality/ethnic origin, age, or gender of individuals. Chapter 14 applies this model of culture to understand the varied cultural perspectives on the meanings of icons and images used in North American academic websites to determine whether the participants' interpretations were influenced by culture.

Addressing language learning with technology, Levy (2007) developed five facets of the culture concept: culture as elemental, culture as relative, culture as group membership, culture as contested, and culture as individual (variable and multiple). This articulation helps us to think about the role of the individual in a given group culture, the different cultures to which an individual may belong, and culture as multiple and layered and introduces the notion that culture can be contested. Each perspective aims to provide a focus for thinking about culture and thereby to provide a valid and useful point of departure for thinking about the practice of culture learning and teaching with new technologies.

Baumgartner (2003), on the basis of the analysis of studies on cultural dimensions and the expert questionnaire, came up with 29 cultural factors that affect the user-interface design in an online environment. He ranked these factors and suggested the five most important factors to be considered in designing a user interface: context, technological development, uncertainty avoidance, time perception, and authority conception. For example, the dimension of context influences the user-interface design in such a way that in high-context cultures the use of high-context graphics without precise explanations support navigation and interaction, whereas in low-context cultures a great deal of explicitness is important in online user-interface design. Taking another example of time orientation, in a culture where people tend to do one thing at a time and stay on schedule (a monochronic culture, linear time perception, related to the concept of low context [Hall, 1983]), people prefer precise directions for information retrieval, whereas in a culture where people do several things at a time and tend to change plans rather easily (a polychronic culture, cyclic time perception, related to the concept of high context [Hall, 1983]), people prefer browsing through information on a web interface. Even though Baumgartner's five dimensions need to be further validated in various cultural contexts and with diverse learner groups, they could be used to support decision making during the localization of a global user-interface design or during the user-interface design of an online course in a specific culture.

More recently, Parrish and Linder-VanBerschot (2010) proposed the Cultural Dimensions of Learning Framework (CDLF), adapted from the models of Hofstede, Hall, and other scholars, to identify cultural dimensions that impact online teaching and learning situations. CDLF identifies eight cultural dimensions across three areas (social relationships, epistemological beliefs, and temporal perceptions) that need to be considered in the design and implementation of online education. In the area of social relationships, three dimensions are included: equality versus authority, individualism versus collectivism, and nurture versus challenge. In the epistemological beliefs area, three dimensions are listed: stability seeking versus uncertainty acceptance, logic argumentation versus being reasonable, and causality versus complex systems (or analysis versus holism). In the area of temporal perceptions, two dimensions—clock time versus event time, and linear time versus cyclical time—are identified. Parrish and Linder-VanBerschot argued that these dimensions can help online educators develop a better understanding of the cultural differences among online learners and become aware of their own cultural orientations and biases embedded in their online teaching.

Moving Toward Culture as Negotiated Online

Responding to the need for a new understanding of culture in the online learning context, Goodfellow and Lamy (2009) problematized the very notion of "culture" in online learning environments by advancing the idea of "learning cultures" where technology is a player in the social interaction through which online learning cultures are built. They viewed "learning cultures" as the "area of emergent, informal, often innovative, collective approaches to learning in conditions that are wholly or partially characterized by remote communication" (p. 173). As online educators, we need to examine this concept of "learning culture" further. For example, the wiki has changed our learning culture from reading and writing by an individual to participatory cowriting, codeveloping, and reconstructing knowledge by a group of individuals, as evidenced in the work of Chao and Huang (2007) and Lykourentzou, Papadaki, Vergados, Polemi, and Loumos (2010). Various tools such as hypertext, mobile devices, social media, podcasting, and Web 2.0 have all contributed to the creation of learning cultures in an online learning environment.

To conceptualize cultures that emerge online and accommodate the notion of culture as negotiated by online participants whose ethnic, gender, and religious identities are enacted, concealed, or merged into hybrid identities, Gunawardena and colleagues (Gunawardena, Idrissi Alami, Jayatilleke, & Bouachrine, 2009) adopted the definition of *idioculture*, a concept developed by Gary Alan Fine (1979) and cited by Cole and Engestrom (2007), in their work:

> Idioculture consists of a system of knowledge, beliefs, behaviors, and customs shared by members of an interacting group to which members can refer and employ as the basis of further interaction. Members recognize that they share experiences in common, and these experiences can be referred to with the expectation that they will be understood by other members, and further can be employed to construct a social reality. (Fine, 1979, p. 734)

This definition focuses on the interacting unit, that culture is experienced as part of a communication system of a small group. It accommodates the idea of culture as emerging from a local activity system such as Internet chat (Cole & Engestrom, 2007), where multiple cultural selves and hybrid identities interact with each other to form unique cultures of their own. Cole and Engestrom noted that by focusing on the interacting unit, Fine showed that each group has to some extent a culture of its own, which he refers to as the idioculture. The definition allows for the development of culture through communication, by dialoguing, sharing experiences, and interacting with each other. It supports the concept of a "discourse community," groups that have goals or purposes and use communication to achieve these goals (Swales, 1990). The definition of *idioculture* fits well with the ephemeral, fluid nature of the Internet that fuels the development of cybercultures, cultures that emerge among those who use the Internet to communicate, developing their own etiquette, norms, customs, ethics, and mythology, just as an idioculture does. This notion of an idioculture is taken up in chapter 4 to discuss identity creation and identity play in cybercultures.

Another useful concept for understanding culture in the online environment is that of flow developed by Breslow and Mousoutzanis (2012) in their definition of *cybercultures* as cultures of flow:

> Cybercultures know neither boundaries, nor limitations, nor inhibitions. They are the *ne plus ultra* expression of flow spreading as, when, and how they can. Cybercultures do not follow predetermined paths, nor do they exist in predetermined states. . . . Cyber-cultures do not articulate themselves according to a specific logic, fixed identity, or set of rules determined by one space or another. They flow from place to place, from node to node, from site to site. In so doing, they rewrite the logics, relationships, meanings, behaviors and subjectivities, heretofore found within any locale, any node, and any site, on the Internet. (p. xii)

We, therefore, need to come to terms with the complexity of culture online, by defining it from the perspective of the Internet as a culture in its own right, blurring the boundaries between the real and virtual worlds, where participants develop their own rules for what is appropriate behavior online. Wang and Reeves (2007) showed what increased global online access is beginning to mean for participants in online education and explored the nature of cyberculture and how it affects the online learning experiences of international students. In the context of transnational, cross-border education, cultures travel with students and through technologies and create new cultures (Lam, 2006). Thus, online learning has the great potential to motivate and engage students in participating in cross-national exchanges of cultures and the creation of new cultures.

We ask you to be mindful of these diverse perspectives on culture and online learning as you peruse our book. We now present the organization and structure of the book and provide you with a glimpse of the variety of ways in which our authors address culture and online learning.

Organization of the Book

We discuss the chapters in this section, grouping them into eight themes. Several of these chapters discuss research on a specific aspect of culture and online learning.

Learners, Learning, and Learner Support

Understanding learners and learning from a cultural perspective is the critical foundation necessary to build online learning environments that appeal to diverse audiences. Culture online, as we have seen, is complex, dynamic, and ephemeral. These complexities shape our perceptions of learning and how we teach and learn online. In chapter 2, Jung takes up the challenge of exploring learners and learning from a cultural perspective and provides many examples of cultural traits that influence the learning process. One of the major challenges is to know where universals apply and where cultural differences and subcultures will influence the learning processes and outcomes. The major task for online educators is to make sure that they are well aware of the multiple and complex nature of cultural and subcultural influences on learners' learning behaviors and on their own teaching and utilize these cultural understandings to tactically devise learner support strategies, ensuring that learners from different cultural contexts achieve their particular learning objectives, as well as the more universal educational objectives.

In chapter 8, Gunawardena picks up the theme of supporting diverse online learners by exploring aspects of diversity that need to be considered when designing a learner support system to bridge different types of distance in an online environment. Observing that learner support is the critical link in online education, she presents examples from her own online designs to show how learner support can be integrated into courses to support diverse learners. This chapter presents a framework that can be adapted by readers to design learner support for diverse online learners.

Nonnative Speakers

Barrett in chapter 13 extends the exploration of the experiences of nonnative speakers by discussing a qualitative study of the experience of Taiwanese students, Taiwanese teaching assistants, and North American instructors in a synchronous second-language teaching environment. She discusses eight themes that emerged and shows how transformational learning occurred at some level for all of the participants as a consequence of the cross-cultural interactions that took place in the online class. She concludes her discussion by offering guidelines for instructors, students, support staff, and administrators on how to address cultural challenges in online learning.

Facilitating Learning, Mentoring, and Professional Development

The paradigm shift from teacher-centered classrooms to learner-centered networked learning has engendered many questions about the role of the teacher in an online learning environment. In chapter 7, Gunawardena and Jayatilleke explore the role of the teacher and show how it has changed to one of facilitation and mentoring. They discuss cultural issues that should be considered when designing the sociocultural environment and facilitating social construction of knowledge online. On the basis of a cross-cultural study between U.S. e-mentors and Sri Lankan protégés who engaged in an online inquiry-based learning activity, they discuss cultural issues that emerged during the learning process and challenges to cross-cultural e-mentoring.

Focusing on the theme of professional development for online educators, Tu and McIsaac, in chapter 10, present a model that would support educators to develop Global Digital Citizens (GDC), promote global citizenship through mutual understanding and respect for cultural diversity, and create a collaborative global knowledge network. They discuss two European projects and show how educators should aim to transform digital learners into competent Global Digital Citizens by helping them to become social collaborators, cultural constructivists, and community collaborators.

Learning Design, Identity, Gender, and Technology

Despite significant advances in education and technology, most learning designs for the online environment continue to account only for Western-centric ways of teaching, often at the expense of global students. In chapter 6, Frechette, Layne, and Gunawardena attempt to account for culture in instructional design and review one design model, WisCom (Wisdom Communities), that can facilitate these objectives by helping instructors—and learners—explore their culturally derived beliefs and values as they design for online learning. They show how to apply WisCom to design online learning communities, present evidence of its efficacy, and make recommendations for designing culturally inclusive online courses. They conclude that to better meet the needs of diverse learners, instructional designers need to reflect on their cultural biases (while encouraging continuous self-reflection among learners), design for cultural inclusivity (not neutrality), and work to recognize and delineate, not eliminate, cultural influences from their course designs.

In chapter 4, Gunawardena examines an important factor that impacts the design of online learning communities: how cultural identities are constructed and negotiated by online participants. Discussing a study of communication processes employed by Internet chat users in Morocco and Sri Lanka, Gunawardena examines what happens when individuals whose self-images are characterized by a sense of group identity use the culturally heterogeneous and technically ephemeral spaces of the Internet to pursue personal communication goals. She examines identity and its associated constructs, as well as gender and face negotiation, and discusses implications for designing the social environment for online learning communities.

In chapter 12, Latchem discusses important gender considerations in online learning environments that influence communication, learning processes, and outcomes. He argues that although we should avoid gender stereotyping and acknowledge variations within each gender and particular context, we also have to be aware of the existence of gender differences in communication and learning and ensure that each gender's learning preferences, needs, and circumstances are considered when we design and support online learning. He introduces innovative cases where women have contributed to the development of online education and training for women and emphasizes the need to familiarize oneself with the cultures of others for more gender-considerate online teaching and learning.

Designing for learning in the online environment means that one needs to carefully examine the role that technology plays in mediating the learning process. In chapter 3, Jung shows that culture is an important factor that plays a role in how technology will be adopted and used. Culture influences the way learners and teachers perceive online learning, and those perceptions may slow down or advance adoption and utilization. Jung examines acceptance of various technologies in different cultures by discussing three models and concludes that online educators and researchers should consider cultural influences in planning and researching the adoption of online learning.

Visual Culture

In chapter 5, Rha takes us on a journey to examine an intriguing area of online learning design by exploring emerging visual culture. He observes that emerging visual culture in an online learning context shows four key characteristics: (a) It promotes a participatory culture where both learners and teachers can actively participate in both the consumption of and the creation of visual data, (b) it supports the development of diversified forms of visual objects, (c) it facilitates new ways of visual expressions that blend spoken and written languages or orality and literacy in communication, and (d) it views texts as an integral part of visual representations. This chapter provides guidance for interface design by showing how features of online visual culture can be incorporated into designing and supporting online learning.

In chapter 14, a collaborative study by Knight, Gunawardena, Barberà, and Aydın conducted in Turkey, Spain, Sri Lanka, and the United States extends understanding of visual culture by discussing the varied cultural interpretations of icons and images used in North American academic websites. They show that both the visual form of an icon or image and the attributes associated with participants' sociocultural context influenced perceptions of the visual meaning. Photographs were difficult to use across cultural contexts because the photographic form is information dense. Attributes associated with participants' sociocultural context such as their social orientation and cognitive style, cultural values, age, gender, religious practices, and ethnic origin were as important to the perceived meaning as the visual form of the icon or image. They conclude that in devising the visual form of an icon or image, designers must consider the political, ethnic, and economic contexts that will impact the viewer's interpretation of meaning.

Leadership

To address the growing demand for online education across the globe, leaders of distance education programs must be sensitive to the cultural and institutional contexts within which programs are designed and delivered and be prepared to bring about transformative change. In chapter 11, Beaudoin examines these leadership challenges as they relate to the diffusion of online education in transcultural settings. Specifically, the chapter examines the challenges that online education leaders face in establishing collaborative organizational arrangements, addressing differing teaching-learning styles in cross-cultural settings, and maintaining ethical behavior in these activities. Viable models and suggested strategies are offered to online education leaders.

Quality

Considering the complexity and value-laden nature of quality, Sangrà, Porto, and Jung, in chapter 9, explore the diversity of expectations, experiences, and meanings of quality and assessment in online learning at different levels (institutional, program, and course levels) and from different perspectives (students, teachers, and administrators). The chapter highlights similarities and differences in assessing the quality of online learning in three cultural contexts (Asia, Europe, and the United States) and provides several examples, such as the perception of assessment. In the Asian context, examinations are seen as a means to demonstrate virtue and merit. In the American and European contexts, students give more value to alternative and continuous assessment methods compared with traditional examinations. The authors offer implications of these diverse perceptions of quality for online learning providers.

In chapter 16, Chen, Shen, Fukuda, and Jung extend the discussion on quality by discussing a comparative study of Asian learners' perceptions of quality distance education, conducted in three Asian countries that have been influenced by Confucianism: China, Japan, and South Korea. Their study identified cultural differences and similarities in the perception of quality by the different groups of Asian learners and revealed that quality concerns of the learners are not quite the same as those of the providers or developers. They conclude that to offer learner-centered and flexible online learning, developers need to understand and incorporate the learners' views on quality online learning.

Research

Addressing the dearth of research on issues of culture and online learning, Al-Harthi in chapter 15 examines how much, to what extent, by whom, and in what aspects research on cultural issues has been conducted in the field of open, distance, and online education by conducting a content analysis of three international journals over the past decade, from 2001 to 2011: *The American Journal of Distance Education*; *Distance Education*; and *Open Learning: The Journal of Open, Distance and e-Learning*. The representation of cultural issues in these three journals was considered adequate, although the quality of the representation raised some concerns because of the limited number of empirical studies. Al-Harthi concludes that cultural researchers in open and online education should ask serious questions and answer them using empirical data rather than simply describe and share their experiences.

In chapter 17, the final chapter, Jung and Gunawardena address the need to ask serious questions and conduct quality research studies by proposing a cultural approach to research in online learning. They propose four types of research—exploratory research, cross-cultural research, explanatory research, and design research—and present research questions for each category and discuss methods for gathering and interpreting data in a cultural approach to research. In addition, this chapter brings together the implications for design and practice addressed by each author of this book and encourages readers to begin conducting research on culture and online learning and plan for improved online learning practices.

We believe that the greatest strength of this book is in the diversity of perspectives presented by our collection of international authors who have created a "gathering place" to examine issues of culture. We hope these diverse perspectives engage our readers and expand as they take up the challenge of examining and exploring issues of culture and online learning.

References

Baumgartner, V. J. (2003). *A practical set of cultural dimensions for global user-interface analysis and design* (Master's thesis). University of Vienna. Retrieved from http://mavas.at/val/downloads/ValBaumgartner_PracticalSetOfCulturalDimensions.pdf

Bell, D. (2001). *An introduction to cybercultures*. London: Routledge.

Breslow, H., & Mousoutzanis, A. (2012). Introduction. In H. Breslow & A. Mousoutzanis (Eds.), *Cybercultures: Mediations of community, culture, politics* (pp. vii–xx). Amsterdam, the Netherlands: Editions Rodopi B. V.

Callahan, E. (2005). Cultural similarities and differences in the design of university websites. *Journal of Computer-Mediated Communication, 11(1),* Article 12. Retrieved from http://jcmc.indiana.edu/vol11/issue1/callahan.html

Chao, Y. C. J., & Huang, C. K. (2007). The effectiveness of computer-mediated communication on enhancing writing process and writing outcomes: The implementation of blog and wiki in the EFL writing class in Taiwan. In C. Montgomerie & J. Seale (Eds.), *Proceedings of World Conference on Educational Multimedia, Hypermedia and Telecommunications 2007* (pp. 3463–3468). Chesapeake, VA: AACE.

Cole, M., & Engestrom, Y. (2007). Cultural-historical approaches to designing for development. In J. Valsiner & A. Rosa (Eds.), *The Cambridge handbook of sociocultural psychology* (pp. 484–507). New York, NY: Cambridge University Press.

Cronjé, J. C. (2011). Using Hofstede's cultural dimensions to interpret cross-cultural blended teaching and learning. *Computers and Education*, 56(3), 596–603.

Ess, C. (2009). When the solution becomes the problem: Cultures and individuals as obstacles to online learning. In R. Goodfellow & M. Lamy (Eds.), *Learning cultures in online education* (pp. 15–29). London, UK: Continuum.

Ess, C., & Sudweeks, F. (2005). Culture and computer-mediated communication: Toward new understanding. *Journal of Computer-Mediated Communication, 11*(1), Article 9. Retrieved from http://jcmc.indiana.edu/vol11/issue1/ess.html

Fine, G. A. (1979). Small groups and culture creation: The idioculture of little league baseball teams. *American Sociological Review, 44*(5), 733–745.

Fougere, M., & Moulettes, A. (2007). The construction of the modern West and the backward rest: Studying the discourse of Hofstede's culture's consequences. *Journal of Multicultural Discourses, 2*(1), 1–19. doi:10.2167/md051.0

Goodfellow, R., & Hewling, A. (2005). Reconceptualising culture in virtual learning environments: From an "essentialist" to a "negotiated" perspective. *E-Learning, 2*(4), 355–367. doi:10.2304/elea.2005.2.4.355

Goodfellow, R., & Lamy, M. N. (Eds.). (2009). *Learning cultures in online education*. London, UK: Continuum.

Gunawardena, C. N. (2013). Culture and online distance learning. In M. G. Moore (Ed.), *Handbook of distance education* (3rd ed., pp. 185–200). New York, NY: Routledge.

Gunawardena, C. N. (2014). Globalization, culture, and online distance learning. In O. Zawacki-Richter & T. Anderson (Eds.), *Online distance education: Towards a research agenda*. Athabasca, Edmonton, Canada: Athabasca University Press.

Gunawardena, C. N., Idrissi Alami, A., Jayatilleke, G., & Bouachrine, F. (2009). Identity, gender, and language in synchronous cybercultures: A cross-cultural study. In R. Goodfellow & M. N. Lamy (Eds.), *Learning cultures in online education* (pp. 30–51). London, UK: Continuum.

Gunawardena, C. N., & LaPointe, D. (2007). Cultural dynamics of online learning. In M. G. Moore (Ed.), *Handbook of distance education* (2nd ed., pp. 593–607). Mahwah, NJ: Lawrence Erlbaum.

Gunawardena, C. N., & LaPointe, D. (2008). Social and cultural diversity in distance education. In T. Evans, M. Haughey, & D. Murphy (Eds.), *International handbook of distance education* (pp. 51–70). Bingley, UK: Emerald.

Gunawardena, C. N., Nolla, A. C., Wilson, P. L., López-Islas, J. R., Ramírez-Angel, N., & Megchun-Alpízar, R. M. (2001). A cross-cultural study of group process and development in online conferences. *Distance Education, 22*(1), 85–121.

Hall, E. T. (1959). *The silent language*. New York, NY: Doubleday.

Hall, E. T. (1976). *Beyond culture*. New York, NY: Doubleday.

Hall, E. T. (1983). *Dance of life: The other dimension of time*. Yarmouth, ME: Intercultural Press.

Hofstede, G. H. (1980). *Culture's consequences, international differences in work-related values*. Beverly Hills, CA: Sage.

Hofstede, G. H., & Bond, M. H. (1988). The Confucius connection: From cultural roots to economic growth. *Organizational Dynamics, 16*(4), 5–21.

Hofstede, G. H., Hofstede, G. J., & Minkov, M. (2010). *Cultures and organizations: Software of the mind* (3rd ed.). New York, NY: McGraw-Hill.

Ishii, S. (1982). Thought patterns as modes of rhetoric: The United States and Japan. *Communication, 11*(3), 81–86.

Jung, I. S. (2012). Asian learners' perception of quality in distance education and gender differences. *The International Review of Research in Open and Distance Learning, 13*(2), 1–25. Retrieved from http://www.irrodl.org/index.php/irrodl/article/view/1159/2128

Jung, I. S., Kudo, M., & Choi, S. (2012). Stress in Japanese learners engaged in online collaborative learning in English. *British Journal of Educational Technology, 43*(6), 41016–41029. doi:10.1111/j.1467-8535.2011.01271.x

Jung, I. S., & Lee, Y. K. (2013). YouTube acceptance by university educators and students: A cross-cultural perspective. *Innovation in Education and Training*. Advance online publication. doi:10.1080/14703297.2013.805986

Jung, I. S., & Suzuki, Y. (2014). *Scaffolding wiki-based collaboration in a multicultural language learning context*. Manuscript submitted for publication.

Lam, W. S. E. (2006). Culture and learning in the context of globalization: Research directions. *Review of Research in Education, 30*, 213–237. Retrieved from http://www.sesp.northwestern. edu/docs/publications/2024761014463247786e208.pdf

Levy, M. (2007). Culture, culture learning and new technologies: Towards a pedagogical framework. *Language Learning and Technology, 11*(2), 104–127.

Lykourentzou, I., Papadaki, K., Vergados, D. J., Polemi, D., & Loumos, V. (2010). CorpWiki: A self-regulating wiki to promote corporate collective intelligence through expert peer matching. *Information Sciences, 180*(1), 18–38.

McSweeney, B. (2002). Hofstede's model of national cultural differences and consequences: A triumph of faith—A failure of analysis. *Human Relations, 55*, 89–118.

Mead, M. (1932). *Cooperation and competition among primitive peoples.* New York, NY: Mead Press.

Miike, Y. (2002). Theorizing culture and communication in the Asian context: An assumptive foundation. *Intercultural Communication Studies, 11*(1), 1–21.

Miike, Y. (2004). Rethinking humanity, culture, and communication: Asiacentric critiques and contributions. *A Journal of the Pacific and Asian Communication Association, 7*(1), 67–82.

Parrish, P., & Linder-VanBerschot, J. (2010). Cultural dimensions of learning: Addressing the challenges of multi-cultural instruction. *International Review of Research in Open and Distance Learning, 11*(2), 1–19. Retrieved from http://www.irrodl.org/index.php/irrodl/ article/view/809/1497

Raffaghelli, J. E., & Richieri, C. (2012). A classroom with a view: Networked learning strategies to promote intercultural education. In L. Dirckinck-Holmfeld, V. Hodgson, & D. McConnell (Eds.), *Exploring the theory, pedagogy and practice of networked learning* (pp. 99–119). New York, NY: Springer.

Reid, E. (1995). Virtual worlds: Culture and imagination. In S. G. Jones (Ed.), *CyberSociety: Computer-mediated communication and community* (pp. 164–183). Thousand Oaks, CA: Sage.

Ross, R., & Faulkner, S. (1998). Hofstede's dimensions: An examination and critical analysis. In K. S. Sitaram & M. Prosser (Eds.), *Civic discourse: Multiculturalism, cultural diversity, and global communication* (pp. 31–40). Stanford, CT: Ablex Publishing.

Shaw, J. B., & Barrett-Power, E. (1998). The effects of diversity on small work group processes and performances. *Human Relations, 51*(10), 1307–1325.

Swales, J. (1990). *Genre analysis: English in academic and research settings.* Cambridge, UK: Cambridge University Press.

Tuleja, E. A. (2005). *Intercultural communication for business* (2nd ed.). Mason, OH: South Western Cengage Learning.

Wang, C., & Reeves, T. C. (2007). Cyberspace and online education: The influences of global cyberculture on international students. In K. St. Amant (Ed.), *Linguistic and cultural online communication issues in the global age* (pp. 239–252). Hershey, PA: Idea Group.

Wheeler, S. (Ed.). (2009). *Connected minds, emerging cultures: Cybercultures in online learning.* Charlotte, NC: Information Age Publishing.

2

CULTURAL INFLUENCES ON ONLINE LEARNING

Insung Jung

As far as anthropologists and other behavioral scientists are concerned, culture is the full range of learned human behavior patterns (O'Neil, 2006). Culture is a human tool for survival; for example, it is reflected in the way we organize our social, economic, and political systems; work and play; share knowledge and skills with others; and so on. But it is also a fragile phenomenon, constantly changing and easily lost, because it exists only in our minds. Nieto (2010) described culture as "dynamic, multifaceted, embedded in context, influenced by social, economic, and political factors, created and socially constructed, learned, and dialectical" (p. 137).

In considering cultural influences in teaching, learning, and online learning, we must recognize that there are in fact three layers or levels of culture that influence our learned behavior patterns and perceptions.

First, there are the cultural traditions that distinguish a specific society—the shared and inherited language, traditions, and beliefs that set people apart from others. Second, within complex, diverse societies there are identifiable subcultures that display subcultural traits that set them apart from the rest of society, for example, in the way they dress, communicate, relate to each other, and relate to other subcultures and society as a whole. Third, there are cultural universals, learned behavior patterns that are shared by all of humanity, for example, the construction of language; the classification of people by age, gender, or kinship (young, old, male, female, father, mother); the organization of families and social groups; and the establishment of some form of leadership roles for making community decisions.

As this chapter shows, one of the challenges in sharing or adopting teaching and learning patterns across cultures is knowing where cultural universals apply and where cultural differences and subcultures will influence the processes and outcomes. For example, it might be commonly assumed that most young people are computer literate. But even though the Internet and the web are universal, it would be a serious error to assume that there are cultural universals in e-readiness and e-learning readiness.

Consider new groups of students from different backgrounds and of different ages enrolling in an educational institution or program. Some may be *digital natives* (persons who understand the value of digital technology and seek out every opportunity to use it), whereas some may be *digital immigrants* (late, recent, and perhaps even reluctant adopters of the new technology) (Prensky, 2001). There may also be digital natives and immigrants in the teaching force. The ideological, as well as the knowledge and skills, divide that may exist between these subcultures—the digital natives and digital immigrants and the different generations of learners and teachers—may well lead to uncertainty, misunderstandings, tensions, and even conflict. Consider too the culture of chat and the culture of the tutorial and you will start to appreciate the implications for online learning.

This chapter discusses how these often contradictory attributes of culture affect approaches to teaching and learning in different cultural contexts in order to help educators develop better understandings of cultural influences on learning and online learning. It first explores how culture with both static and dynamic features influences learning. It then looks at how the multifaceted nature of culture promotes multicultural and diverse experiences of learners in learning and online learning, with a special focus on gender differences. It also discusses the bilateral interaction between culture and learning context, followed by socially constructed and changed concepts of culture in learning and online learning. It concludes with recommendations for online educators.

Culture and Learning

Examining culture from a static perspective, we note that deeply held values transmitted from generation to generation remain constant and do not change readily as a result of multicultural experiences. Our basic psychological processes such as perception, cognition, memory, and problem solving are influenced by culture (Matsumoto, 1996). But at the same time, people from different cultural backgrounds receive and process information in quite different ways. Using the well-known Müller-Lyer figure (see figure 2.1), Henrich, Heine, and Norenzayan (2010) and Matsumoto (1996) found that perceptions of this optical illusion varied by culture. Most Westerners, well used to observing human-made, rectangular-shaped objects, perceived Line A to be shorter than Line B, whereas Indians and New Guineans, who are more familiar with natural, rounded, and irregular surroundings, perceived them to be the same length.

In another example, Kearins (1986) examined the visual spatial location and memorization skills of Australian outback aboriginal children and White metropolitan children using a version of Kim's game, which involved rearranging objects on a grid and then requiring the two groups of children to recall their original location. On all occasions, the aboriginal children performed significantly better than the White children. They sat

Figure 2.1 The Müller-Lyer illusion. Created in 1889, Creative Commons Attribution-Share Alike 2.5 Generic License.

very still, concentrated on the task, took their time in rearranging the objects, and clearly employed visual means to solve the problems. By contrast, the White children fidgeted, rearranged the objects hastily, and muttered to themselves, using a verbal strategy that was inappropriate to this particular task. It was concluded that the aboriginal children were influenced by different inherited cultural practices and that their superior visual spatial memory skills were part of a wider cognitive skill set necessary in a natural world where survival depends on the ability to hunt, gather foodstuffs, and find water. As studies by Gauvain (2001) reveal, cultural factors influence not only what children learn but also how they apply different strategies of attention, memory, planning, and problem solving.

Cultural influences are also evident in the differences between long-held Western and Eastern ways of thinking and knowing. Spronk (2004) observed that Western cultures tend to adopt an analytical approach, dividing reality into its parts, whereas Eastern cultures favor more synthetic approaches, focusing on the whole over the parts. Nisbett (2003) characterized Western thought as seeking consistency and stressing the object and Asian thought as accepting contradiction and being more concerned with context. Others such as Hofstede (1991) and Hall (1976) defined Western cultures as individualistic, logical, precise, action oriented, and low context and Asian cultures as collective and high context, for example, being more concerned with the nonverbal behaviors and status of the speakers. These differences help to explain why some Asian students tend to plagiarize. Quoting from well-known and highly respected sources is a sign of deep respect for the authority. Altering the authority's words would be a sign of disrespect. And in Asian societies that value societal independence over individual rights and ownership, knowledge is regarded as belonging to the society as a whole, so one's duty is to share it with others (Introna, Hayes, Blair, & Wood, 2003; McDonnell, 2003).

Joy and Kolb (2009) examined the impact of culture on learning styles. They used 10 culture clusters derived from a decade-long empirical study involving 170 scholars from 62 societies to categorize and test cultural dimensions at societal and organizational levels: Anglo, Latin Europe, Nordic Europe, Germanic Europe, Eastern Europe, Latin America, sub-Saharan Africa, Middle East, Southern Asia, and Confucian Asia. To assess the differences in learning styles of 1,292 individuals from these cultures, the researchers used the Kolb Learning Style Inventory, a 12-item instrument that measures the degree to which individuals show different learning styles (Abstract Conceptualization vs. Concrete Experience, and Active Experimentation vs. Reflective Observation). They found that Confucian Asia, including China, Japan, and South Korea, scored the highest in Abstract Conceptualization, whereas the Latin and Anglo cultures such as France, Spain, Australia, and the United States rated highest in terms of Concrete Experience. No cultural differences were identified in the preference of Active Experimentation over Reflective Observation. These results suggest that Confucian Asian culture has a strong preference for abstraction, whereas the Latin and Anglo cultures prefer concreteness over abstraction in learning. Joy and Kolb also calculated how much culture and other factors (age, gender, level of education, and educational specialization) explained learning style and found that educational specialization or study field (which of course represent subcultures) ranked first, accounting for the most variance in Abstract Conceptualization versus Concrete Experience, and culture second. Further data analyses revealed that people from countries with high scores in uncertainty avoidance, future orientation, performance orientation, and collectivism such as Singapore and Germany tended to have abstract learning styles.

Although all of these studies may have their methodological limitations, they all concur that culture is an important, if not the primary, factor influencing how people develop strategies to perceive or receive information from the world around them, process information and learn specific strategies for remembering information, interpret the world around them, and learn the rules and strategies for planning and problem solving.

But, as observed at the start of this chapter, culture is dynamic and ever changing. In today's global, mobile, and online society, people interact with people from other cultures and, in so doing, absorb something of these different cultures. The former territories of the British Empire, such as India, Singapore, Hong Kong, and the West Indies, have long shown many adopted Western cultural traits, and today, Asian countries such as Japan, South Korea, and China are rapidly absorbing many Western ideas and ways of doing things often due to commercial imperatives. As Nisbett (2003) observed, increasing numbers of Asian organizations, institutions, and individuals are bicultural, able to switch their worldviews to Western or Asian according to context and need. Globalization and the online environment are also accelerating cultural change in education, which holds both promise and challenges.

Culture and Online Learning

It is important to stress that although the following observations have diagnostic value, caution should always be exercised in stereotyping students based on country of origin or a static notion of culture.

Cultural Experiences

In the individualistic Western cultures where an "I-You" stance reflects mutual respect and equal status, and online learning typically entails text, independent learning, and the use of metacognitive skills, in Asia, as Özkul and Aoki (2006) found in Japan, teachers and students prefer TV and videoconference lectures to impersonal text on the Internet and asynchronous online space. This is explained by the fact that in Asia, the "We-They" stance prevails, age and social status are determiners of appropriate behavior for learners, and the students deem the knowledge and opinion of the instructor to be more worthy than theirs. Also, the learners are accustomed to the instructor providing clear instructions and closely monitoring their progress. This is why Wang (2006) observed that Chinese online teachers struggle to achieve a balance between teacher-centeredness and embracing the more learner-centered and self-directed learning approaches that online learning environments offer.

Interviewing an international group of instructors, Downey, Wentling, Wentling, and Wadsworth (2005) identified a positive relationship between national culture and the usability of an e-learning system. They suggested that e-learning providers targeting the global market need to consider the level of leadership expected by the learners, and the level of group interaction and support offered to learners, in order to improve the usability of their systems. For example, learners from power-centric cultures may expect greater guidance from their teachers and prefer a more teacher-centered approach to online learning. On the contrary, learners from more power-distributed cultures may wish to adopt a more student-centered approach. In collectivistic societies, learners may desire strategies that promote group work, collaboration, and social activities, whereas learners from more individualistic societies may prefer an e-learning system where learners can exercise greater control over their own learning pace and method and where a principle of competition is promoted during instruction and assessment.

Multicultural Experiences

In a multicultural and collaborative online learning environment, both students and teachers are exposed to cultural differences in teaching and learning and, in some cases, the need to communicate in an unfamiliar language. During this process, as shown in chapter 13, both sets of participants begin to develop new values and habits and question their previous assumptions in regard to teaching and learning and their fellow learners. As a result, a reasonably homogeneous online teaching and learning culture emerges, and as Anderson (2004) observed, regardless of racial, ethnic, or linguistic backgrounds, the participants experience a "profound and multifaceted increase in communication and interaction capability" (p. 42). There are clearly many advantages to using the Internet to provide students with opportunities to extend their experiential learning spaces and learn and interact with those of other cultures (Jung & Latchem, 2011), but careful planning is necessary to ensure that the content, use of technology, role of the instructors and learners, and management of the learning process enable participants from different cultures to reflect on knowledge, opinions, and assumptions about educational practices and shed light on some important issues at the interface of technology, culture, and pedagogy.

The Issue of Subcultures

As already noted, within any nation, ethnic group, or society, different subcultures exist. They may be generational, social, or political. So although it holds true that in many educational contexts, students in high-context Asian cultures prefer face-to-face contact with their teachers and a group-oriented environment, a different learning culture may be observed in online education. Examining predictors of learner satisfaction in online learning in Japan where teacher-centered face-to-face learning was highly valued, Bray, Aoki, and Dlugosh (2008) discovered that students experienced in distance education revealed a preference for online learning because it accorded with a newly adopted learning style of independent study and self-directed learning. Chen and Wang (2010) noted similarly that today's Chinese online learners ask for more interactions and flexible learning activities guided by instructors, whereas their institutions place more emphasis on the provision of video lectures and multimedia resources.

Culture and Gender Differences

Again caution is needed in regard to gender stereotyping, but in a meta-analysis of research into gender differences in learning styles, Severiens and Ten Dam (1994) concluded that males tend to be more interested in learning for the sake of gaining qualifications offered, whereas females are more interested in learning for learning's sake. They also found that males were more likely to employ deep learning approaches than their female counterparts. Hayes and Smith (1994) and Lie, Angelique, and Cheong (2004) found that because females focus more on interpersonal relationships, they tend to prefer collaborative learning, whereas males prefer independent learning.

In regard to online learning, a number of studies indicate that male and female students differ in their experiences, perceptions, motivation, preferred learning and communication styles, and performance (Blum, 1999; Chyung, 2007; Gunn, McSporran, Macleod, & French, 2003; Rovai & Baker, 2005; Sullivan, 2001; Tekinarslan, 2009). For example, Sullivan (2001) discovered that overall, female students in one U.S. community college were more favorably disposed toward online learning than were male students. Chyung (2007) found female students in a U.S. university's online course scored higher than males in self-efficacy and exam results. Rovai and Baker (2005) found that female students felt more connected and learned more than males in 12 graduate-level online courses. After reviewing international literature and practices on gender issues in computer-supported learning, Gunn et al. (2003) concluded that female students both posted and read more messages on course bulletin boards and generally performed better than their male counterparts. And Bellman, Tindimubona, and Arias (1993) found that in both African and Latin American contexts, female students who were reticent in offering their opinions in face-to-face situations tended to make strong assertive comments in online environments when their anonymity was ensured.

However, other studies report inconsistent or contrary results in gender differences. For example, Yükseltürk and Bulut (2009) found no gender differences in motivational beliefs, self-regulated learning, and achievement in an online class in Turkey; Barrett and Lally (1999) found that male students in an online graduate course posted more and longer messages and made more socioemotional contributions to the online community than did females; and Tekinarslan (2009) revealed male students' higher self-efficacy in web-based learning in a study of Turkish undergraduate students.

These inconclusive results suggest that context is an important variable in judging gender differences in face-to-face and online learning.

Culture and Learning Context

A number of studies confirm the bilateral interaction of culture and context. Jung and Suzuki (2014) analyzed the behaviors and motivations of students who made no contributions to editing other students' writing in a wiki-based Japanese language course. They deduced the main reasons for their inactivity were a lack of confidence and avoiding "loss of face." These could of course be attributed to the Confucian values instilled in these learners since early childhood: "Accept things as they are, don't try to stand out in the group, don't speak up until you're spoken to, and respect those who lead, are older, or have superior knowledge." Silence in the typical Japanese classroom is generally attributed to these factors. But in fact all of these students were non-Japanese and mostly from Western countries. So why was their behavior similar to that of the Japanese students? It was concluded that inactivity or silence is more closely related to the contextual expectations of the Japanese classroom than the students' personal or cultural backgrounds. In some Middle Eastern countries, women's access to higher education is either openly or by tacit discrimination limited. So in some cases, distance and online education becomes the only opportunity. This is why 68% of the students at Payame Noor University, the state distance education university in Iran, are females (Povey & Rostami-Povey, 2012). On the other hand, in Saudi Arabia, women are admitted to the conventional universities but cannot be seen unveiled by men in public places, so they study on separate parts of the campuses. So in addition to online course material distribution, discussions, quizzes, and assessment for female students, videoconferencing is often used for simultaneous course delivery to both male and female students, with the latter being able to see, hear, and interact with the male teachers and students while remaining hidden from their gaze. These two examples show how culture and context can shape the nature and application of online learning (Latchem & Jung, 2012).

Socially Constructed Culture of Learning

As we have shown, culture can be socially constructed and changed, but this does not occur easily and needs to be carefully planned and supported.

The following example from Asia shows that policy support, strategic planning, shared responsibilities, encouragement, and continuous support are needed to construct new cultures of teaching and learning. Like many of its neighbors, South Korea is a high-context culture wherein communication is less verbally specific, meaning and context are equally important, harmony is preferred to confrontation, and paralanguage plays an important role. This explains why many Korean students prefer face-to-face learning and many online courses make extensive use of TV broadcasts, streamed video lectures, and blended learning. However, as a result of a combination of government and institutional policies, encouragement and support, and the development of sophisticated technology infrastructure in all higher education institutions, a new teaching and learning culture has emerged in the university and professional development sectors. As noted in Latchem, Jung, Aoki, and Özkul (2008), many Korean universities' web pages give prominence to innovative learning approaches, including online learning, and all universities have centers for teaching and learning whose main roles include technology and pedagogy support for innovative teaching and learning. Over 80% of the 4-year universities offer online or blended learning courses and programs, every university has created an average of 29 wholly online courses (Kim, Leem, Chung, & Choi, 2010), and as of 2011, there are 20 virtual universities offering 245 majors fully online (Ministry of Education, Science and Technology [MEST] & Korea Education and Research Information Service [KERIS], 2011). These developments appear to have in turn brought changes to the teaching and learning culture in university classrooms, with faculty members combining Twitter and other social networking tools in both face-to-face and online classes, using e-portfolios to provide continuous learning support and integrating open educational resources into their online or blended courses, and creating multicultural learning environments by inviting participation by external experts and students from other countries via networking technologies (KERIS, 2010). All of which can occur only in an open culture and a culture open to change.

Cultural change can also be unconsciously learned. Indeed it may be more common to learn and adapt culture without any conscious effort. As Nieto (2010) pointed out, culture is learned subconsciously through interactions with others in the community and in informal environments. She went on to say that most people do not think about their culture unless their culture is in conflict with, or under the influence of, another culture. People who belong to a majority culture do not seem to consciously ponder culture. Maybe this is why most of the culture-focused articles are written by authors who have been a part of two or more cultures or do not belong to a majority culture, as depicted in chapter 15 of this book.

By studying in online learning environments, students learn not only the content but also the culture that is unique to online learning (see chapters 4, 5, and 9). Think about students who have studied only in a face-to-face learning environment and have never been exposed to online learning. They belong to the majority culture of learning and thus may have difficulties in understanding and applying the new ways of learning that are required in the twenty-first century. So in achieving change in online learning, online learners require more than training and instruction in the technology and methods. They require initiation into the new and different cultural norms and values and induction into the thought systems and culture of interactive, interdependent, and self-directed learning by means of direct and immersive involvement in online learning. Although sensitivity to traditional and different cultures is very important, to be prepared for study, work, and life in the twenty-first century and be competent lifelong learners, all students need to become bicultural, internalizing these two cultures of learning: the conventional and the virtual.

Conclusion

Culture is often referred to as the concept with two faces: "the known meanings and directions, which its members are trained to; and the new observations and meanings, which are offered and tested" (Williams, 1958, p. 6). On the one hand, culture can lead us to follow common approaches and directions that we have acquired, whereas on the other hand, it can offer new and rich experiences and opportunities for constant change. These complexities of culture shape our perceptions of learning and online learning and how we teach and learn. The major challenges for online educators are to make sure that they are well aware of the multiple and complex nature of cultural and subcultural influences on learners' learning behaviors and on their own teaching and utilize these cultural understandings to tactically devise learner support strategies, ensuring that learners from different cultural contexts achieve their particular learning objectives and the more universal educational objectives. The art of achieving this lies in avoiding indoctrination and manipulation and induction into knowledge of culture as a thinking system (see also chapter 8).

References

Anderson, T. (2004). Toward a theory of online learning. In T. Anderson & F. Elloumi (Eds.), *Theory and practice of online-education* (pp. 33–60). Athabasca, Canada: Athabasca University.

Barrett, E., & Lally, V. (1999). Gender differences in an online learning environment. *Journal of Computer Assisted Learning*, *15*, 48–60. Retrieved from http://www.qou.edu/arabic/researchProgram/distanceLearning/genderDifferences.pdf

Bellman, B., Tindimubona, A., & Arias, A., Jr. (1993). Technology transfer in global networking: Capacity-building in Africa and Latin America. In L. Harasim (Ed.), *Global networks: Computers and international communications* (pp. 237–254). Cambridge, MA: MIT Press.

Blum, K. (1999). Gender differences in asynchronous learning in higher education. *Journal of Asynchronous Learning Networks, 3*(1), 46–47.

Bray, E., Aoki, K., & Dlugosh, L. (2008). Predictors of learning satisfaction in Japanese online distance learners. *International Review of Research in Open and Distance Learning, 9*(3), 1–24.

Chen, L., & Wang, N. (2010). Attitudes to distance education in China. In J. Baggaley & T. Belawati (Eds.), *Distance education technologies in Asia* (pp. 111–126). New Delhi, India: Sage.

Chyung, S. Y. (2007). Age and gender differences in online behavior, self-efficacy and academic performance. *Quarterly Review of Distance Education, 8*(3), 213–222.

Downey, S., Wentling, R. M., Wentling, T., & Wadsworth, T. (2005). The relationship between national culture and the usability of an e-learning system. *Human Resource Development International, 8*(1), 47–64.

Gauvain, M. (2001). Cultural tools, social interaction, and the development of thinking. *Human Development, 44*, 126–143.

Gunn, C., McSporran, M., Macleod, H., & French, S. (2003). Dominant or different? Gender issues in computer supported learning. *Journal of Asynchronous Learning Networks, 7*, 14–30. Retrieved from http://www.cs.lamar.edu/faculty/osborne/COSC1172/v7n1_gunn.pdf

Hall, E. T. (1976). *Beyond culture.* New York, NY: Doubleday.

Hayes, E. R., & Smith, L. (1994). Women in adult education: An analysis of perspectives in major journals. *Adult Education Quarterly, 44*(4), 201–219.

Henrich, J., Heine, S. J., & Norenzayan, A. (2010). The weirdest people in the world? *Behavioral and Brain Sciences, 33*, 61–83.

Hofstede, G. H. (1991). *Cultures and organizations: Software of the mind.* New York, NY: McGraw-Hill.

Introna, L., Hayes, N., Blair, L., & Wood, E. (2003). *Cultural attitudes towards plagiarism: Developing a better understanding of the needs of students from diverse cultural backgrounds relating to plagiarism.* Lancaster, UK: Plagiarism Advisory Service, Lancaster University.

Joy, S., & Kolb, D. A. (2009). Are there cultural differences in learning style? *International Journal of Intercultural Relations, 33*(1), 69–85.

Jung, I. S., & Latchem, C. (2011). A model for e-education: Extended teaching spaces and extended learning spaces. *British Journal of Educational Technology, 42*(1), 6–18.

Jung, I. S., & Suzuki, Y. (2014). *Scaffolding wiki-based collaboration in a multicultural language learning context.* Manuscript submitted for publication.

Kearins, J. (1986). Visual spatial memory in Aboriginal and White Australian children. *Australian Journal of Psychology, 38*, 203–214.

Kim, J., Leem, J., Chung, J., & Choi, M. (2010). *A policy study on the result analysis of e-learning in higher education and for the improvement of the university e-learning support center.* Seoul, Korea: Korea Education and Research Information Service.

Korea Education and Research Information Service. (2010). *2010 best practices in technology integration in higher education.* Seoul, Korea: Author.

Latchem, C., & Jung, I. S. (2012). Cultural perceptions of flexibility in Asian higher education. In E. Burge, C. C. Gibson, & T. Gibson (Eds.), *Flexible pedagogy, flexible practice: Notes from the trenches of distance education* (pp. 79–92). Edmonton, Canada: Athabasca University Press.

Latchem, C., Jung, I. S., Aoki, K., & Özkul, A. E. (2008). The tortoise and the hare enigma in e-transformation in Japanese and Korean higher education. *British Journal of Educational Technology, 39*(4), 610–630.

Lie, L. Y., Angelique, L., & Cheong, E. (2004). How do male and female students approach learning at NUS? *CDTL Brief, 7*(1), 1–3.

Matsumoto, D. (1996). *Culture and psychology.* Pacific Grove, CA: Brooks/Cole.

McDonnell, K. E. (2003). *Academic plagiarism rules and ESL learning: Mutually exclusive concepts?* Unpublished manuscript, TESL 501 English Language Teaching I (Summer 2003, Professor Karen Taylor), American University, Washington, DC.

Ministry of Education, Science and Technology & Korea Education and Research Information Service. (2011). *White paper: Adapting education to the information age.* Seoul, Korea: Author.

Nieto, S. (2010). Culture and learning. In S. Nieto (Ed.), *Language, culture, and teaching: Critical perspectives* (pp. 135–159). New York, NY: Routledge.

Nisbett, R. E. (2003). *The geography of thought: How Asians and Westerners think differently . . . and why.* New York, NY: Free Press.

O'Neil, D. (2006). *What is culture.* Retrieved from http://anthro.palomar.edu/culture/culture_1 .htm

Özkul, A., & Aoki, K. (2006, September). *E-learning in Japan: Steam locomotive on shinkansen.* Proceedings of the 22nd ICDE World Conference on Distance Education: Promoting Quality in On-line, Flexible and Distance Education, Rio de Janeiro, Brazil.

Povey, T., & Rostami-Povey, E. (Eds.). (2012). *Women, power and politics in 21st century Iran.* London, UK: Ashgate.

Prensky, M. (2001). Digital natives, digital immigrants. *On the Horizon, 9*(5). Retrieved from http://www.marcprensky.com/writing/Prensky%20-%20Digital%20Natives,%20Digital%20 Immigrants%20-%20Part1.pdf

Rovai, A. P., & Baker, J. D. (2005). Gender differences in online learning: Sense of community, perceived learning, and interpersonal interactions. *The Quarterly Review of Distance Education, 6*(1), 31–44.

Severiens, S. E., & Ten Dam, G. T. M. (1994). Gender differences in learning styles: A narrative review and quantitative meta-analysis. *Higher Education, 27,* 487–501.

Spronk, B. (2004). Addressing cultural diversity through learner support. In J. Brindley, C. Walti, & O. Zawacki-Richter (Eds.), *Learner support in open, distance and online learning environments* (pp. 169–178). Oldenburg, Germany: Bibliothecks-und Informationssystem der Universität.

Sullivan, P. (2001). Gender differences and the online classroom: Male and female college students evaluate their experiences. *Community College Journal of Research and Practice, 25,* 805–818.

Tekinarslan, E. (2009). Turkish university students' perceptions of the World Wide Web as a learning tool: An investigation based on gender, socio-economic background, and web experience. *International Review of Research in Open and Distance Learning, 10*(2), 1–19.

Wang, V. (2006). The instructional patterns of Chinese online educators in China. *Asian Journal of Distance Education, 4*(1). Retrieved from http://www.asianjde.org/2006v4.1.Wang.pdf

Williams, R. (1958). *Culture and society.* London, UK: Chatto & Windus.

Yükseltürk, E., & Bulut, S. (2009). Gender differences in self-regulated online learning environment. *Educational Technology and Society, 12*(3), 12–22.

3

CULTURE AND TECHNOLOGY

Insung Jung

Over the past few decades, researchers have tried to understand why individual users adopt or do not adopt certain technologies (e.g., Davis, Bagozzi, & Warshaw, 1989; Rogers, 1995; Teo, Lee, Chai, & Wong, 2009; Venkatesh, Morris, Davis, & Davis, 2003). Some have argued that users' perceptions of usefulness and ease of use with technology play a key role in its adoption. Others have considered personal factors of users, such as one's job, personal performance expectations, or self-efficacy, as an important influence in explaining an individual's level of technology acceptance. Yet still others have argued that social influences and environmental conditions are important in predicting individuals' acceptance of technology. It has also been revealed that culture plays a large part in an individual's perception of and reaction to new technology, which is evident in several studies of technology acceptance, including that of N. Li and Kirkup (2008) and Teo et al. (2009).

This chapter examines the acceptance or adoption of various technologies in different cultures and factors related to such technology acceptance. It begins with an overview of selected technology acceptance theories and models, and it details cultural influences in the process of technology adoption. It concludes with the implications for cultural influences on online learning.

Theories and Models of Technology Acceptance

There have been efforts to explain how an individual or a group adopts or accepts new technology from various perspectives, including communications, psychological, and social viewpoints.

Rogers's Diffusion of Innovations

Rogers's diffusion model (1983, 1995) provides a framework to examine the effects of various components involved in the communication process on the rate of adoption of innovations. In particular, the model argues that how an individual perceives attributes of an innovation strongly affects the process of diffusion and adoption. Previous studies have shown that the primary characteristics of an innovation itself are not necessarily influential in technology adoption, and the focus has shifted from the intrinsic traits of a certain innovation to the perceived attributes of that innovation.

Considering an individual's perception of an innovation, Rogers (1995) identified five factors explaining the process of innovation adoption:

1. *Relative advantage:* The degree to which an innovation is perceived as better than the object or idea it supersedes influences how rapid the innovation is adopted. Relative advantage can be measured in terms of economic benefits, social prestige, convenience, and satisfaction. An innovation with greater perceived relative advantage is more quickly adopted.
2. *Compatibility:* The degree to which an innovation is perceived as being consistent with the existing values, past experiences, and needs of potential adopters also affects the process of adoption. An innovation with greater perceived compatibility is more quickly adopted.
3. *Complexity:* The degree to which an innovation is perceived as difficult to understand and use has an effect on the adoption process. A complex innovation is more slowly adopted than a simpler innovation.
4. *Trialability:* The degree to which an innovation may be experimented with on a limited basis influences the adoption process. An innovation that can be tried out in the form of a free sample or a trial use is more quickly adopted than an innovation that cannot be experimented with on a limited scale.
5. *Observability:* The degree to which the results of an innovation are visible to others affects the adoption rate. The easier it is for people to see the results of an innovation, the faster its rate of adoption.

Rogers (2003) also attested cultural influences on adoption of innovation through various cases, including boiling water in Peru, bar code readers in the United States and Italy, and Lotus 1-2-3 in India. These cases illustrate that different cultural beliefs and values lead to different ways of perceiving the innovation and affect individuals' adoption decision.

Several studies have applied Rogers's model in examining the adoption of recent technologies. T. Lee's (2004) qualitative study on analyzing nurses' perceptions about using a computerized care plan system using Rogers's diffusion model revealed that nurses' behavior during the process of adopting the new technology can be accurately explained by the model's five innovation characteristics. However, recent studies have shown somewhat different results. For example, Duan, He, Feng, Li, and Fu (2010) examined Chinese students' perceptions regarding innovative attributes of e-learning when choosing online programs offered by U.K. universities. Survey results from 215 students revealed that two factors of Rogers's model—perceived compatibility and trialability—were particularly influential in Chinese students' adoption of online degree programs. However, trialability was negatively related to the adoption of online education, and the other three factors—relative advantage, complexity, and observability—did not appear to be important for Chinese students to accept the innovative education format. Although no explanation was given in the study regarding the negative relationship between trialability and the adoption of online education, it may be that the Chinese online learners would not want to pay for online degree programs that are open for free tryouts and prefer online degree programs to be more exclusive. The researchers noted that for the young generation in China, whether a new technology or innovation is complex is not an issue and thus they are not afraid of trying it out as long as it meets their learning needs, lifestyles, and career goals. This study showed the limited explanatory power of Rogers's model in predicting innovation adoption by the younger generation in certain cultures and suggested a need for exploring factors other than perceived attributes of innovations.

Technology Acceptance Model

The technology acceptance model (TAM) was initially designed to infer technology acceptance and usage in the workplace (Davis et al., 1989). Like Rogers's diffusion of innovations model, TAM also focuses on the perception of a user in explaining technology acceptance. TAM assumes that a user's perceived usefulness and perceived ease of use are two major factors for technology acceptance. *Perceived usefulness* is defined as the extent to which using a technology is perceived as helpful to one's job performance, whereas perceived ease of use refers to the extent to which a technology is perceived as not requiring much effort or is free of effort. These two factors influence an individual's attitude toward the use of technology. When an individual has a positive attitude, he or she forms an intention to use a technology that will eventually lead to the actual adoption or usage of that technology. The arrow between perceived usefulness and behavioral intention shows that if an individual believes that a certain technology will help his or her job performance, then he or she will form an intention to adopt or use that technology, without forming a positive attitude toward the actual technology use.

TAM is applicable to various contexts with different technologies and users, and numerous studies (e.g., Adams, Nelson, & Todd, 1992; Pai & Huang, 2011; Selim, 2003; Taylor & Todd, 1995) have tested TAM with a wide range of new technologies and proved that perceived usefulness and perceived ease of use explains about 40% to 50% of the variance in the intention to use a technology. However, several researchers including Legris, Ingham, and Collerette (2003) have pointed out that some significant factors related to both human and social change processes are missing in TAM. Venkatesh and Davis (2000) extended TAM to three external variables affecting perceived usefulness, ease of use, and behavioral intention: social influence processes (subjective norm, voluntariness, and image), cognitive instrumental processes (job relevance, output quality, result demonstrability), and experience. When tested in four organizations, the extended model, or TAM2, was strongly supported, accounting for 40% to 60% of the variance in perceived usefulness and 34% to 52% of the variance in behavioral intentions to use. But the main focus of TAM2 is still on users' perceptions of an innovation.

Social Cognitive Theory

Social cognitive theory (SCT) attempts to explain human behaviors not just from individual perspectives but also from the social aspects of human decisions. Within the notion of triadic reciprocality, Bandura (1986) explained the complexity of human functioning via the interactions between three factors: (a) personal factors such as cognition, emotions, and self-efficacy; (b) behavior; and (c) the environment in which an individual is engaged. These three factors constantly influence and interact with each other much like the points of a triangle (Compeau, Gravill, Haggerty, & Kelley, 2006).

According to SCT, people watching others performing a behavior (e.g., using a new computer) will be influenced by what others do, form perceptions of their own ability to perform the behavior (e.g., computer self-efficacy), perceive the expected outcomes, and think about strategies for effective performance. Compeau and Higgins (1995) and Compeau, Meister, and Higgins (2007) applied SCT in explaining technology acceptance and found that personal factors, such as job and personal performance expectations or self-efficacy, play important roles in individuals' computer acceptance behaviors. In these studies, self-efficacy that reflects a future-oriented belief about what one can accomplish appears to be more important for the adoption of a technology than the actual capability to use that technology.

The Unified Theory of Acceptance and Use of Technology

Rogers's diffusion of innovations model, TAM, and SCT have been criticized for their narrow focus on personal variables, as indicated in Y. Lee, Kozar, and Larsen (2003), and for often ignoring organizational influences on technology adoption in social settings such as in schools and companies, as discussed in Shen, Laffey, Lin, and Huang (2006). To address these issues, several other theories and models, such as the model of PC utilization, theory of reasoned action, motivational model, theory of planned behavior (TPB), combined TAM and TPB, and innovation distribution theory, have included social influences and environmental conditions for predicting technology acceptance to some extent.

Venkatesh et al. (2003) proposed the unified theory of acceptance and use of technology (UTAUT) where both personal and social factors are tightly connected in explaining technology acceptance. Venkatesh et al. (2003) empirically compared the existing models of technology acceptance, developed the UTAUT to integrate key personal and social elements across those models, and validated their new model in six organizations. The UTAUT explains performance expectancy (PE), effort expectancy (EE), social influence (SI), and facilitating conditions (FC) as direct determinants of individuals' intention to adopt technology. PE refers to "the degree to which an individual believes that using the system will help him or her to attain gains in job performance" (p. 447) and includes the perceived usefulness of a certain technology. EE refers to "the degree of ease associated with the use of the system" (p. 450) and concerns the perceived ease of use of a certain technology. SI refers to "the degree to which an individual perceives that important others believe he or she should use the new system" (p. 451) and includes an individual's perception of norms in his or her social environment regarding the use of a certain technology. FC refers to "the degree to which an individual believes that an organizational and technical infrastructure exists to support use of the system" (p. 453) and includes support, infrastructure, knowledge, and training related to the use of a certain technology.

Since its development, the UTAUT and its four determinants have been validated in several studies across various contexts. In the context of online education, Sundaravej (2010), in a study on the acceptance of a learning management system with 262 college students in the United States, reported satisfactory validity and reliability of the UTAUT constructs and a significant degree of correlations between the four determinants. Similarly, in a study conducted with weblog systems, J. P. Li and Kishore (2006) found that scales for the four key constructs in the UTAUT have constant true scores across most subgroups. In Saudi Arabia, Al-Gahtani, Hubona, and Wang (2007) reported the appropriateness of the UTAUT constructs in explaining around 40% of variance of behavioral intention to use technology. Im, Hong, and Kang (2011) also confirmed how well the UTAUT fits the data observed on the acceptance of the MP3 player and Internet banking in Korea and the United States. Similarly, Oshlyansky, Cairns, and Thimbleby (2007), in a study validating the UTAUT in nine countries across different continents, confirmed that the UTAUT is robust enough to uncover important factors affecting technology acceptance cross-culturally.

The aforementioned studies have also found the impact of culture on specific determinants of technology acceptance. Im et al. (2011) revealed that although the effect of performance expectance and social influence on behavioral intention is similar in the United States and Korea, the effect of effort expectancy is greater in the United States. These findings led them to conclude that the degree of impact of the four key determinants in the UTAUT vary from culture to culture. Oshlyansky et al. (2007) also showed that different constructs have different levels of influence across the nine countries investigated in their study.

Influence of Culture on Technology Acceptance

Previous studies that applied various theories and models of technology acceptance have found that culture can slow down or promote technology acceptance or implementation efforts because of differences in the way technology is perceived and interpreted in different sociocultural contexts (Robey, Gupta, & Rodriguez-Diaz, 1990). For example, if a technology is perceived compatible with the existing culture, it is more likely to be quickly adopted and implemented, as argued by Rogers (1995).

A large-scale study conducted by Bagchi, Hart, and Peterson (2004) showed the impact of culture on technology adoption. They proposed three types of indicators for information technology adoption—cultural, institutional, and economic—by analyzing data from the study of national culture and the adoption of six information technologies—the PC, telephone, cell phone, fax, Internet, and pager—over a decade in 31 countries across North America, South America, Europe, and Asia-Pacific regions. They discovered that even after controlling for national economic and social differences, Hofstede's national cultural indicators predict most technology adoptions. In particular, they revealed that the diffusion of information technologies is greater in nations with higher levels of individualism, lower power distance, and cultural femininity. However, caution is needed to interpret this finding, as those six technologies tend to require individual decisions rather than organizational or national ones.

Hasan and Ditsa (1999) argued that information technology tends to expand quickly in nations with low uncertainty avoidance for information technology, which is evident in studies by Straub (1994) and Singh (2006) in the way that high uncertainty avoidance cultures like Japan (even though it is a high-tech country) lead to lower levels of new technology adoption compared with low uncertainty avoidance cultures like the United States. Png, Tan, and Wee (2001) also found similar results and concluded that high uncertainty avoidance cultures show a tendency to wait longer for technology adoption and rely more on observing early adopters' experiences.

As seen previously, uncertainty avoidance is singled out more frequently than any other of Hofstede's cultural dimensions, and results showing its impact on technology acceptance are not always consistent. Although other studies have argued that high uncertainty avoidance cultures tend to show a resistance to adopting the technology, Cardon and Marshall (2008) found that when uncertainty avoidance is in practice, these cultures are more likely to embrace technology as a means to reduce uncertainty. In a meta-analysis conducted with 95 TAM articles, they showed that correlations between the TAM constructs (perceived ease of use and perceived usefulness, perceived ease of use and behavioral intension, perceived usefulness and behavioral intension) are lower in cultures where the rules and procedures are already institutionalized and implemented to deal with uncertainty. Those cultures where uncertainty avoidance is in practice or high tend to welcome technological solutions and promote the learning of science and technology to reduce the inevitable uncertainty associated with new technology adoption by individuals. Thus, in these societies, perceived ease of use is less influential because the formal mechanisms for learning new technologies are already established.

Other studies have identified the impact of culture on specific determinants of technology acceptance, applying one or more of the previously mentioned adoption models. For example, Im et al. (2011) revealed that although the effect of performance expectance and social influence on behavioral intention are similar in Korea and the United States, the effects of effort expectancy is greater in the United States. These findings led them to conclude that the degree of impact of the four key determinants in the UTAUT vary from culture to culture. In another study conducted with college students in Japan and the United States, Jung and Lee (2013) revealed that the facilitating condition is a more important factor for participants from Japan, a high uncertainty avoidance culture, in accepting technology than it is for their counterparts from the United States, a low uncertainty avoidance culture. Japanese culture is also high in power distance, meaning that Japanese students, compared with their teachers, are more pressured into conformity with other people and apt to follow the teachers' guidance when learning (Hofstede, 2001). Thus, social influence, the tendency to consider the opinions of peers or teachers, is likely to have an impact on students' new technology use and may be even stronger in Japanese culture.

All these studies show that national culture is an important factor in explaining technology adoption, and different cultural dimensions have different magnitudes of influence across countries and technology types. They also indicate that there are other factors influencing the technology adoption as shown in the Chinese study (Duan et al., 2010).

Implications for Online Learning

Online learning is often perceived by both learners and teachers as a new and innovative approach and an alternative to traditional face-to-face teacher-dominant instruction. The studies discussed tell us that how learners and teachers perceive online learning plays an important role in the adoption and effective utilization of it. In addition, culture influences those perceptions and thus may delay or advance adoption and utilization of online learning. The following list provides some suggestions derived from studies on technology acceptance that online educators might want to consider introducing into their online learning practice:

- It would be effective to communicate advantages of online learning to the learners in relation to their own learning styles and needs.
- It is important to demonstrate how online learning is compatible with, and how it is not compatible with, the values existing within the learners' culture, as well as with the learners' past experiences.
- Allowing the learners to experience online learning on a trial basis will foster the adoption of online learning, especially in high uncertainty avoidance cultures. This shows the importance of developing orientation programs or modules prior to engaging students in online learning.
- Making the process and result of online learning observable will have a positive impact on the rapid adoption of online learning.
- Learners will more readily accept online learning if they see favorable facilitation conditions such as support, infrastructure, and training related to the adoption of online learning, especially in high uncertainty avoidance cultures.
- Role modeling by teachers in the use of online technology and mentoring, encouragement, and guidance will promote learners' acceptance of online learning.

Although Hofstede's dimensions of national culture have been widely used in studies of technology acceptance, it is important to be aware of some of the limitations of Hofstede's model and think about cultural factors more broadly. Researchers should consider the following:

- Culture does not necessarily fall along national borders, as emphasized by Ford, Connelly, and Meister (2003). It is important for researchers to remember that different cultures exist within nations, within societies, and within family units. In an online context, these factors may be influenced by the dynamics of the cultures that emerge as a result of online interactions.
- Culture changes over time. It is not static. Thus, it is important to identify cultural changes within a nation and across generations when carrying out studies in technology acceptance.
- Culture as represented by quantified cultural dimension indexes may be inadequate in understanding culture in online learning. Other determinants such as personal competencies, technical development, and political influences are closely related to online learning, and there is a need to develop a systematic modeling of these characteristics of online learning using personal, educational, technical, social, economic, and political data, as suggested by Baskerville (2003).

References

Adams, D. A., Nelson, R. R., & Todd, P. A. (1992). Perceived usefulness, ease of use, and usage of information technology: A replication. *MIS Quarterly, 16*(2), 227–247.

Al-Gahtani, S. S., Hubona, G. S., & Wang, J. (2007). Information technology (IT) in Saudi Arabia: Culture and the acceptance and use of IT. *Information and Management, 44*(8), 681–691.

Bagchi, K., Hart, P., & Peterson, M. (2004). National culture and information technology product adoption. *Journal of Global Information Technology Management, 7*(4), 29–46.

Bandura, A. (1986). *Social foundations of thought and action: A social cognitive theory.* Englewood Cliffs, NJ: Prentice Hall.

Baskerville, R. F. (2003). Hofstede never studied culture. *Accounting, Organizations and Society, 28,* 1–14.

Cardon, P. W., & Marshall, B. (2008). National culture and technology acceptance: The impact of uncertainty avoidance. *Issues in Information Systems, IX*(2), 103–110.

Compeau, D. R., Gravill, J., Haggerty, N., & Kelley, H. (2006). Computer self-efficacy: A review. In P. Zhang & D. Galletta (Eds.), *Human-computer interaction in management information systems: Foundations* (pp. 225–261). New York, NY, and London, UK: M.E. Sharpe.

Compeau, D. R., & Higgins, C. A. (1995). Application of social cognitive theory to training for computer skills. *Information Systems Research, 6*(2), 118–143.

Compeau, D. R., Meister, D., & Higgins, C. A. (2007). The perceived characteristics of innovating: A reconsideration. *Journal of the Association for Information Systems, 8*(8), 409–439.

Davis, F. D., Bagozzi, R. P., & Warshaw, P. R. (1989). User acceptance of computer technology: A comparison of two theoretical models. *Management Science, 35*(8), 982–1003.

Duan, Y., He, Q., Feng, W., Li, D., & Fu, Z. (2010). A study on e-learning take-up intention from an innovation adoption perspective: A case in China. *Computers and Education, 55*(1), 237–246.

Ford, D., Connelly, C., & Meister, D. (2003). Information systems research and Hofstede's cultures' consequences: An uneasy and incomplete partnership. *IEEE Transactions on Engineering Management, 50*(1), 8–25.

Hasan, H., & Ditsa, G. (1999). The impact of culture on the adoption of IT: An interpretive study. *Journal of Global Information Management, 7*(1), 5–15.

Hofstede, G. (2001). *Culture's consequences* (2nd ed.). Beverly Hills, CA: Sage.

Im, I., Hong, S., & Kang, M. S. (2011). An international comparison of technology adoption: Testing the UTAUT model. *Information and Management, 48*(1), 1–8.

Jung, I. S., & Lee, Y. K. (2013). YouTube acceptance by university educators and students: A cross-cultural perspective. *Innovation in Education and Training.* Advance online publication. doi:10.1080/14703297.2013.805986

Lee, T. (2004). Nurses' adoption of technology: Application of Rogers' innovation-diffusion model. *Applied Nursing Research, 17*(4), 231–238.

Lee, Y., Kozar, K. A., & Larsen, K. R. T. (2003). The technology acceptance model: Past, present, and future. *Communications of the Association for Information Systems, 12,* 752–780.

Legris, P., Ingham, J., & Collerette, P. (2003). Why do people use information technology? A critical review of the technology acceptance model. *Information and Management, 40*(3), 191–204.

Li, J. P., & Kishore, R. (2006). How robust is the UTAUT instrument? A multigroup invariance analysis in the context of acceptance and use of online community weblog systems. *Proceedings of the 2006 ACM SIGMIS CPR Conference on Computer Personnel Research,* 183–189.

Li, N., & Kirkup, G. (2008). Gender and cultural differences in Internet use: A study of China and the UK. *Computers and Education, 48,* 301–317.

Oshlyansky, L., Cairns, P., & Thimbleby, H. (2007). Validating the unified theory of acceptance and use of technology (UTAUT) tool cross-culturally. *Proceedings of the 21st British HCI Group Annual Conference on People and Computers, 2,* 83–86.

Pai, F. Y., & Huang, K. I. (2011). Applying the Technology Acceptance Model to the introduction of healthcare information systems. *Technological Forecasting and Social Change, 78,* 650–660.

Png, I. P. L., Tan, B. C. Y., & Wee, K. L. (2001). Dimensions of national culture and corporate adoption of IT infrastructure. *IEEE Transactions on Engineering Management, 48*(1), 36–45.

Robey, D., Gupta, S., & Rodriguez-Diaz, A. (1990). Implementing information systems in developing countries: Organizational and cultural considerations. In S. C. Bhatnagar & N. Bjorn-Andersen (Eds.), *Information technology in developing countries* (pp. 41–50). North-Holland: Elsevier Science.

Rogers, E. M. (1983). *Diffusion of innovations* (3rd ed.). New York, NY: Free Press.

Rogers, E. M. (1995). *Diffusion of innovations* (4th ed.). New York, NY: Free Press.

Rogers, E. M. (2003). *Diffusion of innovations* (5th ed.). New York, NY: Free Press.

Selim, H. M. (2003). An empirical investigation of student acceptance of course web sites. *Computers and Education, 40*, 343–360.

Shen, D., Laffey, J., Lin, Y., & Huang, X. (2006). Social influence for perceived usefulness and ease of use of course delivery systems. *Journal of Interactive Online Learning, 5*(3), 270–282.

Singh, S. (2006). Cultural differences in, and influences on, consumers' propensity to adopt innovations. *International Marketing Review, 23*(2), 173–191.

Straub, D. W. (1994). The effect of culture on IT diffusion: E-mail and fax in Japan and the U.S. *Information Systems Research, 5*(1), 23–47.

Sundaravej, T. (2010). *Empirical validation of unified theory of acceptance and use of technology model.* Retrieved from http://wenku.baidu.com/view/f9e3592acfc789eb172dc8e1.html

Taylor, S., & Todd, A. (1995). Understanding information technology usage: A test of competing models. *Information Systems Research, 6*(2), 144–176.

Teo, T., Lee, C. B., Chai, C. S., & Wong, S. L. (2009). Assessing the intention to use technology among pre-service teachers in Singapore and Malaysia: A multigroup invariance analysis of the technology acceptance model (TAM). *Computers and Education, 53*, 1000–1009.

Venkatesh, V., & Davis, F. D. (2000). A theoretical extension of the technology acceptance model: Four longitudinal field studies. *Management Science, 46*, 186–204.

Venkatesh, V., Morris, M. G., Davis, G. B., & Davis, F. D. (2003). User acceptance of information technology: Toward a unified view. *MIS Quarterly, 27*(3), 425–478.

4

ONLINE IDENTITY AND INTERACTION

Charlotte Nirmalani Gunawardena

The increasing interest in developing online learning communities and communities of practice has generated the exploration into issues of identity that impact online communication. "As we engage in communities of discourse and practice, our knowledge and beliefs are influenced by those communities. So is our identity formation, which is also a major outcome of learning" (Jonassen & Land, 2012, p. x).

Shuter (2012) observed that cultural identity, according to social identity theory, is derived from membership in social groups, the self in relation to others, and a social identity that is based on group contact fixed in space and time, producing "discernable social identity(ies) that varies in salience depending on the social context(s)" (p. 221). However, he noted that in this age where people live in virtual spaces with myriad others, this perspective may not be relevant and sufficient for explaining the development and maintenance of cultural identity. Shuter offered three areas for consideration when studying twenty-first-century identity theory that go beyond past cultural identity theory studied in face-to-face communities: (a) How are cultural identities constructed in virtual communities? (b) How are hybrid cultural identities created in virtual and face-to-face communities? (c) Compared with face-to-face communities, what are the differences in the dynamics of maintaining cultural identity in virtual communities?

This chapter aims to develop our understanding of Shuter's first question, that of identity creation and negotiation in virtual interaction, by reporting on a study the author conducted to examine the sociocultural processes of synchronous online communication from the perspective of two different cultural contexts: Morocco and Sri Lanka. To better understand the sociocultural processes that play a role in identity formation in online interactions, we need to examine the informal use of the medium in different cultural contexts. Determining how identity is negotiated in informal Internet interactions enables us to infer how various individuals will adapt their communication styles to more formal computer-mediated, text-oriented communication.

The study discussed in this chapter asked the following question: What happens when individuals whose self-images are characterized by a sense of group identity (mainly in face-to-face contexts) based on factors such as nationality, ethnicity, religion, gender, language, and socioeconomic status use the culturally heterogeneous and technically ephemeral forums of the Internet to pursue personal communication goals? It was undertaken with the intention of understanding the sociocultural environment of an online community based on factors that emerged from the communication processes employed by Internet chat users in Morocco and Sri Lanka. Such a framework would enable us to suggest implications for online interaction and community formation in more formal academic settings. The study discussed in this chapter was conducted collaboratively with colleagues in Morocco and Sri Lanka. An initial analysis of the data can be found in Gunawardena, Idrissi Alami, Jayatilleke, and Bouachrine (2009). This book chapter draws on a modified analysis of the data, focusing on identity and interaction.[1]

Design of the Study

The study adopted a qualitative ethnographic perspective when conducting interviews with participants and examining their communication processes in synchronous chat. Grounded theory building (Strauss & Corbin, 1998) was used to develop a conceptual framework for understanding expression of identity and the role it played in online interactions. This collaborative design involved four researchers who offered an interdisciplinary perspective and understood the cultural contexts studied. Interview questions were translated into Moroccan Arabic, French, Sinhala, and Tamil. Interviews were conducted in these languages and English.

Individual and focus group interviews were conducted in Internet cafés and university computer labs in four different locations in the Middle Atlas region of Morocco between September 2004 and January 2005 and in small and large towns in the western, southern, and eastern parts of Sri Lanka from February 2005 to July 2005. This study focused primarily on participants who used chat forums to engage in conversation and build relationships with people they did not know. Data were gathered from 55 adults in Morocco, which included 36 males and 19 females, and from 50 adults in Sri Lanka, which included 33 males and 17 females. At these given points in time, Internet adoption in these two countries was in its early stages.

Morocco and Sri Lanka exemplify two very different cultural contexts. Morocco is an Arab, Berber, Muslim, and Mediterranean African country, more recently colonized by the French, speaking standard Arabic, Moroccan Arabic, Berber, and French. Sri Lanka is a Sinhalese, Tamil, and Muslim country, which is predominantly Buddhist and more recently colonized by the English, speaking Sinhala, Tamil, and English. Both countries are similar in that they have diverse minority groups with different languages and religions represented in the population. In both these countries, fewer women frequented Internet cafés, reflecting social taboos. In Morocco, cafés were the domain of men, which applies to Internet cafés as well. In Galle, a midsize, fairly conservative town in Sri Lanka, only 1 in 10 users were women.

Definition of *Culture*

Although Sri Lankan and Moroccan societies would be classified in Hofstede's (1980) framework as high power distance societies, participants from these countries look to the online medium as a liberating environment that equalizes status differences, thereby providing them with a level playing field. Therefore, their interactions online would not necessarily reflect high power distance communication. Graiouid (2005) took this point further by stating that Internet chat and discussions are dismantling the traditional power structures in Morocco by allowing previously disenfranchised groups to publicize their concerns. The use of social media during the more recent "Arab Spring Movement" exemplifies this phenomenon.

Very often, those who communicate online identify with multiple frames of reference. Ess and Sudweeks (2005) noted that Hofstede's (1980) framework and to a lesser extent Hall's (1976) conceptualization of culture appear to be limited to national cultural differences and thus less well suited for understanding and researching multiple cultural differences within nation-states, including the "third" or hybrid identities that are themselves fostered by the cultural flows facilitated by the Internet and the web.

However, for our study, we found Hall's (1976) conceptualization of high-context (direct) and low-context (indirect) communication styles useful for analyzing cultural differences in communication online. Both Morocco and Sri Lanka are described as high-context cultures (Hall, 1976). In both Moroccan and Sri Lankan cultures, context is important in understanding messages and their connotations. Many Moroccans and Sri Lankans adopt an indirect communication style in face-to-face interactions.

Coming to terms with the complexity of online culture meant that we had to define it in its own right. Therefore, we adopted the definition of *idioculture* developed by Fine (1979) and discussed in chapter 1 as our definition of *online culture*. This definition includes multiple cultural selves and hybrid identities on the Internet that interact with each other cross-culturally to form unique cultures online.

Emerging Themes and Conceptual Framework

Expression and formation of identity online emerged as a major theme when we examined the sociocultural processes that shaped informal online interactions in Morocco and Sri Lanka. Associated with this major theme were three subthemes: trust building, self-disclosure, and face negotiation. Gender differences were observed in the expression of identity in these subthemes. The following sections discuss these themes in detail. The results of our analyses indicated that men and women employ and value different communication styles when chatting. The online environment gives them the anonymity and freedom to act out gender roles and experiment with gender identity.

Identity Online

In chat sessions, communicators express identity by disclosing their age, sex, and location. Depending on the context, chatters either reveal their true identity, create a different identity, or blend or communicate their identity using a pseudonym (referred to as an ID) that expresses their true or imagined character. The chatter uses this information to create an image about his or her interlocutor. Ahmed stated that the revelation of his identity depends on the first question. If he feels the chatter is truthful, he would give his real name. It appears that of the three elements of identity expression, age and sex are more important than location. Hamid gives his real age and sex: "If the other person is not interested in your location, you do not tell." Giving the location can sometimes hinder access to chatters. Lal, a Sri Lankan male, noted that although he wanted to chat with Western females, they would not respond; only women from the Philippines did.

Cultural and social stereotyping occurs through names, nicknames, and pseudonyms. Mohammed used to have an ID "Mohammed" but decided to change it because when he entered American and British chat rooms, he was accused of terrorism and was verbally assaulted. He feels his new ID "Green Python" is attractive enough to gain access to people. Other IDs used by female participants included "Scarlet," "Diva," and "Tzay." Sarath, a Sri Lankan male, noted that to appeal to different audiences, he changes his identity. As in the example of "Mohammed," disclosing real names that are strongly associated with a religious, racial, or ethnic group could hinder communication online, whereas a nickname can enable a chatter to stay in an online relationship. Joinson (2003) observed that constructing identity through text provides opportunity for people to craft an identity that exists quite apart from the usual pressures of real life and impression management.

In both countries, chatting is perceived as playful activity, a form of entertainment, a therapeutic agent, and a game that does not require the disclosure of true identity from the beginning. It is also perceived as an addiction, as many individuals were described as "chat addicts." Graiouid (2005) showed that for some Moroccan study participants, chat had become an essential part of life, and like morning coffee a chat session was necessary to start the day. On the other hand, asynchronous discussion forums, on a topic of interest, are regarded as more serious because they represent an arena for debating ideas and defending opinions. Therefore, respondents would feel more comfortable divulging their true credentials in such forums. The participants made a clear distinction between identity expression in anonymous chat and identity expression in a more serious forum discussion.

The sociocultural context influences online communication, which in turn is influenced by the virtual culture that develops online. "Whereas the Western concept of 'self' is based on the individual, the Moroccan concept of self is based on the Islamic notion of *jamaçah* 'community/group' and is, thus inherently plural" (Sadiqi, 2003, p. 65). One aspect of the collective self is the difficulty that Moroccans have in talking about themselves in public, as it is generally considered as a "lack of modesty" (p. 67). Sadiqi noted that the language of introductions reveals many aspects of a Moroccan's self. Introductions involve interplay of cultural, social, situational, and identity variables, which range from gender, local geographical origin, class, setting, participants, age, and self-interest. In Sri Lanka, the major forms of social identity are Sinhala, Tamil, and Muslim, and in addition there are hybrid identities signaling a mix of these three, even though there are other forms of identity meaningful to people such as caste, region, and religion (Silva, 2004). Given the two sociocultural contexts, it was interesting to observe the freedom with which many participants played with their identity online.

Identity and Gender

Sadiqi (2003) pointed out the dichotomy between public space and private space in Morocco. Public spaces (the streets and the marketplace) are the domain of men, whereas women are expected to remain in private spaces (the home). In general, although women have access to public spaces, stepping out into the street is still considered by many as an act of trespassing, into a hostile male domain. Sadiqi further elaborated that Moroccan culture strongly constrains the behavior of men and women and listed eight influences on gender perception, gender subversion, and language use: history, geography, Islam, orality, multilingualism, social organization, economic status, and political system. Given this sociocultural context, Internet communication provides tremendous opportunities to create virtual identities that can breach the dichotomy of public and private space that exists in Moroccan society. Graiouid (2005) noted that this might explain why female chatters enjoy the anonymity of the Internet, which allows them to build relationships without compromising themselves.

As reflected in the following perspectives from Moroccan participants, gender stereotypes prevail in the creation of identity. Jamal admitted that it is easy to disguise himself as a woman. In posing as a woman, he talks about women's topics such as dress and fashion. Hamid thinks that women rarely discuss social issues. They are mostly interested in personal experiences and love affairs. When asked about how he can tell if a man is posing as a woman, he said that exaggeration is what gives away a man posing as a woman. Hassan thinks that women tend to discuss their daily schedules and errands more than men do. He thinks that chat is like a game that could turn into a healthy relationship or end quickly.

Analysis of interviews from Sri Lanka also indicated gender differences in the expression of identity. Generally males disclose their true identity (age, sex, location) from the start, irrespective of the purpose and type of the communication (chat or academic forums). A 23-year-old male student observed,

> I'll tell that I am a webmaster from Sri Lanka and this is my website. I also tell my age and gender. Usually when males get to know that I am a male, they won't continue. But if someone is interested in my research area then they will continue. Usually chatting among males is less. But females prefer to chat with females.

Sri Lankan females were much more cautious than males and did not reveal their true identity in unknown communities. They either give their first name or use a pseudonym and do not reveal much personal information. They tend to talk more about their personal lives once they have established the relationship. On the other hand, if women are chatting to get academic help, then they usually reveal their true identity. Women in both Morocco and Sri Lanka were more cautious than men in revealing their identity online for fear of being harassed. This seems to be a cultural feature of online communication that transcends nationality. Harassment online is a serious concern not only for women but also for children.

A majority of Sri Lankan females prefer to communicate only with females. They are reluctant to talk with male counterparts unless they have been introduced by one of their friends or relations, reflecting social norms and practices. Most of them chat with local and Asian communities, as they feel more secure in these circles.

Gender differences emerge when chatters establish social presence. Many feel that they need to choose adequate and suitable topics when communicating their presence to someone of the opposite sex. Tone is also important. Male participants claim that they do not talk in the same way to males and females. With females they are more cautious and more flattering. As to communicating with females, most respondents suggest that they depend on establishing social presence by asking about tastes in music, movies, reading, sports, and dress styles. They feel that women tend to communicate their presence through description of their daily lives and their personal problems. When males chat with other males, subjects of discussion tend to be about political, social, and abstract problems.

Therefore, the expression of identity online showed the interplay of real and imagined identities and gender differences in the projection of identity based on the context of the communication.

Trust Building

Identity is closely linked to building trust. Many chatters will not reveal their true identity until they feel they can trust the other person. From the initial encounter, chatters spend their time trying to determine the trustworthiness of others. The most common trust-building technique is to ask a series of questions in the initial online contact and ask the same questions again later to determine the consistency or inconsistency in the answers. Many mentioned time as an important factor for building trust.

If in the same country, some chatters will give out their mobile phone numbers in order to verify the trustworthiness of the other. Most respondents prefer e-mail when the online relationship grows stronger over time. They feel that e-mail communication is more serious and honest than chat. Another advantage of e-mail is that there is less time pressure to answer immediately. The speed at which chatters type affects the flow of communication and possibly the chatter's level of interest and trust. The use of mobile phones and e-mail is significant because it suggests the ways in which chatters view the development of cyber relationships and how they "hierarchize" the methods of communication: chatting: low risk and easy to dismiss; e-mail: more personal and involving larger risk; mobile phones: higher risk and requiring a degree of trust.

Self-Disclosure

Self-disclosure is associated with trust building and the expression of identity. Many participants indicated that the trustworthiness of others is expressed through their disclosure of their private life. They insist that the disclosure of personal experiences and intimate problems allows people to get to know each other better and strengthens the relationship. Anonymity increases participants' ability to self-disclose. Joinson (2003) confirmed this by showing how visually anonymous computer-mediated communication (CMC) leads to higher levels of self-disclosure. Where there is an unequal distribution of power in society, such as in Sri Lanka and Morocco, anonymous online communication equalizes participants. Respondents felt that talking online can break barriers of communication between people of different classes, professions, and sexes. On the other hand, anonymity also encourages relationships that are superficial. A male participant noted that it is not necessary to reveal the truth, because he does not have any intention of continuing the friendship. When trust is established, participants are more likely to reveal their true identity.

Self-Disclosure and Gender

Generally, both females and males have reservations about revealing their personal details to an unknown person or group. Both do not reveal their personal information until they build up the relationship. Relationship building takes time and several messages. Much of the relationship-building process is based on intuitions, as it often relates to the "feelings" participants get from reading others' messages and the extent to which they "feel" the others or their "social presence" in mediated communication.

Some males do not hesitate to place their own photograph on the web. One particular male uses different font sizes and colors to make it more attractive: "I use a webcam and give a profile with the picture. I usually use 14–16 font with shaded colors." Females hardly ever send their photographs. But some who are familiar with computers use different fonts, colors, and emoticons (smileys) when they send messages: "I use emoticons. Those are quick. Use font[s] like Comic Sans for friends and Arial and [Century] Gothic with official group[s]. Use short cuts like Y, U, etc. Different techniques for different people." Chat users have developed various conventions to present their identity and persona in chat sessions and will reveal their true identity depending on the context.

Face Negotiation

Face is an identity phenomenon. Ting-Toomey (1994) defined *face* as "the presentation of a civilized front to another individual within the webs of interconnected relationships in a particular culture" (p. 1). In this study, *face negotiation* is defined as the individual's intentions to portray his or her self-image in a positive manner to others by utilizing verbal, nonverbal, and self-representation methods to support his or her conception of face.

In online chat sessions, the nature of the relationship determines reactions to insults and the negotiation of face. Chatters will close the window if the relationship is weak, and they will employ a variety of techniques to resolve misunderstandings and negotiate face if the relationship is strong. A 35-year-old Sri Lankan male respondent observed, "It depends on the friendship. . . . If the friendship is deep then you feel that the person is next to you. In that instance you would like to continue the friendship."

Generally, if respondents feel insulted, they first seek an explanation. Then they decide on other courses of action, such as shutting down the communication, ignoring the person, insulting back, or asking for an apology. An apology is requested if the person or the relationship is valued. Participants will resort to e-mail to clarify the situation, settle misunderstandings, and present apologies. E-mail is preferable if the relationship has been going on for a long time and if the insulted person thinks that it is not intentional but a result of a misunderstanding.

In Morocco and Sri Lanka, face-to-face communication patterns are more high context and less direct than they are in the United States. Generally, it is difficult to communicate context in an online medium. In Morocco, for example, there are many taboos and behaviors that imply *hchouma* or "shame" and should be avoided during communication. Many questions do not get answered because chatters cannot be very direct and tell them to the face of the other. This opens up room for interpretation and sometimes miscommunications. Sadiqi (2003) observed that the concept of collective self is so rooted into the Moroccan psyche that an individual's self-image is not cultivated internally but rather derived from others' opinions and attitudes, which is manifested clearly in the concept of *hchouma*, which may be defined as the "fear of losing face in front of others" (p. 67). This explains the heavy pressure within Moroccan families to protect all its members, because bad behavior from one member affects the reputation of all. To avoid shame, Moroccans may refrain from admitting blatant realities in public if it involves the risk of losing face.

According to Ting-Toomey (1988), low-context cultures emphasize individual identity, self-face concern, and direct verbal and nonverbal expression. In contrast, high-context cultures emphasize group identity, other-face concerns, and indirect verbal and nonverbal expressions. However, when people are online, whether they are from a high-context or low-context culture is not critical, as anonymity is a factor in the attempt to negotiate face. The elimination of title, gender, and other status cues can create a more neutral atmosphere. If a stranger threatens the concept of face, he or she will be ignored. Therefore, attempts to negotiate face depend on the strength of the relationship that has been built. Face-saving strategies are adopted when there is a bond and when there is an interest in maintaining the relationship. If this is not the case, in the real-time world of chat, the general tendency is to close the window and forget the person.

Gender and Face Negotiation

Both female and male respondents in our study noted that they take extra care to resolve their online misunderstandings and negotiate face if the relationship is strong. If they fail online, they will telephone and explain the situation. Females are more likely to negotiate even when the relationship is not that strong. Usually males chat for entertainment and do not expect long-lasting relationships online. Therefore, when there is a misinterpretation, they do not make an extra attempt to resolve the conflict. On the other hand, females take the extra initiative to resolve the misunderstanding. Davidson and Schofield (2002) supported this finding by showing that women are more relational than men in virtual interactions. They highlighted that women are more likely to approach the world as an individual within a social network, more likely to acquire skills in developing and sustaining personal connections, and more likely to seek out situations and develop behaviors that foster relationships.

Implications for Designing the Social Environment for Online Learning Communities

From these findings of informal synchronous communication in the early days of Internet adoption in two different cultural contexts, we can draw implications for designing the social environment in transnational online learning. Results showed that CMC is not a mere neutral technological innovation. Rather, it is a practice affected by the culture and society of its users. Expression and formation of one's online identity emerged as a major theme when we examined the sociocultural processes that influence informal online interactions in Morocco and Sri Lanka. Associated with this major theme were three subthemes: trust building, self-disclosure, and face negotiation. Gender differences were observed in the expression of identity. Given the unique online cultures developed by interacting groups, and the themes that emerged, we draw the following implications for designing the social environment to foster online learning communities:

- Participants learn about themselves by creating and playing with their online identity. This is a psychological tool that helps individuals to experience the real world in a new way. The ability to change one's environment and try out different ways of being lends itself well to role-play activities and computer simulations as learning strategies in online learning environments.
- The expression of self-identity through introductions is important for building relationships and generating social presence in online learning communities. However, because self-disclosing and posting photographs may not be easy for some participants, protocols should be provided for how introductions should be done, allowing for some degree of anonymity. Alternative techniques include having participants introduce each other online or post an image that represents them, along with an explanation of why the image represents them.
- Building trust and relationships is crucial for the health and well-being of an online learning community. Pre-course activities or an orientation can help participants build trust and become more comfortable interacting with each other.
- Attempts to negotiate face and resolve conflict depend on the strength of the relationship that has been built. Therefore, face-saving strategies should be part of the communication protocols developed for online learning communities. Women are more likely to make an attempt to resolve misunderstandings and negotiate face and should be encouraged to take up facilitating roles in team interactions.
- Netiquette (a communication protocol) that is both culture and gender sensitive should be developed for online learning communities. This protocol must clearly define what is expected in academic discussions, versus in informal chat or virtual spaces such as a cybercafé, and delineate what tools or medium to use for different communication functions.
- Online designs should allow for an element of multilingual communication and diversity in the expression of English, which will promote cross-cultural understanding and increase comfort levels.
- The distinction between public space and private space in Morocco highlights the extent to which cultural context is an important factor in understanding messages. Therefore, participants should be encouraged to provide context for their messages, enabling others to easily decipher them.
- Moderators or facilitators should play an active role in the relationship-building process. Frequent online presence and one's ability to nurture a healthy and productive online community can maintain a safe and conducive environment for all participants. Where there is unequal power distribution in a society such as in Sri Lanka and Morocco, online communication equalizes participants. Moderators should pay attention to power dynamics among participants and try to maintain an equitable learning environment that encourages everyone to participate and contribute.

- In many developing countries, the Internet café may be the only resource center where learners can gather to participate in online learning. Academic institutions wishing to provide access to learners in geographically isolated locations should make arrangements with Internet cafés to provide access to technology and resources necessary for their academic programs.

These implications provide guidelines for the development of conducive social environments to support online learning. Issues of identity, gender, and language will continue to provide impetus for further research in our efforts to understand the cultures that develop in virtual environments. The data reported in this study were collected in the early days of Internet diffusion. It would be worthwhile to engage in studies to determine how communication patterns have changed with the advent of social networking sites and the impact of this change on the creation of online identity and virtual cultures.

Author's Note

[1] This research study was supported by a Fulbright Regional Research Scholarship award by the U.S. Department of State, 2004–2005. Special thanks go to Ahmed Idrissi Alami, Gayathri Jayatilleke, and Fadwa Bouachrine-Brady for participation in the initial data collection and analysis.

References

Davidson, A. L., & Schofield, J. W. (2002). Female voices in virtual reality: Drawing young girls into an online world. In K. A. Renninger & W. Shumar (Eds.), *Building virtual communities: Learning and change in cyberspace* (pp. 34–59). Cambridge, UK: Cambridge University Press.

Ess, C., & Sudweeks, F. (2005). Culture and computer-mediated communication: Toward new understandings. *Journal of Computer-Mediated Communication, 11*(1), 179–191. doi:10.1111/j.1083-6101.2006.tb00309.x

Fine, G. A. (1979). Small groups and culture creation: The idioculture of little league baseball teams. *American Sociological Review, 44*(5), 733–745.

Graiouid, S. (2005). Social exile and virtual *H'rig*: Computer-mediated interaction and cybercafé culture in Morocco. In M. Wiberg (Ed.), *The interaction society: Practice, theories, and supportive technologies* (pp. 57–92). Hershey, PA: Idea Group.

Gunawardena, C. N., Idrissi Alami, A., Jayatilleke, G., & Bouachrine, F. (2009). Identity, gender, and language in synchronous cybercultures: A cross-cultural study. In R. Goodfellow & M. N. Lamy (Eds.), *Learning cultures in online education* (pp. 30–51). London, UK: Continuum.

Hall, E. T. (1976). *Beyond culture*. Garden City, NY: Anchor Books.

Hofstede, G. (1980). *Culture's consequences: International differences in work-related values*. Newbury Park, CA: Sage.

Joinson, A. N. (2003). *Understanding the psychology of Internet behavior: Virtual worlds, real lives*. Hampshire, UK: Palgrave Macmillan.

Jonassen, D., & Land, S. (Eds.). (2012). *Theoretical foundations of learning environments* (2nd ed.). New York, NY: Routledge.

Sadiqi, F. (2003). *Women, gender and language in Morocco* (Vol. 1 of *Women and gender, the Middle East and the Islamic World*). Leiden, the Netherlands: Brill.

Shuter, R. (2012). Intercultural new media studies: The next frontier in intercultural communication. *Journal of Intercultural Communication Research*, *41*(3), 219–237. Retrieved from http://dx.doi.org/10.1080/17475759.2012.728761

Silva, N. (2004). Introduction: The hybrid island. In N. Silva (Ed.), *The hybrid island: Culture crossings and the invention of identity in Sri Lanka* (pp. i–vii). Colombo, Sri Lanka: Social Scientists' Association.

Strauss, A., & Corbin, J. (1998). *Basics of qualitative research: Techniques and procedures for developing grounded theory* (2nd ed.). Thousand Oaks, CA: Sage.

Ting-Toomey, S. (1988). Intercultural conflict style: A face-negotiation theory. In Y. Y. Kim & W. B. Gudykunst (Eds.), *Theories in intercultural communication* (pp. 213–235). Newbury Park, CA: Sage.

Ting-Toomey, S. (1994). Face and facework: An introduction. In S. Ting-Toomey (Ed.), *The challenge of facework: Cross-cultural and interpersonal issues* (pp. 1–14). Albany: State University NY Press.

5

EMERGING VISUAL CULTURE IN ONLINE LEARNING ENVIRONMENTS

Ilju Rha

Visual culture begins with human creativity and intention to communicate visually, but in the end it requires a complementary relationship with technology that allows such visual expression. Take, for example, paper and pen, which is an early form of technology. The invention of paper and pen allowed us to express, document, and inherit certain visual forms such as letters and still images, and from it, a new culture emerged. Technology invented by human creativity triggered more creative ideas in human beings and, in turn, brought further development of new technologies and further changes in our culture. The development of television and motion picture technologies brought a new visual culture different from that created by paper and pen, allowing us to use moving images. New technologies afford us the chance to diversify our expression methods. These technology-driven changes in visual culture have been observed in many parts of our society, including education.

Although *culture* can be defined in many ways, it is often defined as both the process of meaning-making (Spillman, 2002) and the learned ideas and behaviors that result from such a process (Hofstede, 1991). Applying these concepts of culture, we can view visual culture as the process of making meanings of visual objects and the resulting values and behavioral patterns. This definition of *visual culture* is based on the premise that a visual object does not have physical properties that can be objectively seen through the eyes of its viewers. It is instead understood and interpreted by individual viewers through *visuality*, a concept referring to the cultural ways of "seeing, being able to see, being allowed or made to see, and even seeing the unseen" (Foster, 1988, p. ix).

Online learners come across a variety of visual objects through different devices and deal with these visual objects either consciously or unconsciously. They also perform such activities as visiting websites, texting, taking photos or videos with a smart phone or a tablet PC, playing online games, and watching YouTube videos on a variety of occasions. Instructors also perform similar activities for their own purposes. It is from these very natural, ordinary activities of learners and instructors that visual culture in the online learning environment emerges.

This chapter will discuss the online visual culture that has emerged most recently in the context of online learning. It will first overview the techno-social background of the development of online visual culture. It will then look into the online visual culture that has been observed in online learning environments and, finally, conclude with a set of implications for the emerging visual culture of online learning.

Techno-Social Background of Online Visual Culture

As a new form of visual culture, online visual culture has emerged with the development and daily use of digital technologies. Let us examine some key techno-social factors that have influenced the emergence of recent online visual culture.

Development and Widespread Use of Digital Technologies

As we have defined *online visual culture* as the meaning-making process of visual objects that are presented online or on digital devices and its resulting ideas and behavioral patterns, digital technologies have become an essential basis for online visual culture. Digital technologies that are particularly important in creating online visual culture are information and communications technologies (ICTs) and display technologies. ICTs have made it possible to develop, process, and exchange an enormous amount of data in a short period of time. Computer technologies offer readily available functions for us to create, transform, and store visual and moving images without acquiring sophisticated production skills. Also, with the currently available optical and wireless communications technologies, we can easily transfer high-resolution images and movies in just a few seconds.

Along with ICTs, display technologies also serve the development of online visual culture, as they present visual objects that are created by means of ICTs on a screen. These technologies include not only large screens like HDTVs and computer screens but also medium-sized screens on tablets (e.g., iPad, Nexus) and small-sized screens on smart phones (e.g., iPhone, Galaxy). High-resolution and high-definition images and videos displayed on any of these screens are visual objects, evoking certain interpretations and meanings that are different from those elicited from other types of visual objects.

Mobile devices serve as a good example in that they are now often used in our daily lives more than other technologies. Smart phones and tablet PCs integrate the functions of digital cameras and networking technologies, enable us to create photos and videos and add text messages, and distribute them not only to friends but also to the public via sharing sites or social networking sites. People are constantly creating, re-creating, and sharing visual objects and being exposed to various types of visual objects developed and constructed by others via digital technologies. Such widespread use of these technologies is changing our visual culture. We will see another type of visual culture revealed once recent digital technologies such as ubiquitous, 3D, and flexible display devices become more prevalent in our society.

Growing Technology Affordances

Using the definition of *affordance* as proposed by Gibson (1979) and Gaver (1991), we can define *technology affordances* as properties of technologies that are compatible with and pertinent to people's interactions and communications. Affordances offered by tools and technologies allow users to take some kind of action. Today's digital technologies offer affordances that have not been possible with old media and technologies, and these are closely related to online visualizations. For example, digital cameras generate a picture or a movie clip in an instant. With an editing program such as Photoshop or Maya, one can easily create a high-quality 2D or 3D image. The created images can also be easily modified according to the needs of the users and are displayed in a variety of ways on monitors of varying sizes. Moreover, text messages in various fonts, sizes, colors, and motions can be added to those images. Another example can be found in the affordances provided by display technologies, allowing various multimedia to be displayed on one page concurrently while multiple windows remain open in a cascade format on one screen. These affordances or opportunities provided by digital technologies are leading us to process tasks more visually, flexibly, and interactively.

Another example of new technological affordance can be found in the use of mobile networking devices. An increase in mobile interactions is causing an unexpected cultural phenomenon in human communication. Using mobile phones, people communicate with each other not just via voice but also through text messages, images, videos, or any mixture of these symbols. As visual communication via mobile phones becomes common, a unique visual culture is emerging that uses literacy and orality interchangeably to produce various visual representations while people are on the move. Mobile phone users adapt to a small screen and keyboard-based mobile communication environment and develop certain ways of delivering their messages and expressing emotions using abbreviations (e.g., lol: "laugh out loud," yolo: "you only live once"), hieroglyphics (e.g., xoxo: "hug kiss hug kiss," T_T: "tears," :-): "smiling eyes"), emoticons, and special characters, which are unique visual representations and difficult to classify as either text or image. These changes in communication are happening universally as a result of technological advances provided by mobile phones. They are more visual than ever.

Online Visual Culture

Online visual culture has a functional relationship with affordances provided by digital technologies and with ways in which these affordances are manifested by human beings in visual formats. As previously discussed, digital technologies provide technological affordances and infrastructure for the creation, processing, transformation, storage, and distribution of data. Human beings utilize affordances provided in this technology-rich environment in ways that are personally meaningful and socially acceptable to them. During this process, certain beliefs and behavioral patterns are formed, and a new culture emerges.

As one can easily imagine, online visual culture is not a global phenomenon, as access to digital technologies is at varying stages of access and development in different parts of the world. Yet, in considering the rapid adoption of technologies around the globe, it will be only a matter of time before online visual culture emerges, even in the least developed areas.

Chapter 1 of this book points out the difficulties of defining *culture* in just a few words, and the same applies to *online visual culture*. Thus, in this section of the chapter, instead of defining *online visual culture* in just a few sentences, we will try to discuss major manifestations within this visual culture, which are thought to be important for online learning.

Participatory Culture

Online visual culture is a participatory culture where both learners and teachers can actively participate in both the consumption of and the creation of visual data. There has never been a time in our history like today when so many visual objects are being produced and shared among so many people and in such a short period of time. Considering that until recently only a handful of people with special talent (such as artists) or people with authority (such as teachers) were able to produce visuals, this trend is certainly a revolutionary change. It is revolutionary in the sense that virtually anyone can participate in the creation of visuals on a massive scale and repurpose or alter already existing visuals for their own purposes. In an online learning environment, the distinction between the provider and the consumer of visual objects is blurring, and teachers are not the only group who produce and provide visual objects for learning.

Learners encounter numerous images and videos on YouTube, Flickr, Facebook, and other similar websites and use them for their learning. They also produce and share such visuals. About 3,000 pictures every second, or 250 million pictures every day, are uploaded to Facebook. On YouTube alone, 900,000 hours of video are uploaded daily as of 2012. Many of these visuals are used in various educational contexts. A recent study conducted with American and Japanese faculty and university students (Jung, Ho, & Suzuki, 2013) reported that American faculty used YouTube to search educational content (65%), movies and TV shows (46%), and music videos (31%) for their teaching and to upload their own lectures (35%), whereas Japanese faculty used YouTube mainly to decide on educational content (53%) and movies and TV shows (37%) for teaching. A great number of American students used YouTube to watch educational content (71%) and music videos (61%), whereas fewer Japanese students were using YouTube for educational content (12%). The American students were more active in uploading their own video clips to YouTube (31%) and adding their own video clips to their blogs or websites (32%), whereas only about 4% of Japanese students engaged in such activities. Although this study reveals some cultural differences in YouTube use and its creation, it clearly shows a noticeable trend in participatory online visual culture where both learners and teachers act as producers and consumers of visual data.

Diversified Forms of Visual Objects

Online visual culture promotes the development of diversified forms of visual objects. As digital technologies make it possible to create visual representations of both physical objects and invisible phenomena, various types and formats of visual resources are available to online teachers and learners. Visual resources include photos of real objects, graphs showing logical relationships of numeric values or data sets, moving texts, diagrams, 3D movies, and more. Although some of these visuals can be presented in print, other visuals that require multiple steps of technical transformation and visual expressions of their dynamic processes are possible only in computing environments. Visuals presented in print can be easily elaborated on and reconstructed with the help of digital devices.

Figure 5.1 A mind map drawn by the chapter author using a visualization tool.

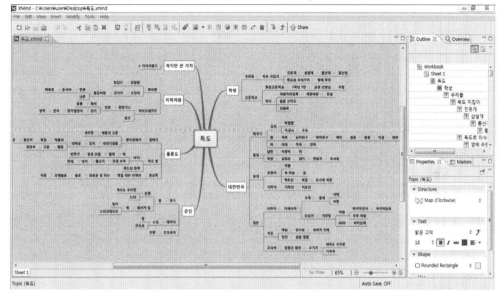

Note. Interface: XMind (Version 3.3.1) [Computer software]. Hong Kong: XMind, Ltd.

Take the example of a mind map, a diagram used to visually outline and organize information, ideas, or concepts. Using visualization tools currently available online (e.g., free and easy mind-mapping tools such as MindMeister and XMind; commercial tools such as Mindjet MindManager and iMindMap), learners are able to draw different formats of a mind map from the same set of information, work as a team to create a mind map together, expand and collapse concept branches, and explore mind maps in other formats such as PDFs, JPEGs, and text outlines. Figure 5.1 illustrates one example of a mind map created by a visualization tool. This kind of data visualization technology is particularly effective for online learning, as it can represent relationships among sets of data visually, displaying differences in information in different colors or shapes, outlining complicated information in a graphic format, presenting invisible scenes or phenomena visually, and/or supporting collaborative creations of visual objects.

Emergence of New Visual Expressions Blending Orality and Literacy

Online visual culture promotes new ways of visual expressions that blend spoken and written languages or orality and literacy in communication. On one hand, spoken languages have oral properties that express ideas and thoughts of a speaker to communicate with a listener using sound. Written language, on the other hand, has literal properties to share information and knowledge. Because people often use spoken language in face-to-face conversation, they often accompany it with nonverbal behaviors so they can communicate more effectively. When spoken language is used, gestures, facial expressions, tone, and other nonverbal elements become part of the communication process. Thus, a spoken language's repetitive, illogical, or uncertain parts can be compensated for by other nonverbal elements. Written language, however, is often used by itself, without the support of such nonverbal elements, and so it must remain logical and concise in order for people to communicate successfully.

Figure 5.2 Examples of emoticons used among Korean youth. (Top row: smile, worrying, no comment, huh!; middle row: wink, arrogance, crying, angry; bottom row: ridiculous, tired, crown, uncomfortable.) Created by Yoomi Cho and used with her permission.

Modern digital technologies make it possible to combine both spoken and written languages, or orality and literacy. In writing e-mail or short messages using a mobile phone, learners frequently insert special characters or emoticons to express emotions or to highlight certain points. They also tend to use shortened expressions rather than complete sentences. As Thurlow and Brown (2003) argued, on the basis of the point made by cultural critic Umberto Eco, our learners are "Generation Txt," are tied to their mobile, and value "the diminutive, the brief and the simple in communication."

The frequent mixture of spoken and written languages has stimulated the development of new emoticons (see figure 5.2), characters, abbreviations, and pictograms that are now evident in online texting, and as a result of this phenomenon, new linguistic practices are becoming visible in an online environment. A student might send a message to another student with the following pictogram, phonogram, and abbreviations: "hahaha.. hi y'all. ^-^ thnx for sendin the file *-) xoxo."

Text as Visual Object

Online visual culture views texts as an integral part of visual representations. Text has been the core medium of communication in traditional printing culture. Text is repositioned as visual objects in online visual culture. That is, with the affordances offered by digital technologies, text is now becoming a visual object that expresses our thoughts and emotions in a variety of ways. When text is presented on a piece of paper, it usually has content to be read and interpreted in a rather objective manner. Of course, even in printed products such as books and newspapers, numerous visual displays of text messages are possible, including spacing, visual grouping, different typefaces, italics, bold, capitalizations, and underlines. But those changes are restricted within pieces of paper that allow for only the static arrangement of the characters.

When text is displayed on a screen or online, it becomes a visual object presenting not only content but also its creator's mind and emotions, which induces a reader's subjective interpretation. As online text can be displayed in various visual ways using different fonts, sizes, shades, colors, and other effects in a dynamic fashion (e.g., hypertext or text movement) in conjunction with other types of visuals, the messages or contents will be interpreted differently by various readers depending on how they are arranged, linked, and visualized. A poem displayed in boldface gothic letters may not evoke the same feeling as the same poem displayed in neat handwriting-style letters.

Online visual culture views text as something that can be altered and adjusted by its readers. For instance, with e-books or digital textbooks, readers can change font sizes and styles, line spacing, page margins, and page breaks, and thus book page numbers. Readers can add underlines and highlight some parts interesting or important to them. This is not the case with printed books.

Although there have been several studies investigating the effects of digital reading (e.g., reading a Word or PDF file on screen) in comparison with print reading, not much research has been conducted into examining learners' reading behaviors and the educational benefits of recent, more flexible, visually presented texts. As Liu (2005) and others pointed out, students reading texts online may spend more time browsing and scanning, spotting keywords, highlighting, doing nonlinear and selective reading, or following hypertext links without particular aim and less time doing in-depth and concentrated reading. However, as shown in Eden and Eshet (2012), some evidence has begun to appear that learners who are familiar with the online visual culture of texts can more actively engage in interpreting, making their own meanings of, and altering digital texts.

Implications for Online Educators

Fred Ritchin (2010), a professor of photography and imaging at New York University, claimed that many journalists still do not take full advantage of digital technologies, which offer effective and innovative models of reporting, illuminating, and discussing the news and engaging readers, because of the lack of serious understanding in differences between digital and analog technologies. He warned that if journalists do not integrate new digital ways of sharing what they know, the importance of their role in digital society will be seriously diminished. In following that, if online educators do not incorporate the aforementioned emerging visual culture, they will not be able to play their roles as effectively. The following suggestions are offered to help online educators consider the features of online visual culture in designing and supporting their online learning:

- Online educators should view learners as both consumers and creators of visual objects and promote a participatory culture in online learning. In online learning, the learners should be the ones who lead the visual culture by actively engaging in interpreting, altering, repurposing, and creating a variety of visual objects, including texts, and using the diversity of available visual tools for their learning.

- Online educators should acquire competencies (attitudes, knowledge, and skills) to utilize a variety of the visual tools available in our society in the pursuit of promoting learning. Those visual tools provide the opportunities that are needed for effective, efficient, and appealing conditions for young learners. In particular, online data visualization tools can be effectively used with different sets of data (facts, numerical data, ideas, concepts, words, etc.) across different subject areas to promote learners' active engagement in the learning process.
- Online learning materials should be produced in such a way that they accommodate all that is offered by digital technologies today and encourage learners to use them in creative and innovative ways. For example, online learning materials could integrate hypertexts to promote more interactive activity-based learning and/or allow learners to underline key concepts or draw diagrams or visual summaries from textual information provided in their materials.
- Online educators should integrate more visuals in their online courses, as most of our learners today are visual learners. The Net Generation grew up with digital devices and feel more comfortable in visually rich learning environments than in purely text-based environments, as Rha (2007) and Oblinger and Oblinger (2005) argued. It is not difficult to find students who do not understand their teacher's lecture and proceed to Google the concept; find video lectures on YouTube, TED, or Khan Academy; and share them with their friends. Online lectures that combine visually advanced elements, summaries, and/or supplementary video clips will certainly better support online learning.

Author's Note

I would like to thank Professor Yoomi Choi for her drawing of icons shown in figure 5.2, and my graduate students Haeseon Yun, Seoyon Hong, and Yoonjung Kim for their support.

References

Eden, S., & Eshet, Y. (2012). The effect of format on performance: Editing text in print versus digital formats. *British Journal of Educational Technology*. doi:10.1111/j.1467-8535. 2012.01332.x

Foster, H. (Ed.). (1988). *Vision and visuality* (Discussions in contemporary culture). New York: New Press.

Gaver, W. (1991). Technology affordances. In S. P. Robertson, G. M. Olson, & J. S. Olson (Eds.), *Proceedings of the SIGCHI Conference on Human Factors in Computing Systems Conference April 28–June 5, 1991, New Orleans, LA* (pp. 79–84). New York, NY: ACM.

Gibson, J. (1979). *The ecological approach to visual perception*. Hillsdale, NJ: Lawrence Erlbaum.

Hofstede, G. (1991). *Culture and organisations*. New York, NY: McGraw-Hill.

Jung, I. S., Ho, C., & Suzuki, K. (2013). YouTube use in colleges in Japan and USA: A comparative look. *Educational Media Studies, 19*(2), 11–24.

Liu, Z. (2005). Reading behavior in the digital environment: Changes in reading behavior over the past ten years. *Journal of Documentation, 61*(6), 700–712.

Oblinger, D. G., & Oblinger, J. L. (2005). *Educating the net generation.* Retrieved from www .educause.edu/educatingthenetgen

Rha, I. (2007). Human visual intelligence and the new territory of educational technology research. *Educational Technology International, 8*(1), 1–16.

Ritchin, F. (2010, Spring). Failing to harness the web's visual promise. *Nieman Reports.* Retrieved from http://www.nieman.harvard.edu/reportsitem.aspx?id=102091

Spillman, L. (2002). *Cultural sociology.* Oxford, UK: Blackwell.

Thurlow, C., & Brown, A. (2003). Generation Txt? The sociolinguistics of young people's text-messaging. *Discourse Analysis Online, 1*(1). Retrieved from http://faculty.washington.edu/ thurlow/research/papers/Thurlow&Brown(2003).htm

6

ACCOUNTING FOR CULTURE IN INSTRUCTIONAL DESIGN

Casey Frechette, Ludmila C. Layne, and Charlotte Nirmalani Gunawardena

This chapter explores how cultural considerations might influence the ways we facilitate online learning and underlying models of instruction. We begin with an examination of the merits of factoring culture into online learning design and review how instructional design models currently account for culture. We then examine one particular model, WisCom, and review evidence of its effectiveness in diverse learning contexts, including online classes in Sri Lanka, Venezuela, and the United States. We conclude with suggestions for designing learning across cultures with WisCom and other design models.

Why Design With Culture in Mind?

Globalization and related advances in education and technology have resulted in a preponderance of Western-centric instruction to learners with wide-ranging cultural experiences (Rogers, Graham, & Mayes, 2007). This trend can be observed most acutely in the rise of MOOCs—massive open online courses—often sponsored, in part, by top U.S. universities and delivered to students around the world. The diversity of cultures observed in online education presents critical considerations for designers and instructors (Olaniran, 2009). Many (e.g., Bielaczyc & Collins, 1999; S. J. Chen, Hsu, & Caropreso, 2006; Swierczek & Bechter, 2010) have argued for closer attention to culture and difference when designing instruction for global learners.

Technology has connected us and enabled cross-cultural educational experiences, but it hasn't mandated the success of those experiences. Perhaps by better accounting for different values, beliefs, and educational preferences, we can ensure higher quality experiences for all learners.

Culture shapes values and drives behavior. In educational contexts, it influences learning preferences and habits. In this regard, culture can be viewed as a learner trait, through the same constructivist lens that encourages designers to acclimate to any individual difference that might influence the effectiveness of an instructional technique.

Many have argued for a holistic view of culture when designing instruction (e.g., Bentley, Tinney, & Chia, 2005; Marlowe & Page, 1998). Cultural imprints can be seen not only on learners but also on teachers, teaching strategies, learning environments, and underpinning design models. As discussed in chapter 2, culture affects everything, often in subtle, interconnected ways. And, beyond influencing every aspect of a learning experience, culture is neither monolithic nor static. Each of us belongs to multiple cultures, and our conceptions of these cultures modulate over different life experiences and sociocultural encounters. Put simply, culture is nuanced and complex, and its effects can be difficult to pinpoint.

Not surprisingly, early efforts to account for culture in learning design sought to mitigate perceived problems with cultural bias by relieving educational experiences of culture altogether. The premise of cultural "neutrality" led designers to scrub overt cultural references, leaving, so they believed, their cultural biases "at the door." However, many scholars now agree it's inevitable to transmit culture through instructional design (e.g., A. Chen & Mashhadi, 1998; McLoughlin & Oliver, 1999), especially online, where the medium itself is culturally derived (Bowers, 2000). Henderson (1996) argued for the embrace of culture in instructional design and delineated overlapping cultural realities, each in need of design considerations. These realities echo the notion that we claim simultaneous membership to multiple cultures, determined, in part, by our nationality, region, ethnicity, gender, and class, to name just a few dimensions. The Internet has itself become an incubator for a shared cultural experience (Slevin, 2000).

Most scholars (e.g., Henderson, 1996; Powell, 1997) now believe that designing effective learning for global audiences requires not cultural neutrality but cultural *inclusivity*. Full inclusiveness demands an embrace of designers', instructors', and learners' cultural influences and an anticipation of how these values and beliefs might impact the learning that unfolds. It also requires an acknowledgment of the dimensions of culture specific to learning, including past educational experiences, learning styles, and language abilities.

How Instructional Design Has Accounted for Culture

In an exploratory case study, Rogers et al. (2007) found that instructional designers had limited awareness of how they differed from the learners for whom they were designing. Interviews revealed many factors competing for designers' time and attention, with cultural understanding falling relatively low in priority, often leading to its exclusion from the design process. Rogers et al. also uncovered a feeling that certain learning design principles are universal, regardless of cultural factors. In some cases, this understanding seemed to prompt a desire to find ways to calibrate the principle to the particular learner population (including their cultures); in others, it prompted an attitude more reminiscent of the aforementioned tendency to "neutralize" culture.

Thomas, Mitchell, and Joseph (2002) argued for a revamping of the classic ADDIE (analyze, design, develop, implement, evaluate) model, proposing a commitment to cultural inclusiveness at every step in the process rather than a halfhearted attempt to account for culture in the initial analysis, with decreasing cultural focus with each passing phase. They characterized culture as a *dimension* of instructional design, one that can run in parallel with efforts to iterate through the process multiples times, in different directions. The cultural dimension captures three layers: (a) *intention* to include cultural realities purposefully, (b) *interaction* with learners to draw them into the design process, and (c) *introspection* that might surface one's own cultural values.

The culture-based model (CBM) designed by Young (2008, 2009) consists of eight interrelated and interactive self-selection processes, allowing the designer to choose which areas best meet the needs of the design project. The CBM is a product-oriented model that is composed of the following eight areas: inquiry, development, team, assessments, brainstorming, learners, elements, and training (ID-TABLET).

S. J. Chen et al. (2006) proposed a model for designing cross-cultural learning experiences. Their approach focused on interactions between teachers, among students, and across the two groups. One-on-one communications, they argued, form a sturdy foundation for cross-cultural leaning on the web, especially when supporting systems and resources are designed to ensure effective interactions. S. J. Chen et al. identified three kinds of support—technical, learning, and social—and three kinds of resources—language, culture and context, and learning content. Within their model, learners are expected to make effective connections across cultures early in their online learning experience.

Rose and Meyer (2000), Eberle and Childress (2006), and others argued for the value of universal design in creating culturally inclusive online course materials. Derived from the fields of architecture and software development, universal design is the principle that spaces and experiences should be constructed to allow for the greatest number of people to participate to the largest degree (Barajas & Higbee, 2003). Applying the concept of universal design to learning emphasizes the importance of making each student as active as possible in the learning process.

Encouraging learners to choose from different methods of instruction (e.g., reading a transcript of a lesson or listening to a recording), modes of expression (e.g., recording a video response or typing a reaction), and means of interaction (e.g., via real-time video chat or asynchronous discussion forums) can incorporate diverse learner needs into learning design. By creating opportunities for student choice, universal design for learning increases the chances the various cultural factors that shape learning habits and preferences will be accounted for in the instruction, without the need for specialized localizations or adaptations of the teaching.

The Value of Choice

Universal design emphasizes the value of choice. Given options, learners are more likely to find a path that meets their needs. However, how can we ensure the right choices are provided? Bentley et al. (2005) argued for a commitment to self-reflection among both designers and students. They pointed to the need to make personal values and beliefs around education explicit as a way to align online learning experiences with students' needs. Alignment, or value matching, may not, however, always be the goal. Gunawardena and LaPointe (2008) highlighted the value in challenging learners to encounter activities that require unfamiliar learning styles as a means to become better equipped to deal with globalized, multicultural communication in its many manifestations. Ultimately, designing for cultural difference requires a commitment to hearing from learners, to the point where their needs and perspectives can shape the design itself (McLoughlin & Oliver, 1999).

Degrees of Cultural Inclusiveness in Instructional Design

On the basis of our review of how instructional design models have accounted for culture and related literature into the role culture plays in all aspects of learning and instructional design, we have identified four levels of cultural inclusivity for instructional design:

> *Level 1:* The model doesn't directly address cultural factors, but it implicitly caters to the cultural values of its creator(s).
> *Level 2:* The model is explicitly designed for a particular culture, which may or may not match the model creator's culture(s).
> *Level 3:* The model is designed for different cultural contexts, though not multiple contexts within a single course or learning experience that has been designed with the model.
> *Level 4:* The model is designed to create multicultural learning experiences.

We conclude that models at the higher levels may be better suited for certain kinds of learner groups, especially those representing diverse cultural backgrounds. We also acknowledge, however, that cultural bias can influence how instructional design models are both constructed and employed. At the same time, we see opportunities to account for culture in most design models, as shown by the work of Thomas et al. (2002), even when initial concepts were devoid of cultural considerations, though we concede cultural inclusivity will come more naturally with some models, especially those that embrace a constructivist-oriented view of learning.

Designing Across Cultures With the Wisdom Communities Instructional Design Model

The Wisdom Communities instructional design model (WisCom) was developed to inform the design of collaborative online learning experiences (Gunawardena et al., 2006). The three authors of this chapter who were part of the initial design and development team discuss how this design model can be used to address culture in online learning designs. The first author, Casey Frechette, developed a revised graphic of the design model (see figure 6.1) to focus on mentoring and learner support as the key elements of the design model. Grounded in socio-constructivist theories and socially constructed meaning (A. Hall, 2007), WisCom places the community at the heart of the online learning experience and prompts the design of course curriculum around this social dynamic.

WisCom involves a community that innovates knowledge through a five-step cycle of inquiry. Knowledge innovation leads to wisdom and transformational learning, and the community is bolstered by mentoring and other forms of learner support.

WisCom is designed to develop two notable outcomes: wisdom and transformational learning. Wisdom is the primary desired outcome when instructors implement

Figure 6.1 The WisCom design model.

the WisCom model. In a WisCom course, wisdom is meaningful learning (Faucher, Everett, & Lawson, 2008; Gan & Zhu, 2007) marked by self-reflection (Segundo, 2002), a balance of knowledge, intent and action (Rowley, 2006), and insight, flexibility, and humility (Gunawardena et al., 2006). Wisdom emerges when efforts to advance individual and group interests converge (Sternberg, 2005), and it can be observed as a quality of both individual achievement and group functioning.

WisCom is created to facilitate creative thinking around context-sensitive, ill-structured problems. It's especially well suited for courses focused on emergent issues, especially when there's a lack of consensus around the "best" solution—or even what "good" solutions look like. With this in mind, WisCom makes several important assumptions about the group communication dynamics likely to lead to meaningful learning around open-ended content domains. First, WisCom assumes multiple perspectives and diverse ideas are essential to understanding—and beginning to approach—complex, real-world problems. Second, WisCom values divergent, interdisciplinary thinking and the integration of seemingly competing ideas. Rather than emphasizing a search for the "right" answer, WisCom encourages the development of multiple promising solutions.

In practice, WisCom courses tend to be rigorous and rewarding. Instructors, students, and other participants tend to get out what they put in to the community. Collaborative learning experiences compose most of the day-to-day activities in a WisCom course, whereas traditional learning and teaching roles are deemphasized. Both process and outcome are valued in a WisCom course, and students are encouraged to extend new values and ideas to their behaviors and thinking outside the course. This final quality speaks to WisCom's focus on transformational learning, a long-lasting outcome marked by self-reflection, challenged assumptions, and new frames of reference (Mezirow, 1997).

In light of our earlier discussion on the qualities of culturally inclusive online instruction, we believe that WisCom is particularly well suited for cross-cultural and intercultural learning for at least six reasons:

1. It promotes self-determined learning cohorts. Wisdom communities define their own identity, especially with regard to how communication unfolds. It takes into account different communication styles, for example, high- or low-context communication (E. T. Hall, 1976), silence, and nonverbal communication (E. T. Hall, 1973).
2. It emphasizes the value of integrating ideas rather than placing them in competition until a "victor" is established.
3. It's learner focused. WisCom is very much rooted in a constructivist paradigm. Learner analysis is key, as recommended by Edmundson (2007), in the cultural adaptation process (CAP) model, for example, taking into account factors such as cultural influences on learning, educational expectations, and help-seeking behaviors.
4. Multiple solutions are sought from diverse perspectives.
5. The individual and group are both valued in assessment policies and practices.
6. It is flexible to accommodate diverse learner needs.

With these qualities as a foundation, WisCom informs the design of three essential components in an online learning experience: a learning group, mentoring and other forms of learner support, and knowledge management. On closer examination, each of these elements reveals itself to support cultural diversity.

Learning Groups

The WisCom model builds courses with strong virtual communities. The student groups work together to meet shared learning goals. Many of the learning tasks in a WisCom course are distributed, building community and pushing toward group goals at different times and in different ways. Typical WisCom activities include discussion forums, wikis, text chats, and videoconferencing to facilitate learning goals.

WisCom group work should lead to specific, focused—but not singular—conclusions. WisCom prioritizes shared trust, respect, and commitment. Within this environment, reflection and dialogue tend to be most effective because "a safe, supportive environment enables learners to engage in a cycle of inquiry, a dynamic learning process grounded in a real-world learning problem, or challenge. Team work, paired with the empowerment of individual members, contributes to this process" (Gunawardena, Layne, & Frechette, 2012, p. 374).

In a WisCom-based course, group identity is largely left to the group itself to define. The cultural values of individual group members have an important role to play in the formation of the group's personality. This allows for different learning cohorts to define themselves quite differently, depending on the experiences and learning preferences of their members. It also creates an environment in which each member has a stake in shaping what the group becomes. Along with forming a self-determined identity, WisCom groups reach outcomes through consensus building and negotiated meaning. By valuing multiple perspectives over "right answers," WisCom promotes thoughtful deliberation of diverse viewpoints, even those that may be at odds with learners' experiences and values. In the end, collaboration trumps competition in a WisCom course.

Mentoring and Learner Support

Apprenticeship and learner support are important sources of scaffolding in a WisCom course, and notions from communities of practice (COPs) and mentoring are leveraged to support this aspect of the model. COPs solve practical problems (Lave, 1991) by focusing on tools, techniques, and results. COPs are informal groups, and their members reflect on the work they do, at best, advancing their craft or trade. Within COPs and other informal and formal learning groups, mentors can provide support to novice members by coaching, guiding, and advising. Effective mentorships can help novices in task performance, acclimation to group social dynamics, and productive interactions (McLoughlin, 2002).

WisCom resists mandating certain kinds of support; rather, it encourages designers to build a range of support options that can be mixed and matched by instructors and students alike, depending on learner needs and preferences. Likewise, the mentoring support is expected to shift depending on learner needs, especially with regard to communication styles and level of involvement. The flexibility built into how mentoring is provided in a WisCom course parallels Gunawardena and LaPointe's (2008) conclusion that help-seeking behaviors, including the kind and extent of help sought, are culturally based.

Knowledge Innovation

WisCom promotes knowledge innovation and knowledge management (KM) to help community members discover and create ideas in a collaborative, ongoing fashion. By not only managing the discovery of knowledge but also innovating the creation of new ideas and concepts, this process moves communities from a focus on data and information to knowledge and, ultimately, wisdom. Shared understanding, reflection, and real-world experiences facilitate this progression (Applehans, Globe, & Laugero, 1999).

The process of knowledge innovation online happens in a cycle of inquiry consisting of six steps: a learning challenge (i.e., problem, case, or question), exploration, resources, reflection, negotiation, and preservation. These steps reflect the process, or phases, of a collaborative learning event, the intent of which is to solve a problem, discover something, or work together to achieve a common learning goal. After viewing the problem, case, or question, the group navigates through a process whereby individual cognitions are shared (initial exploration); multiple perspectives are challenged, accommodated, and negotiated with peer learners and experts (resources, perspectives); and time is allotted for individual reflective restructuring in thinking (reflection, reorganization). This internalization occurs before the group works again in unison to produce shared artifacts to document the knowledge commodities that result from the collaborative learning experience (negotiation, preservation). Thus, the knowledge management system can make available the "collective knowledge" of the group for others to use (Alavi & Leidner, 2005). Figure 6.2 presents a screenshot of the cycle of inquiry in a graduate-level course on culture and global e-learning that we designed in the WebCT learning management system using WisCom.

Figure 6.2 Screenshot of the knowledge innovation cycle of inquiry. Created by Charlotte N. Gunawardena and Jane Erlandson and used with their and the University of New Mexico's permission.

Table of Contents for Module 3
- Overview of Module 3
- Message from Facilitat
- Learning Challenge
- Case Study for Group
- Case Study for Group
- "Can you lead from be
- "Community Informati
- "ICT for Development
- "ICT for Education…" (
- Report Formats
- 6 Evaluation Report St
- Standard format for ev

Activities
- Discussion: ICT access
- Group 1 Discussion Fo
- Group 2 Discussion Fo
- Knowledge Artifacts Fo
- Self/Group Eval Form
- SUBMIT Self/Group Eva
- Private Journal – Modu

Your location: Home Page > Learning Center > Module 3 > Overview of Module 3

6. Engage in critical thinking and problem-solving to develop recommendations for improving ICT access and equity around the globe.

Learning Process and Procedure

1. Read the Purpose and Overview, and Message from Facilitators.

2. Read your Learning Challenge. Inside this document, click on the link to Real Access/Real Impact criteria. On this Web site, read the 12 real access criteria and their descriptions. You will refer to this list often in your discussions throughout this module.

   ○ After you read the criteria, go to the Discussion on "ICT access and its implications" and try to define what it means to have access and not have access to ICT, and the impact it will have on the global economy. Consider the questions in the Learning Challenge, and the criteria outlined in the reading "Real Access/Real Impact." The entire class will participate in this discussion from **September 29–October 4**, which will help you to consider the issues you will address in your group activity.

3. Next, you will work in a group to provide solutions to a case study presented regarding ICT access. To do this group activity, you will engage in the cycle of inquiry learning process as described in the WisCom instructional design model (see Introduction to Modules) to accomplish the tasks for the group. The cycle of inquiry consists of five stages:
   - Presentation of the Case
   - Initial exploration
   - Resources/perspectives
   - Reflection/reorganization
   - Negotiation/preservation

4. **Presentation of the Case** – Read the case study assigned to your group. The case studies are real-life problems that countries developing ICT solutions are currently experiencing. Each case study suggests a different approach to find solutions: problem-solving or case-based reasoning. Using the suggested approach, your task is to recommend solutions to help these countries solve their problems.
   ○ **Group 1** – You will work on the case study entitled "Exposing India's Children to Computers."
   ○ **Group 2** – You will work on the case study entitled "Alleviating Poverty in China."

5. **Initial Exploration** – You will use the Discussion Forum labeled for your group (Group 1 or Group 2) to communicate with your teammates on how you will approach this learning activity. We would suggest that you appoint a moderator/coordinator for your group and discuss how you will undertake the group tasks. The group will decide how to arrange the group discussion space for this activity. Start with what you know about the case, discuss what other information and resources you would need, to find a solution.

6. **Resources/Perspectives** – Read the following resources we have provided to help you with this task, and discuss them in your group. (See left-side Table of Contents for links to these readings.)
   ○ pdf article titled "Can you Lead from Behind?" From the book Global Perspectives on E-Learning Rhetoric and Reality.
   ○ pdf article titled "Community Informatics: Challenges in Bridging the Digital Divide" by Peter Songan, Khairuddin Ab Hamid, Alvin Yeo, Jayapragas Gnaniah, and Hushairi Zen.
   ○ pdf book chapter "ICT for Development: Challenges and Possibilities" by Vrasidas, Zembylas, and Glass. (2009) (coming soon)
   ○ pdf book chapter "ICT for Education, Development, and Social Justice: Some Theoretical Issues" by Zembylas. (2009) (coming soon)

7. **Reflection/Reorganization** – Continue working with your teammates to solve your case study. Reflect on and reorganize your ideas, negotiate issues, and post your draft documents in your group's discussion forum.

8. **Negotiation/Preservation** – By **Friday, October 9**, your group will post a final report outlining the solutions to your case in the Knowledge Artifact Discussion Forum. Your report will be graded on how well you addressed the 12 real access criteria discussed in the Learning Challenge of this module. All members of your group will receive the same grade. Your group grade will be worth 6 points of the module's total 10 points. You are also required to read the other group's report and provide feedback and comment on the solution-finding approach used, and the solutions recommended. Everyone in the class will be expected to participate in this discussion in the Knowledge Artifacts Forum. You will have three days **(October 10–12)** to post your comments in the Knowledge Artifacts Forum and respond to your classmates.

Participate in Discussion Forum "ICT access and implications"	September 29–October 4
Collaborate with your group members on the case study in your group's discussion forum	September 29–October 9
Post final report (as a group) to "Knowledge Artifacts" Discussion forum	October 9
Comment on and provide feedback to the other groups' reports	October 10–12
Make Private Journal entry	October 12

Note. Interface: WebCT [Computer software]. Washington, DC: Blackboard, Inc.

The KM component of WisCom also supports different cultural orientations to knowledge representation by accounting for many forms of archival knowledge, including those that extend beyond linguistics. The long-term storage of discovered and created knowledge is a key step in the KM process, and WisCom allows for many ways to represent knowledge, including text-based definitions and summaries, storytelling, concept maps, flowcharts and other process diagrams, and even poetry and illustrations. By promoting multiple (and multimodal) knowledge representations, WisCom encourages diverse approaches to thinking about and capturing information.

Cultural Biases in WisCom

WisCom, like any instructional design model, is the product of various cultural forces. Although we believe WisCom is particularly well suited for use not only in different cultural venues but in *multicultural* contexts, we also acknowledge its limitations and biases. Most notably, WisCom puts great emphasis on the role of the instructor as a facilitative one, and this may be unfamiliar or unproductive to students with learning experiences grounded in high power distance cultures (Jin & Cortazzi, 1998).

Similarly, WisCom's focus on group-based social learning may put some high-context learners at a disadvantage, whom Swierczek and Bechter (2010) found acclimate less naturally to collaborative learning than their low-context counterparts.

Meanwhile, although individual contributions are counted and valued, WisCom's emphasis on group dynamics may prove counterintuitive to students whose learning has been rooted in individualistic cultural values. However, we also see value in pushing students to the edge of their comfort zones and see opportunities in the presence of unfamiliar ways of learning that WisCom likely presents for at least some students. This is where mentoring and facilitating can play a key role in supporting these students. However, we also reiterate the importance in being clear about what the "problem spots" might be for some students and clearly communicating these issues.

Evidence for the Effectiveness of WisCom as a Cross-Cultural Design Model

WisCom has been used to design online graduate-level classes in various cultural contexts, and we have studied student perceptions of the model's effectiveness in achieving its stated aims, namely, building a learning community, promoting the social construction of knowledge, and fostering collaborative learning. In all courses studied, students reported positive experiences and affirmed the WisCom model's utility in forming a supportive community of learners.

In a course conducted at a university in the southwestern United States in the fall of 2010, 92% of students ($N = 14$) agreed or strongly agreed that a learning community was created. An equal number experienced a sense of a community engaged in reflective dialog. Equal portions of the class—46%—agreed or strongly agreed there was a sense of shared identity and that group interactions resulted in the construction of new knowledge, with 8% strongly disagreeing in each case. All students reported changes in perspective as a result of their interactions in the course, and 83% strongly agreed that the course resulted in new perspectives.

Two graduate-level courses at Venezuelan universities were also designed with the WisCom model. These courses focused on distance education, instructional design models, and the design of online courses. Surveys were administered at the end of each course to gauge students' perceptions about the formation of learning communities, the social construction of knowledge, and the presence of collaborative learning. In the first course, administered in the spring of 2005, 90% of students ($N = 22$) reported a sense of a learning community, 80% felt the community engaged in both collaborative learning and reflective dialog, and 70% felt the social construction of knowledge centered around the community. In a course from 2006 focused on the theory and practice of instructional design models, 80% of students ($N = 22$) reported a sense of community, with the same number believing the course promoted collaboration, and 60% reported a sense of student support. Three activities leading to collaboration within the community were identified: participating in discussion boards, creating collaborative concept maps, and sharing work with collaborative software. Half of the students felt the social construction of knowledge happened through interactions with the community, with 20% specifically citing student-student interactions, 20% citing student-instructor interactions, and 10% attributing interactions with content.

We have also used transcript analysis to measure WisCom's effectiveness in courses with global students. In a study of a faculty development forum in Sri Lanka designed with WisCom (Gunawardena et al., 2011), it was found that an online case-based reasoning activity in three rounds of training reflected the social construction of knowledge, as measured by the interaction analysis model (Gunawardena, Lowe, & Anderson, 1997). Our examination shows that the social construction of knowledge occurred in the course of solving a complex problem: street children in Sri Lanka. Notably, the processes of negotiation and the social construction of knowledge led to perspective transformations. Participants gained new insights into (a) the value of well-designed online learning, (b) themselves as being able to learn online, and (c) the people directly impacted by the societal problems. Participants' new insights were accompanied by changes in feelings and increased caring toward the problem and people involved. Participants began to see themselves as part of the solution. The group process and product (research papers the three groups wrote) showed evidence of socially mediated thinking.

Another analysis using final evaluation surveys of the same faculty development forum in Sri Lanka showed that interaction emerged as a strong predictor of learner satisfaction explaining 50.2% of the variance in learner satisfaction in the regression model. This finding shows the importance of designing interactive learning activities to support learning online and contradicts the general belief that Sri Lankan participants would be less likely to interact online because they come from a traditional education system that encourages passivity and reception of ideas from a more learned teacher. These results suggest that the online learning design based on WisCom led to learner satisfaction and supported interaction and collaborative learning in the Sri Lankan sociocultural context.

Conclusions

WisCom is a design model well suited for culturally diverse learning cohorts. Rather than aiming to neutralize the presence of culture, WisCom encourages participants—both instructors and learners—to explore their culturally derived beliefs and values and integrate them into their experiences. Moreover, every WisCom course pivots on the formation of a new wisdom community, one with its own unique culture and accompanying values. By emphasizing divergent thinking, consensus building, and the exploration of multiple solutions to complex, real-world problems, WisCom maximizes opportunities for students' diverse backgrounds and experiences to be genuinely valued.

Our experiences with WisCom and consideration of related models and theories lead to the following recommendations for designing culturally inclusive online courses:

- Reflect on your own cultural biases and encourage continuous self-reflection among learners.
- Design for cultural inclusivity, not neutrality.
- Acknowledge the challenges in removing cultural influences from a course design and work to recognize and delineate, not eliminate, those factors.
- Create opportunities for learners to choose among learning activities that reflect different ways to communicate, interact, process information, and otherwise experience the instruction.
- Encourage learners to pursue options less familiar or natural.
- Create flexibility around course timelines and, to the extent feasible, allow students some control over the pace of the course.
- Resist attempts to merge or reconcile differences in student-proposed answers and solutions.
- Place value on both learning *processes* and learning *products*.
- To the extent feasible, build opportunities for learners to influence the course design.
- Avoid temptations to treat culture as either monolithic or static. Recognize that every learning experience, including the one you're designing, contributes to the cultural frameworks learners will bring to future experiences.

References

Alavi, M., & Leidner, D. E. (2005). Review: Knowledge management and knowledge management systems: Conceptual foundation and research issues. In I. Nonaka (Ed.), *Knowledge management: Critical perspective on business and management* (pp. 163–202). New York, NY: Routledge.

Applehans, W., Globe, A., & Laugero, G. (1999). *Managing knowledge: A practical web-based approach*. Reading, MA: Addison-Wesley.

Barajas, H. L., & Higbee, J. L. (2003). Where do we go from here? Universal design as a model for multicultural education. In J. L. Higbee (Ed.), *Curriculum transformation and disability: Implementing universal design in higher education* (pp. 285–290). Minneapolis: Center for Research on Developmental Education and Urban Literacy, General College, University of Minnesota.

Bentley, J., Tinney, M. V., & Chia, B. (2005). Intercultural Internet-based learning: Know your audience and what they value. *Educational Technology Research and Development, 53*(2), 117–126.

Bielaczyc, K., & Collins, A. (1999). Learning communities in classrooms: A reconceptualization of education practice. In C. Reigluth (Ed.), *Instructional design theories and models* (Vol. II, pp. 269–292). Mahwah, NJ: Lawrence Erlbaum.

Bowers, C. A. (2000). *Let them eat data: How computers affect education, cultural diversity, and the prospects of ecological sustainability.* Athens: University of Georgia Press.

Chen, A., & Mashhadi, A. (1998, January). *Challenges and problems in designing and researching distance learning environments and communities.* Paper presented at the 1st Malaysian Educational Research Association (MERA) Conference, Penang, Malaysia.

Chen, S. J., Hsu, C. L., & Caropreso, E. J. (2006). Cross-cultural collaborative online learning: When the West meets the East. *International Journal of Technology in Teaching and Learning, 2*(1), 17–35.

Eberle, J., & Childress, M. (2006). Universal design for culturally diverse online learning. In A. Edmundson (Ed.), *Globalized e-learning cultural challenges* (pp. 239–254). Hershey, PA: Idea Group.

Edmundson, A. (2007). The cultural adaptation process (CAP) model: Designing e-learning for another culture. In A. Edmundson (Ed.), *Globalized e-learning cultural challenges* (pp. 267–290). Hershey, PA: Information Science Publishing. doi:10.4018/978-1-59904-301-2

Faucher, J. P. L., Everett, A. M., & Lawson, R. (2008). Reconstituting knowledge management. *Journal of Knowledge Management, 12*(3), 3–16.

Gan, Y., & Zhu, Z. (2007). A learning framework for knowledge building and collective wisdom advancement in virtual learning communities. *Educational Technology and Society, 10*(1), 206–226.

Gunawardena, C. N., Keller, P. S., Garcia, F., Faustino, G. L., Barrett, K., Skinner, J. K., . . . Fernando, S. (2011). Transformative education through technology: Facilitating social construction of knowledge online through cross-cultural e-mentoring. In V. Edirisinghe (Ed.), *Proceedings of the 1st International Conference on the Social Sciences and the Humanities* (Vol. 1, pp. 114–118). Peradeniya, Sri Lanka: The Faculty of Arts, University of Peradeniya.

Gunawardena, C. N., & LaPointe, D. (2008). Social and cultural diversity in distance education. In T. Evans, M. Haughey, & D. Murphy (Eds.), *International handbook of distance education* (pp. 51–70). Bingley, UK: Emerald.

Gunawardena, C. N., Layne, L. C., & Frechette, C. (2012). Designing wise communities that engage in creative problem solving: An analysis of an online design model. In C. Vrasidas & P. Panaou (Eds.), *Design thinking in education, media and society: Proceedings from the 62nd Annual Conference of the International Council for Educational Media (ICEM)* (pp. 369–379). Nicosia, Cyprus: University of Nicosia.

Gunawardena, C. N., Lowe, C. A., & Anderson, T. (1997). Analysis of a global online debate and the development of an interaction analysis model for examining social construction of knowledge in computer conferencing. *Journal of Educational Computing Research, 17*(4), 395–429.

Gunawardena, C. N., Ortegano-Layne, L., Carabajal, K., Frechette, C., Lindemann, K., & Jennings, B. (2006). New model, new strategies: Instructional design for building online wisdom communities. *Distance Education, 27*(2), 217–232.

Hall, A. (2007). Vygotsky goes online: Learning design from a socio-cultural perspective. *Proceedings of the Learning and Socio-cultural Theory: Exploring Modern Vygotskian Perspectives Workshop, 1*(1), 94–107.

Hall, E. T. (1973). *The silent language.* New York, NY: Anchor Books.

Hall, E. T. (1976). *Beyond culture.* New York, NY: Anchor Books.

Henderson, L. (1996). Instructional design of interactive multimedia: A cultural critique. *Educational Technology Research and Development, 44*(4), 85–104.

Jin, L., & Cortazzi, M. (1998). Dimensions of dialog: Large classes in China. *International Journal of Educational Research, 29*(8), 739–761.

Lave, J. (1991). Situating learning in communities of practice. In L. B. Resnick, J. M. Levine, & S. D. Teasley (Eds.), *Perspectives on socially shared cognition* (pp. 63–82). Washington, DC: American Psychological Association.

Marlowe, B. A., & Page, M. L. (1998). *Creating and sustaining the constructivist classroom.* Thousand Oaks, CA: Corwin Press.

McLoughlin, C. (2002). Learner support in distance and networked learning environments: Ten dimensions for successful design. *Distance Education, 23*(2), 149–162.

McLoughlin, C., & Oliver, R. (1999). Designing learning environments for cultural inclusivity: A case study of indigenous online learning at tertiary level. *Australian Journal of Educational Technology, 16*(1), 58–72.

Mezirow, J. (1997). Transformative learning: Theory to practice. *New Directions for Adult and Continuing Education, 74*, 5–12.

Olaniran, B. (2009). Discerning culture in e-learning and in the global workplaces. *Knowledge Management and E-Learning: An International Journal, 1*(3), 180–195.

Powell, G. C. (1997). On being a culturally sensitive instructional designer and educator. *Educational Technology, 37*(2), 6–14.

Rogers, C. P., Graham, C. R., & Mayes, C. T. (2007). Cultural competence and instructional cultural dimensions of learning: Addressing the challenges of multicultural instruction design: Exploration research into the delivery of online instruction cross-culturally. *Educational Technology Research and Development, 55*(2), 197–217.

Rose, D. H., & Meyer, A. (2000). Universal design for learning: Associate editor column. *Journal of Special Education Technology, 15*(1), 67–70.

Rowley, J. (2006). Where is the wisdom that we have lost in knowledge? *Journal of Documentation, 62*(2), 251–270.

Segundo, R. S. (2002). A new concept of knowledge. *Online Information Review, 26*(4), 239–245.

Slevin, J. (2000). *The Internet and society.* Cambridge, UK: Polity.

Sternberg, R. J. (2005). Foolishness. In R. J. Sternberg & A. Collins. (Eds.), *A handbook of wisdom: Psychological perspectives* (pp. 331–352). Cambridge, UK: Cambridge University Press.

Swierczek, F. W., & Bechter, C. (2010). Cultural features of e-learning: A Euro-Asian case study. In J. M. Spector et al. (Eds.), *Learning and instruction in the digital age* (pp. 291–308). New York, NY: Springer.

Thomas, M., Mitchell, M., & Joseph, R. (2002). The third dimension of ADDIE: A cultural embrace. *TechTrends, 46*(2), 40–45.

Young, P. A. (2008). The culture-based model: Constructing a model of culture. *Journal of Educational Technology and Society, 11*(2), 107–118.

Young, P. A. (2009). *Instructional design frameworks and intercultural models.* New York, NY: Information Science Reference.

7

FACILITATING ONLINE LEARNING AND CROSS-CULTURAL E-MENTORING

Charlotte Nirmalani Gunawardena and Buddhini Gayathri Jayatilleke

One unique feature of online learning is its ability to network learners for extended periods of time across geographical boundaries to facilitate collaborative learning. However, many who began teaching online, instead of transforming teaching practice to take maximum advantage of this unique feature, used the online medium to continue their traditional ways of teaching. Although traditional teaching methods are not bad per se, many are often missing the opportunity to teach in ways that can generate novel ways of learning. Harasim (2012) proposed a new theory of learning for the knowledge age, online collaborative learning (OCL) theory, to take advantage of the unique affordances of the network-based medium. The OCL process includes discourse, collaboration, and knowledge building where learners work together online to identify and discuss issues and apply their new understanding and analytical reasoning to solving problems. Harasim identified three intellectual phases as being key to OCL—idea generating, idea organizing, and intellectual convergence (or construction of shared knowledge and understanding)—that clearly indicate the need to transform the role of teaching online into that of facilitation. How, then, does culture play a role in the facilitation of OCL? We need to consider this question in relation to both the development of the sociocultural environment to enhance online learning and the facilitation of the discipline-oriented environment to support knowledge building.

This chapter explores issues of culture that impact facilitation of OCL and the roles facilitators and mentors play in helping diverse learners engage in community and knowledge building online. We focus on cultural issues that impact community and knowledge building, as these two areas are unique to supporting networked learning. We then discuss a study of cross-cultural e-mentoring between the United States and Sri Lanka that was analyzed from a cultural perspective for this book chapter to highlight how mentoring across cultures can facilitate community and knowledge building to support OCL. Previous analysis of these data from other perspectives can be found in two separate studies (Gunawardena et al., 2013; Jayatilleke, Kulasekara, Kumarasinha, & Gunawardena, 2012). Chapter 6 discussed how to consider culture when designing an online environment to facilitate OCL, and in this chapter we focus on how to consider cultural issues when we facilitate learning in such an environment.

Online facilitators must begin by examining and reflecting on their own cultural programming and value systems in order to be mindful of how these systems will influence the interactions they have with culturally diverse learners. One of the most important reasons for understanding cultural factors is the awareness it raises of our own cultural identity (Martin & Nakayama, 2004). Obtaining a better understanding of oneself, as well as alternative approaches to communication and learning, is the first step one must take when embarking on the journey of facilitating learning across cultures.

Developing the Sociocultural Environment for Online Collaboration

Wegerif (1998) argued that the social dimension, especially how students relate to each other, is important to the effectiveness of discussions and student learning, and he provided evidence from an ethnographic study of a computer-mediated course at the Open University, United Kingdom. He found that individual success or failure in the course depended on the extent to which students were able to cross a threshold from feeling like outsiders to feeling like insiders. In this section, we explore three factors that have an impact on the sociocultural environment for OCL: social presence, help-seeking behaviors, and silence.

Social Presence

Social presence is the degree to which a person is perceived as a "real person" in mediated communication. One of our studies (Gunawardena & Zittle, 1997) established that social presence is a strong predictor of learner satisfaction in a computer conference, which was subsequently supported by Richardson and Swan (2003). Further studies have begun to examine cultural perceptions of social presence. Tu (2001) found that Chinese students perceived online communication as a more comfortable medium to express their thoughts because of the lack of confrontation and face-saving concerns and thus increased their social presence in an interactive OCL environment. But, on the other hand, they were concerned that their messages might appear in public areas and cause them to lose face and privacy.

In a cross-cultural study of group process and development in online conferences in the United States and Mexico, we (Gunawardena et al., 2001) found that social presence emerged as a theme addressed by both U.S. and Mexican focus group participants. The U.S. participants felt that social presence is necessary to the smooth functioning of a group, to provide a sense that the group members are real people. The Mexican participants, however, felt that having personal information about fellow classmates was unimportant. For these participants, how peers contribute to the conference is more important than knowing their personal information. The differences in the way that the U.S. participants and the Mexican participants perceived social presence could be attributed to cultural differences related to power distance (Hofstede, 1980) in the two societies. In a high power distance society like Mexico, computer-mediated communication was seen as equalizing power and status differences present in society. Therefore, participants did not want their peers to interject social context cues that would take away the equalizing power of the online environment.

Al-Harthi (2005) conducted in-depth telephone interviews with Arab students in order to understand how they perceived the values related to study in an American distance learning program and found that for Arab students the lack of physical presence in the online environment was seen as a positive feature because, in addition to accessibility advantages, it provided a reduced risk of social embarrassment. Female Arab students in particular felt more comfortable studying online, as it allowed for an easy conformity with the separation of genders that is traditional in Muslim culture.

Therefore, an online facilitator needs to take into consideration the diverse cultural perspectives on social presence when designing the sociocultural environment. Some of the techniques we have used to generate social presence are to (a) create a virtual space devoted only to social interaction, such as a "Virtual Pub"; (b) request students to introduce themselves by providing guidelines for such introductions, being mindful of issues related to self-disclosure as discussed in chapter 4; (c) develop a sense of online community by engaging in community-building activities such as a virtual costume party; (d) encourage participation and reward contributions; (e) facilitate discussions, summarize, and be present online frequently; (f) provide timely feedback; (g) develop formats for interaction that would enhance the presence of others in the community such as storytelling; and (h) provide opportunities for real-time interaction through chat, desktop conferencing, and face-to-face discussions. To build the social environment for OCL, designers must make the concepts of community, collaboration, and interaction central to course design. Assessment must reward collaboration, contribution to community, and products developed within the community.

Help-Seeking Behaviors

Cultures differ in help-seeking behaviors. Help seeking is a learning strategy that combines cognition and social interaction (Ryan, Gheen, & Midgley, 1998) and involves the ability to use others as a resource to cope with difficulty encountered in the learning process. When learners do not seek help, performance and learning can suffer. In formal education contexts that emphasize competition and normative evaluation, students from diverse cultures are often unwilling to seek help, as they fear others may perceive them as lacking in ability (Ryan et al., 1998). But these students would seek help when the socioemotional needs of students and learning for intrinsic reasons are emphasized over performance and competition.

The socioemotional needs of students are often recognized as part of the learning process in some cultures. Chinese students communicate with their teachers outside of class for guidance with personal problems (Zhang, 2006). Teachers in China assume responsibility for educating the whole person instructionally, cognitively, affectively, and morally and are expected to care about students' behaviors and problems inside and outside the classroom. In contrast, Western teachers are expected to perform academic duties and not get involved in students' problems outside of school. Facilitators therefore need to be more cognizant of the expectations of diverse learners related to help-seeking behaviors and make their teaching and learning philosophies, procedures, and practices explicit in course design, the syllabus, and course outlines.

Silence

> *"Communication online involves a minor but real personal risk, and a response—any response—is generally interpreted as a success while silence means failure."*

—Feenberg (1989, p. 23)

Online communication puts a premium on active participation and is often critical of "lurkers," or passive readers. Silence, while frustrating for Americans and Western Europeans, is quite comfortable for those from Asian and Pacific Island cultures (Brislin, 2000). For Americans, silence indicates rudeness, inattention, or uncertainty. However, in some cultures, silence indicates respect (Matthewson & Thaman, 1998). Silence allows people time to collect thoughts, think carefully, listen to others, and reflect before responding. Facilitators, therefore, must be cognizant of what silence might mean to a learner in a specific context and consider how to accommodate silence online.

Culture and Knowledge Construction in OCL

Generally, the primary theory of knowledge construction underlying OCL emphasizes the exchange of ideas and the expressions of agreement and disagreement to construct new meaning. Biesenbach-Lucas (2003), in her survey of the differences between native and nonnative students in their perceptions of asynchronous discussions, found that both groups tended to avoid "challenge and explain cycles" where they had to do more than demonstrate knowledge by also agreeing and disagreeing in nonabrasive ways. She noted that nonnative speakers, particularly Asian students, consider it far less appropriate to challenge and criticize the ideas of others. In addition, they may not know how to express disagreement appropriately in English. She cited similar findings of the absence of challenge to the input of others in Wegerif's (1998) study and Curtis and Lawson's (2001) study of asynchronous discussions, which could be attributed to culturally induced reluctance to debate. Biesenbach-Lucas (2003) also observed that this lack of challenge and disagreement of ideas is troubling, as it is the "resolution of such areas of agreement and disagreement that 'results in higher forms of reasoning' because 'cognitive development requires that individuals encounter others who contradict their own intuitively derived ideas'" (p. 37). Jonassen and Kim (2010) supported this view by saying, "Meaningful learning requires deep engagement with ideas. Deep engagement is supported by the critical thinking skill of argumentation. Learning to argue represents an important way of thinking that facilitates conceptual change and is essential for problem solving" (p. 439).

The point we need to consider here is whether such challenges to ideas expressed by others and discussion of disagreement at the level of ideas in online discussions is a necessary condition for higher forms of reasoning or knowledge construction or whether it is merely an expectation from a Western point of view, particularly American. Furthermore, we need to think about whether higher cognitive reasoning and knowledge construction can happen without such open disagreement of ideas. The following discussion of studies from Mexico and Sri Lanka provides a different perspective.

Lopez-Islas (2001) analyzed knowledge construction in online discussion forums at Monterrey Tech–Virtual University in Mexico, using Gunawardena, Lowe, and Anderson's (1997) interaction analysis model (IAM) that describes five stages in the process of knowledge construction: (a) sharing, comparing, and agreement; (b) cognitive dissonance or disagreement of ideas; (c) negotiation of meaning and coconstruction of knowledge; (d) testing and modification of proposed coconstruction; and (e) application of newly constructed meaning. Lopez-Islas observed that open disagreement with ideas expressed by others is not appropriate in the Mexican context, and therefore participants moved to knowledge construction without moving through the cognitive dissonance phase as described in the IAM.

In our study that employed the IAM to examine social construction of knowledge in asynchronous discussions between American e-mentors and Sri Lankan protégés (Gunawardena et al., 2008), we found a similar result. The Sri Lankan participants did not openly disagree at the level of ideas but moved to negotiation of meaning and coconstruction of new knowledge based on consensus building. Therefore, we had to redefine *dissonance* as specified in the IAM in cultural terms. The Sri Lankan participants were often very polite and indirect when providing a different point of view.

In further exploration of the online asynchronous interactions, we found that although the academic discussion was very polite and lacked open disagreement of ideas, strong opinions and disagreements were expressed by the same participants in the informal "virtual café," where they engaged in a heated debate about gender issues. This finding led us to reflect on the role of culture in academic online discussions. It is possible that collectivist traits in both Sri Lankan and Mexican cultural contexts may have transferred to online group interaction in an academic setting where open disagreement of ideas would make the participants uncomfortable, especially when a teacher is present. Yet, these very same participants as noted in the Sri Lankan context would engage in a heated debate in an informal discussion space. Because the teacher was not present in the informal discussion space, this makes us wonder about teacher presence and whether it can inhibit online interactions in specific sociocultural contexts. So, the context, or in this case the type of online discussion and where it takes place, whether in an informal social space such as a virtual café or in a more serious academic discussion, is key to the expression of open disagreement.

From his study of a global e-mail debate on intercultural communication, Chen (2000) showed that differences in thinking patterns and expression styles influence student reactions to teaching methods. The debate format caused orientation problems for some participants, as the "debate" is a product of low-context culture that requires a direct expression of one's argument by using logical reasoning. Many students who come from high-context cultures in Asia and Latin America find an argumentative format uncomfortable in an academic context, and this discomfort is exacerbated when the debate is facilitated through a medium devoid of nonverbal cues. Students from Asian countries are more likely to build consensus when they are confronted with two opposing points of view, often trying to determine to what degree they can support the opposing point of view, as discussed from the context of a Sri Lankan and American case-based reasoning learning activity (Gunawardena et al., 2013).

This difference between Western and Asian worldviews was explained by Nisbett (2003), who showed how the ecologies of ancient Greece and China led to different economic, political, and social arrangements and corresponding worldviews. The development of personal freedom, individuality, and objective thought in Greece was partly influenced by its unique political system and partly explained by the many foreign influences and worldviews as a result of its maritime location. The ecology of Greece favored hunting, herding, fishing, and trade, whereas the ecology of China was more homogeneous, was less open to outside influences, and favored agriculture that put a premium on living harmoniously with one another. The Chinese had to look outward toward their peers and upward toward authority, and their sense of self was linked in a network of relationships and social obligations. The Greeks were able to act on their own to a greater extent than the Chinese. Not feeling the necessity to maintain harmony, the Greeks were in the habit of arguing with one another in the marketplace and debating one another in the political assembly. For the Chinese, on the other hand, social existence depended on harmony, and therefore they were less likely to develop a habit of confrontation and debate, and "when confronted with a conflict of views, they might be oriented toward resolving the contradiction, transcending it, or finding a 'Middle way'—in short, to approach matters dialectically" (p. 37). This difference in worldviews is exemplified by the Aristotelian tradition that continues in the West and the Confucian tradition that continues in the East. Nisbett, therefore, argued that ecology has influenced the application of dialectical approaches, with Easterners being more inclined to seek the middle way when confronted with apparent contradictions, and Westerners being more inclined to insist on the correctness of one belief versus another.

Given this understanding of cultural approaches to knowledge construction, how do we as facilitators support the negotiation of meaning and shared understanding in our online courses? Next, we discuss a study that examined the role of e-mentoring in facilitating social construction of knowledge in a cross-cultural context.

Cross-Cultural E-Mentoring to Facilitate Knowledge Building and Community Building

The study reported here focuses on the online mentoring experience between e-mentors in the United States (volunteer graduate students at the University of New Mexico) and protégés in Sri Lanka (academics from universities and professionals from organizations) who were in training to become online tutors and mentors for the newly established National Online Distance Education Service (NODES) in Sri Lanka. The e-mentors and protégés engaged in an inquiry-based learning (IBL) activity in small groups (6–11 participants per group) for a period of 3 weeks using Moodle. Each group used a different IBL strategy to solve a social problem in the city of Colombo: problem solving (cleaning up garbage), role-play (traffic congestion), and case-based reasoning (street children). For the protégés, the goal was to learn through critical inquiry in an online environment and develop skills in knowledge construction, community building, and cross-cultural learning and communication. The goals for the e-mentors were to tutor, mentor, and facilitate an IBL activity through the interplay of diverse cultural perspectives and problem resolution through negotiation of meaning.

Study Approach

The questions examined (a) the role of e-mentoring, (b) cultural issues that emerged during the process of e-mentoring, and (c) challenges to cross-cultural e-mentoring. Qualitative analysis of computer transcripts and both quantitative and qualitative analyses of final evaluation surveys were employed. For analysis of computer transcripts, a message was used as the unit of analysis in accordance with the argument put forward by Gunawardena, Lowe, and Anderson (1997). The grounded approach used by Lincoln and Guba (1985) was used to identify the initial categories of e-mentor facilitation techniques. There were a total of 118 protégés in the five rounds of training analyzed for this study. One international e-mentor was assigned to one of the three groups in each round, totaling 15 international e-mentors (6 males and 9 females). In addition to the international e-mentor, one Sri Lankan e-mentor served as the e-mentor-at-large supporting both the international e-mentors and protégés.

E-Mentor Roles

Analysis of the transcripts showed that the international e-mentors demonstrated different facilitating techniques to help the protégés construct knowledge and build the learning community. These techniques were categorized into six e-mentoring roles: social, pedagogical, managerial, technical, collaborative, and inspirational (Jayatilleke et al., 2012). Figure 7.1 shows the roles that emerged in the three IBL designs. The social

Figure 7.1 E-mentor roles in three inquiry-based learning activities

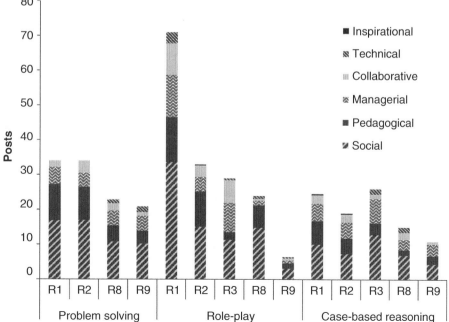

strategies included self-introductions, greetings, and encouragement and praise of the participants who helped to build the community. The pedagogical strategies involved providing guidance on how to conduct IBL activities, as most of the protégées were new to IBL; asking thought-provoking questions; paraphrasing; summarizing; and so on. The strategies related to conducting and completing the activity within the stipulated time were categorized as "managerial" and included giving instructions, assigning roles, stipulating timelines, and so on. The technical category included providing technical help or directing to a technical expert. The strategies used for promoting group collaboration were grouped as "collaborative." Sometimes, there was a tendency for roles to overlap, especially the social and collaborative roles. For instance, "encouraging team members," which was categorized under "social," also has an impact on group cohesion. The "inspirational" category emerged when the protégés clearly indicated that the interactions with the e-mentor changed their way of thinking or influenced them to change their attitudes. The "inspirational" category was inferred unlike the other categories, which could be aligned to a direct utterance from the e-mentor.

As observed in figure 7.1, the most prominent role was the "social" role, highest in all rounds. The second most prominent role was "pedagogical," followed by "managerial." The "collaborative" role was fairly prominent and was exhibited by all e-mentors to a certain degree.

Earlier studies conducted with online tutors and teachers have identified similar roles (Berge, 1995; Kim, Lee, & Lim, 2010): pedagogical, cognitive, intellectual; social; managerial, organizational; and technical. However, our study identified two additional e-mentoring roles: inspirational and collaborative.

Cross-Cultural E-Mentoring Techniques to Facilitate Community and Knowledge Building

In analyzing e-mentor roles further, we were able to identify culture-specific e-mentoring techniques that could be grouped as social and community building, and pedagogical and knowledge building, as described as follows.

Social and community-building e-mentoring techniques included

- greetings,
- self-introductions,
- acknowledgment of each other, and
- polite expressions.

Pedagogical and knowledge-building e-mentoring techniques were

- directly questioning the issues in a protégé's own country (curiosity and openness);
- explaining cultural attitudes in a protégé's own country in relation to the culture of the other protégés;
- elaborating on unique culture-specific terms;
- making comparisons with other countries on the basis of protégés' experiences;

- relating authentic examples, stories, and so on; and
- simplifying and paraphrasing.

In relation to the social role, it was apparent from the postings that both the e-mentors and the protégés showed mutual respect and were culturally sensitive. An e-mentor posted,

I am excited to be working with each one of you. I am here to help you in any way I can. There are just a few things I would ask that we all try to do.

- Let us all be open to learning from one another
- Let us all have fun while we are learning
- Let us always remember that there are no right or wrong answers

So, let the work begin! Please post any questions you may have about this activity or myself and I will do my best to provide answers.

Respectfully, [Name of the e-mentor]. (Round 8, Group 2, Post 1)

The following quote by one of the protégés clearly expressed her gratitude at the end of the learning experience:

Thank you very much for your support. We were fortunate to have you as our mentor. You guided us well in focusing our discussion and directing us in the correct path. (Protégé, Round 2, Group 1, interactive forum Post 41)

In relation to the pedagogical role, the following quote shows how an e-mentor asked thought-provoking questions to build knowledge:

[Name of the protégé], what was the result of President Premadasa's "Kepakaru Mapiya" scheme? Was it successful? How did the population react to it? (E-mentor, Round 1, Group 3, Talk, Post 10)

In another example, the international e-mentor brought his U.S. experience into the IBL activity and invited group members to discuss it in relation to their own context, thereby merging two roles, pedagogical and collaborative:

In the U.S. when a city has a traffic problem, concerned parties might make their views known to the city council, which is a group of elected officials responsible for running the city and which holds regular meetings where the citizens are invited. Does Colombo have something similar? One possibility is that we could organize an online city council meeting to give everyone a chance to make their contribution. Does anyone in the group have any thoughts about this? (E-mentor, Round 2, Group 2, Post 16)

Because there were both U.S. e-mentors and a Sri Lankan e-mentor-at-large, we compared their facilitation styles and found differences in the way they provided guidance to their protégés. Often, indirect coaching was used by U.S. e-mentors to get the protégés to think through the problem and come up with their own solutions. On the other hand, the Sri Lankan e-mentor provided more direct advice to solve a problem. Sri Lankan protégés often expected direct guidance, as they were more accustomed to a teacher-led instructional style.

Lessons Learned and Implications for Designing Cross-Cultural E-Mentoring

On the basis of this study, we present areas that should be addressed in the future design of cross-cultural e-mentoring experiences:

- *Identification of protégé characteristics:* One strategy used by an e-mentor was to review the profiles of the protégés before starting the discussion.
- *Linguistic difficulties:* Those with limited language proficiency participated less. Specific communication protocols that encourage nonnative speakers to contribute, such as writing in conversational language and acknowledging the use of online translators, can encourage those with limited proficiency to participate. But participation to the learners' maximum potential may not be possible if they are not proficient in the language of the course.
- *Expectation of direct guidance from protégés who are more accustomed to teacher-centered learning:* Facilitating to meet this expectation initially and gradually encouraging self-direction and autonomy may be one way to address this.
- *Finding time to provide timely feedback to each protégé during initial postings.*

Conclusion

This chapter highlighted the paradigm shift in teaching from information dissemination focused on knowledge to online facilitation focused on collaborative knowledge construction to support learners in a networked learning environment. The facilitator plays a key role in addressing cultural factors to support the diverse learner when building the social environment and facilitating knowledge construction. We showed from our study how facilitation and e-mentoring across cultures can support OCL. A response to an open-ended question in the final evaluation survey in this study pointed out the value of cross-cultural e-mentoring:

> Yes, I thought that a person who'd be total stranger to our culture won't be able to have good insight into problems pertaining to our country. But I realized online learning bridges the gap between different cultures to a considerable level. (Protégé, Round 3)

References

Al-Harthi, A. S. (2005). Distance higher education experiences of Arab Gulf students in the United States: A cultural perspective. *The International Review of Research in Open and Distance Learning, 6*(3), 1–14.

Berge, Z. L. (1995). Facilitating computer conferencing: Recommendations from the field. *Educational Technology, 35*(1), 22–30.

Biesenbach-Lucas, S. (2003). Asynchronous discussion groups in teacher training classes: Perceptions of native and non-native students. *Journal of Asynchronous Learning Networks, 7*(3), 24–46.

Brislin, R. (2000). *Understanding culture's influence on behavior* (2nd ed.). Fort Worth, TX: Harcourt.

Chen, G. M. (2000). Global communication via Internet: An educational application. In G. M. Chen & W. J. Starosta (Eds.), *Communication and global society* (pp. 143–157). New York, NY: Peter Lang.

Curtis, D. D., & Lawson, M. J. (2001). Exploring collaborative online learning. *Journal of Asynchronous Learning Networks, 5*(1), 21–34. Retrieved from http://sloanconsortium.org/publications/jaln_main

Feenberg, A. (1989). The written world: On the theory and practice of computer conferencing. In R. Mason & A. Kaye (Eds.), *Mindweave* (pp. 22–39). Oxford, UK: Pergamon.

Gunawardena, C., Faustino, G., Keller, P., Garcia, F., Barrett, K., Skinner, J., . . . Fernando, S. (2013). E-mentors facilitating social construction of knowledge in online case-based reasoning. In *Proceedings of the Sixth Annual Mentoring Conference* (pp. 60–68). Albuquerque: University of New Mexico, The Mentoring Institute.

Gunawardena, C. N., Lowe, C. A., & Anderson, T. (1997). Analysis of a global online debate and the development of an interaction analysis model for examining social construction of knowledge in computer conferencing. *Journal of Educational Computing Research, 17*(4), 395–429.

Gunawardena, C. N., Nolla, A. C., Wilson, P. L., López-Islas, J. R., Ramírez-Angel, N., & Megchun-Alpízar, R. M. (2001). A cross-cultural study of group process and development in online conferences. *Distance Education, 22*, 85–121.

Gunawardena, C. N., Skinner, J. K., Richmond, C., Linder-Van Berschot, J., LaPointe, D., Barrett, K., & Padmaperuma, G. (2008, March). *Cross-cultural e-mentoring to develop problem-solving online learning communities.* Paper presented at the 2008 Annual Meeting of the American Educational Research Association, New York.

Gunawardena, C. N., & Zittle, F. (1997). Social presence as a predictor of satisfaction within a computer mediated conferencing environment. *The American Journal of Distance Education, 11*, 8–25.

Harasim, L. (2012). *Learning theory and online technologies.* New York, NY: Routledge.

Hofstede, G. (1980). *Culture's consequences: International differences in work-related values.* Beverly Hills, CA: Sage.

Jayatilleke, B. G., Kulasekara, G. U., Kumarasinha, M. C. B., & Gunawardena, C. N. (2012). Cross-cultural e-mentor roles in facilitating inquiry-based online learning. *Proceedings of the 26th Annual Conference of Asian Association of Open Universities* (pp. 60–68). Chiba: The Open University of Japan.

Jonassen, D. H., & Kim, B. (2010). Arguing to learn and learning to argue: Design justifications and guidelines. *Educational Technology Research and Development, 58*, 439–457.

Kim, Y. J., Lee, S., & Lim, M. (2010). An analysis on tutor's roles for facilitating critical thinking in online discussion. In Z. Abas, I. S. Jung, & J. Luca (Eds.), *Proceedings of Global Learn Asia Pacific 2010* (pp. 4232–4241). Waynesville, NC: Association for the Advancement of Computing in Education.

Lincoln, Y. S., & Guba, E. G. (1985). *Naturalistic inquiry.* Beverly Hills, CA: Sage.

Lopez-Islas, J. R. (2001, December). *Collaborative learning at Monterrey Tech–Virtual University.* Paper presented at the Symposium on Web-based Learning Environments to Support Learning at a Distance: Design and Evaluation, Asilomar, Pacific Grove, CA.

Martin, J. N., & Nakayama, T. K. (2004). *Intercultural communication in contexts* (3rd ed.). New York, NY: McGraw-Hill.

Matthewson, C., & Thaman, K. H. (1998). Designing the rebbelib: Staff development in a Pacific multicultural environment. In C. Latchem & F. Lockwood (Eds.), *Staff development in open and flexible learning* (pp. 115–126). New York, NY: Routledge.

Nisbett, R. E. (2003). *The geography of thought: How Asians and Westerners think differently and why.* New York, NY: Free Press.

Richardson, J., & Swan, K. (2003). Examining social presence in online courses in relation to students' perceived learning and satisfaction. *Journal of Asynchronous Learning Networks, 7*(1). Retrieved from http://sloanconsortium.org/publications/jaln_main

Ryan, A. M., Gheen, M. H., & Midgley, C. (1998). Why do some students avoid asking for help? An examination of the interplay among students' academic efficacy, teachers' social-emotional role, and the classroom goal structure. *Journal of Educational Psychology, 90,* 528–535.

Tu, C. H. (2001). How Chinese perceive social presence: An examination of interaction in online learning environment. *Education Media International, 38*(1), 45–60. doi:10.1080/09523980010021235

Wegerif, R. (1998). The social dimension of asynchronous learning networks. *Journal of Asynchronous Learning Networks, 2*(1), 34–49. Retrieved from http://sloanconsortium.org/publications/jaln_main

Zhang, Q. (2006). Immediacy and out-of-class communication: A cross-cultural comparison. *International Journal of Intercultural Relations, 30,* 33–50.

8

SUPPORTING DIVERSE ONLINE LEARNERS

Charlotte Nirmalani Gunawardena

Learner support is the critical link in online education. A learner support system is composed of human and nonhuman resources that contribute to the learning process of an online course and should be designed as an integral part of the course. For example, if the online course requires students to access library resources to complete a research paper, then easy access to library resources must be provided as part of the learner support system for that course. Learner support for online learners will differ based on the context; learner characteristics such as needs, expectations, prior learning experiences, and so on; and the learning process. Online learners are not homogeneous. They differ in age, gender, culture, education, language, social and economic background, family and employment commitments, goals, objectives, needs, and desires. Each individual has his or her own needs that have to be met.

In an online environment, in addition to geographical distance, there are different types of distance that need to be bridged to support the learner, such as the distance between (a) the learner and teacher or tutor, (b) the learner and other learners, (c) the learner and access to technology, and (d) the learner and the institution. Moreover, there may exist psychological distance (e.g., feelings of isolation), sociocultural distance (e.g., power distance and differences in social class and culture), and technical distance (e.g., lack of necessary technical skills). The challenge then is to determine how to design a learner support system that narrows these types of distances to support diverse learners in a technology-mediated learning environment.

This chapter explores aspects of diversity that one needs to consider when designing a learner support system to bridge different types of distances in an online environment. It also presents a framework for addressing diverse needs of online learners and offers examples to guide the design and integration of learner support into online learning.

Aspects of Diversity

Educational Expectations

Different cultures have different attitudes toward education and its purpose. In a review of studies on questions of culture, Uzuner (2009) concluded that the diverse cultural assumptions students bring to online learning concerning how teaching and learning should be done bring about conflicts, disagreements, and frustrations. What then are some of these diverse cultural assumptions?

Li (2012) provided insight into how educational expectations are influenced by different beliefs about learning, and from her research with college students comparing European American and Chinese learning models, she showed how these beliefs differ in terms of the purpose of learning, the agentic process of learning, the kinds of achievement, and affect. For example, in the European American model, three main purposes of learning emerged: (a) cultivating the mind and understanding the world, (b) developing one's ability and skill, and (c) reaching personal goals. In the Chinese learning model, the three main purposes were (a) perfecting oneself morally and socially, (b) acquiring knowledge and skills for self, and (c) contributing to society. Although the second purpose is similar in both societies, Chinese respondents stressed mastery of knowledge, whereas European Americans emphasized developing ability. Li then showed how the Chinese purposes of learning are inherently related and have been part of Confucian values regarding learning. One needs to engage in personal skill learning and moral development before one can meaningfully contribute to society.

Turkey's culture of patronage, which fosters values of obedience, honor, and respect for authority, and oral traditions has emphasized the sacredness of the text, honored the responsibility of the professor to interpret the text, and expected students to memorize the professor's words (Gursoy, 2005). In an oral tradition, the inability to interact with an esteemed professor is a challenge that one should account for when designing a learner support system. On the other hand, Murphy (1991) pointed out that Turkish culture itself fosters interaction among learners through their work sites, in face-to-face classes, and in outside (supplementary) classes. The need for affiliation is critical for distance learners who tend to be isolated and for Turks in particular, who share values of group ethos and close kinship ties. The outside classes offer more than just the skills and knowledge that students sought; they also provide the possibility for students to develop bonds with fellow classmates and with their instructor. Both forms of bonding are integral aspects of educational patronage. Turkish students tend to find substitutes for teachers (patrons) among their classmates, showing the importance of developing online peer support networks and face-to-face sessions for these learners.

The cultural values of individualism, secularism, and feminism are not recognized as desirable in many cultures that place higher value on religion, group efforts, and well-defined gender roles (McIsaac, 1993). Most Western learners and instructors believe that each learner is a distinct individual, controls his or her behavior, is responsible for outcomes of behavior, is oriented toward personal achievement, and frequently believes group membership compromises goal achievement (Nisbett, 2003). Many learners from Asian countries, on the other hand, believe success is a group goal and a national goal. Attaining group goals is tied to maintaining harmonious social relations.

To address diverse cultural assumptions and expectations, instructors can take the early step to make the criteria and expectations of an online course obvious. In the course syllabus, specific explanations on the teaching-learning philosophy and the hidden culture of the course; specific communication protocols detailing formats and expectations for communication online; and clear guidelines for individual and group responsibilities, collaborative processes, and evaluation criteria in group activities need to be included to address the learners' diverse expectations.

Other ways of designing appropriate learner support is to offer options to meet the diverse educational expectations of the learners. Some online courses have tried to accommodate this demand for traditional teacher-centered instructional methods by offering video lectures online and on demand, so learners can continue to "see and hear" their instructors. Eye movement, gestures, gaze, and the human voice provide the contextual information that learners from high-context cultures rely on to interpret meaning. Thus, online learning is sustaining rather than challenging traditional ways of teaching by focusing the design on teacher-centered instructional methods. When diverse learners and diverse educational expectations are present in an online class, it is prudent to offer options, and having recorded video or podcasts that students can review at their own pace are worthwhile forms of learner support.

Learner Preferences

Learning styles describe learner preferences for different types of learning and instructional activities. These styles are generally measured by instruments that ask individuals how they think they prefer to learn rather than by observing an individual's learning process in a learning task, which would be a better gauge of learning preferences. Chapter 2 discusses the impact of culture on learning styles. In our study using nine instruments to analyze Hispanic learning styles (Sanchez & Gunawardena, 1998), we found that Hispanic adult learners in a northern New Mexico community college showed a preference for collaborative instead of competitive activities, reflectivity in task engagement, and an action-based, active approach to learning. On the basis of this finding, we recommended a learner support system to facilitate real-world problem solving or case-based reasoning in asynchronous learning environments that provide opportunities for reflection and active collaborative learning. Although the value of learning styles instruments lies in understanding the various learning styles represented in a group of learners as in our study, it is a given that a variety of learning styles will be present in an online class, and therefore in designing learner support, we need to look beyond learning styles to understand how culture impacts the learning environment and the teaching and learning process online. In this regard, the Cultural Dimensions of Learning Framework, developed by Parrish and Linder-VanBerschot (2010), is a more useful tool to understand the spectrum of cultural differences that impact the teaching and learning process online.

Another aspect in which individual learners differ is in the prior knowledge, skills, and experience that they bring to a learning environment. Prior knowledge or what the student already knows can be a predictor of how well a student will learn in a new situation. Students from different cultures may have varying levels of prior knowledge and experience even though they have studied the same subject matter. Designing peer mentoring networks that match those who have less prior knowledge and experience with those who have more is a worthwhile form of learner support in this instance.

As we design learner support, it is important to consider that within cultural groups, individuals differ significantly from each other, and therefore it is equally important to identify and respond to an individual's learning preference. Although matching teaching and learning styles may yield higher achievement in test scores, providing learners with activities that require them to broaden their repertoire of preferred learning styles and approaches more fully prepares them to function in our diverse and global society. There is a need to provide a delicate balance of activities that give opportunities to learn in preferred ways and activities that challenge the learner to learn in new or less preferred ways.

Online Interaction and Knowledge Construction

Online teachers and tutors play a key role in supporting interaction and knowledge construction among diverse learners. Chapter 7 discussed the cultural issues that impact knowledge construction online. Studies have reported differences in the way diverse learners engage and participate in online discussions. In a comparative analysis of teacher and student interactions in two distance teaching universities, Shanghai TV University in China and Wawasan Open University in Malaysia, Wu and Teoh (2008) revealed that learners from higher power distance societies were often concerned with fewer face-to-face contacts and found it hard to adapt to interaction in an online environment. Also, learners from higher uncertainty avoidance societies needed to be constantly motivated and assured of their progress. To support these learners, the authors suggested that tutors use motivational strategies by setting out clear objectives for online communication. Although tutors in more individualistic societies can adopt an approach of allowing students to voice their opinions, tutors in more collectivist societies need to constantly invite students to participate in discussions.

Rourke and Coleman (2010) showed the need to provide scaffolding to support knowledge construction in digital environments and discussed a case study where they used a pedagogical model for online collaborative learning (OCL) and computer-mediated peer review (CMPR) to provide scaffolds for knowledge construction in a graduate-level class. Results showed that students actively participated in the learning processes and engaged in both self and peer review, and the scaffolds encouraged the use of multiple modes of representation and self-awareness during the knowledge construction process. The authors noted that OCL and CMPR as a scaffolded process has allowed the students to become more autonomous and independent in their learning as they gradually have this support system removed to allow them to stand on their own feet.

In a mixed-method study of 28 online courses to examine interaction and participation across different ethnic and age groups, Ke and Kwak (2013) found that minority students (predominantly Hispanic and Navajo) were less satisfied with online education in general and felt less confident and comfortable about taking courses online compared with their Anglo counterparts, even though they were more positive about instructor support. The minority students also voiced a need for social presence and a long-term "bond" (i.e., learning partnership) that is developed through a cohort group or program that should last beyond a single course. These findings help to explain why minority students have expressed less satisfaction with overall web-based distance education. According to Ke and Kwak, the findings provide empirical evidence that online learning environments should be adaptive or inclusive to support diverse ethnic and cultural groups of learners, and they suggested balancing high-context and low-context culture norms and, particularly, encouraging long-term learning interactions among learners (e.g., via cohort groups and a program curriculum that highlights the interconnection among courses). Ke and Kwak also revealed that online learners of different age groups valued intergenerational interactions, thus showing the importance of developing intergenerational peer support networks for online classes.

Van Rosmalen et al. (2008) encouraged the use of peer tutoring as a learner support system after they developed and tested a model of peer tutoring to determine how to help students answer content-related questions in online classes via interactions with their peers. In this model, a small group of students is created, which consists of the student who asks the question and peers who should be able to answer it. Criteria used to compose the group are the content of the question in relation to the knowledge and skills of the peers. A specially designed module embedded in the Moodle learning management system exposes students to a learning network, its activity nodes, and a question module (named AskCQ) that organizes and structures the question-answering process. The 8-week experiment with two groups of approximately 50 students showed that students resolved a substantial number of questions using the peer tutoring model and positively valued the model. In another study, Kelly and Stevens (2009) showed how different types of e-learner support—e-messages, the strengthening of subject identity and community, and discussions—through information and communications technology (ICT) can support diverse learner needs online. These studies provide direction for the kinds of software development and ICT utilization that are necessary to customize learning for students with different levels of knowledge in online learning environments.

Gender

In a study of gender differences in a self-regulated online environment in Turkey, Yükseltürk and Bulut (2009) found that there was no significant difference in achievement with respect to gender other than test anxiety. Test anxiety caused a significant amount of variance in female students' achievement. Female students with higher levels of anxiety received lower grades in the online programming course. Reasons for this finding in the Turkish sociocultural context should be explored further, as students' prior experience in the subject matter of the course and/or the educational preparation of female students in general may have had an impact on the findings. One of the suggestions made by the authors to reduce this test anxiety is to include alternative assessment techniques.

On the other hand, a study by Price (2006) showed that women studying the online version of a social science course at the Open University in the United Kingdom scored significantly higher than men on assessments and on the examination and were more academically engaged, self-confident, and willing to learn from other students. In this instance, the results contradict the belief that women are disadvantaged by technology in education and show that women are confident independent learners who are academically engaged and may outperform their male counterparts online. Both studies point to the need to understand the needs of both men and women online learners as we design learner support systems.

Language and Second-Language Speakers

Although English is increasingly recognized as the international *lingua franca*, it puts nonnative learners at a disadvantage. Often English is the learners' second, third, or fourth language, and they might have little opportunity to actually use English daily. English-as-a-second-language (ESL) learners need additional time to read and refer to dictionaries and content provided in a variety of formats such as written lectures, audio recordings, and concept maps.

When computer users from different cultures communicate with each other, they may not be aware of each other's discourse conventions or genres that are culturally appropriate for interactions. Kramsch and Thorne (2002) offered a good example of how miscommunication in an intercultural asynchronous online dialogue between American and French students was caused not so much by deficient individual linguistic styles or code (French or English) but mostly by a lack of understanding "cultural genres" in each other's discourse.

Smith (2005) revealed that a lack of awareness of cultural differences and generalizations about others who use English as a second language may prompt learners from dominant cultures to unknowingly deauthorize group members with group coping strategies that, although well intended, limit opportunities for discussion. Groups assigned minimal responsibilities to their nonnative English-speaking members because they felt these learners faced unusual challenges of adapting to the U.S. culture and completing their studies. These nonnative English speakers then felt uncomfortable and unproductive. This crystallized the recognition of difference among group members: Nonnative speakers were perceived as "others" and treated as a threat to the group in ways that mirror hierarchical structures within a larger society, creating unsafe learning spaces (Smith, 2005).

This discussion shows that as online learning cultures develop, students and facilitators have to adjust to new modes of communication and interaction. Developing communication protocols that serve as a guide for communication online and providing guidelines for teamwork with group members who are nonnative speakers of the language are needed forms of learner support.

Learners With Disabilities

Glazatov (2012) identified several challenges faced by students with disabilities when exploring how online designers are complying with the Americans with Disabilities Act (ADA). These included dealing with the inaccessibility of the website; having technical difficulties; being misunderstood, which led to students not requesting accommodations; needing to work harder than others; and not seeking legally mandated accommodations that could ease their workload. In a survey of online students in five highly ranked U.S. colleges, Roberts, Crittenden, and Crittenden (2011) found that the majority of students chose not to disclose their disabilities and ask for accommodations. Students perceived their disabilities as negative factors to be academically successful and identified special technologies in order to work effectively in an online environment, such as technologies to magnify or enlarge on-screen text, larger monitors, speech-recognition software, oversized keyboards, special mouse technologies, and screen readers. Developing courses based on the Universal Design of Learning (UDL) principles can allow for inclusion of different media and learning preferences for instructional activities that are beneficial to students with and without disabilities (Glazatov, 2012).

Crow (2008) discussed four types of disabilities (visual impairments, hearing impairments, motor impairments, and cognitive impairments) and suggested strategies that designers can use to support students with such disabilities. Students with visual impairments should be provided with meaningful alternate or long descriptions for each non-text element on the website, and the use of layout tables should be minimized, as the screen-reading device typically reads from top left to bottom right. It is also prudent to avoid the use of background images to convey meaningful information, to use a sans serif font, and to avoid the use of any information that relies exclusively on color or color recognition. Students with hearing impairments can be helped if designers provide real-time text captioning for all audio, video, and multimedia presentations in online courses and provide the text transcripts of the audio content. Limiting the use of synchronous (real-time) chat-based assignments, games, and simulation activities that require high degrees of motor dexterity can assist students with motor impairments. Incorporating some practical and cost-effective universal design practices can make the online course more accessible to learners who have cognitive impairments.

In discussing a framework for supporting online learners with psychiatric disabilities, Grabinger (2010) showed how designers can support metacognition by including examples of prior work, focusing on multiple versions of content presentations with a variety of multimedia, highly structured directions, and open, well-organized screens. Giving time to students in the first week and in subsequent weeks to form relationships and learn about each other and encouraging students to use visual and aural media are other methods of supporting these learners online. As implied in our discussion, disability is a type of diversity that designers need to pay attention to in order to support online learning.

Designing Learner Support for Diverse Learners

Framework

Dillon and Blanchard (1991, p. 3) proposed a learner support system for distance learners that takes into account four types of support that is relevant even today as we design learner supports for diverse online learners. These four types of support are as follows:

1. learner support that addresses learner needs (such as cultural background, expectations, learning styles, motivation, confidence, self-concept, self-efficacy, belonging, and financial needs),
2. learner support that addresses the needs of the content (such as support for learning activities and laboratory experiences),
3. learner support related to the institutional context (such as enrollment, library access, use of facilities), and
4. learner support related to technology and communication (such as orientation programs in the use of technology and communication protocols).

All four types of support are necessary in the online context. Offering orientation programs prior to offering a course that helps the learner understand the technical interface, the types of communication, how to learn skills, and the course expectations and requirements will put the learner at ease and encourage participation in interactive learning activities.

On the basis of the experience with interuniversity online collaborations, McIsaac (1993) observed that a number of issues need to be addressed when the electronic classroom cuts across national boundaries. These issues relate to (a) pedagogy, to determine that educational assumptions are mutually agreeable; (b) motivation, to determine differences in online participation between students in various cultures; (c) access to computer facilities; (d) technical difficulties such as frequent power outages and malfunctioning equipment; and (e) language, when communication takes place in writing in a second or third language without any nonverbal signals. One needs to consider these issues when designing support systems for diverse learners.

Taking into consideration the various types of support discussed so far, I provide a framework (see table 8.1) for designing a learner support system to address diverse

TABLE 8.1
Framework for Addressing Diverse Learner Needs in an Online Course

Stage	*Information on Course-Specific Support*	*Information on General Learning Environment Support*
Preentry to course	<ul><li>Course description and expectations</li><li>Teaching and learning philosophy, culture of course</li><li>Synchronous and asynchronous sessions</li><li>Entry requirements</li><li>Registration procedures</li><li>Advisement on available course options and related job skills</li><li>How special needs will be met</li><li>Advice to international and second-language students</li></ul>	<ul><li>Alternative options to a course or degree</li><li>Advice to special needs students</li><li>Counseling for those who return to academics after being away from it</li></ul>
Entry, prerequisites, and orientation	<ul><li>Course requirements</li><li>How to access instructors and tutors</li><li>Institutional regulations and procedures (e.g., incompletes, withdrawals)</li><li>Assignment submission deadlines</li><li>Time management</li><li>How to access library resources and databases</li></ul>	<ul><li>Orientation to course</li><li>Technical system</li><li>Technical skills</li><li>How to solve technical problems</li><li>Navigation and structure of interface</li><li>Support for students with disabilities</li><li>Communication protocols and netiquette</li><li>Learning how to learn skills</li><li>Collaboration and team building</li><li>Writing support and labs</li><li>Mobile support</li><li>24-hour access</li></ul>

(Continues)

TABLE 8.1

Framework for Addressing Diverse Learner Needs in an Online Course (Continued)

Stage	Information on Course-Specific Support	Information on General Learning Environment Support
During the course	<ul><li>Alternative learning activities</li><li>Instructor support</li><li>Mentor support</li><li>Peer support</li><li>Guidelines for collaborative learning and knowledge construction</li><li>Advice on group projects</li><li>Synchronous sessions to discuss course content and issues</li><li>Support at study centers if available</li><li>Individual mobile phone support</li></ul>	<ul><li>Dealing with problems between tutor and learner, and learner and learner</li><li>How to address isolation</li><li>Peer support networks (consider intergenerational networks)</li><li>Networks of support for female students</li><li>How to address changes in life circumstances and economic, financial, and political difficulties</li><li>Counseling on personal difficulties</li></ul>
Assessment (exams, group projects, alternative forms of assessment)	<ul><li>Alternative assessment options</li><li>Time, place, and procedures related to exams</li><li>Advice on taking exams, managing stress, and dealing with group problems</li></ul>	<ul><li>Special support available for exams</li><li>Extra time for learners with disabilities, older learners</li><li>Exam anxiety counseling</li><li>Group problem solving</li></ul>

Note. Created by Charlotte N. Gunawardena, Chulantha Kulasekara, and Shantha Fernando, in the Moodle learning management system for the NODES Online Tutor Mentor Development Program, in Sri Lanka, and used with their permission.

learner needs in an online course from preentry to final assessment. For the four stages listed, types of learner support are distinguished as course-specific support and general learning environment support. Designers can add to, or delete from, this framework to create a learner support system for the diverse learners they expect to have in their online courses.

Examples

In this section, two examples of learner support systems designed for two different sociocultural contexts are discussed to illustrate how learner support systems can be integrated into online course design, taking into consideration diverse learner needs in each context. Figure 8.1 shows the learner support system I designed for a faculty development program in Sri Lanka using Moodle to train online tutors and mentors for the National Online Distance Education Service (NODES) of the Ministry of Higher Education. Figure 8.2 shows the learner support system I designed in WebCT Vista for a graduate-level course on culture and global e-learning (OLIT 537) at the University of New Mexico in the United States. Comparison of these figures will show the similarities and differences in the two systems, with one of the main differences being the availability of regional access centers in the Sri Lankan system to serve the needs of remote learners who do not

Figure 8.1 Learner support system for the Online Tutor Mentor Development Program in Sri Lanka. Originally created by Charlotte N. Gunawardena and Chulantha Kulasekara in the Moodle learning management system for the NODES Online Tutor Mentor Development Program, in Sri Lanka, and used with their permission.

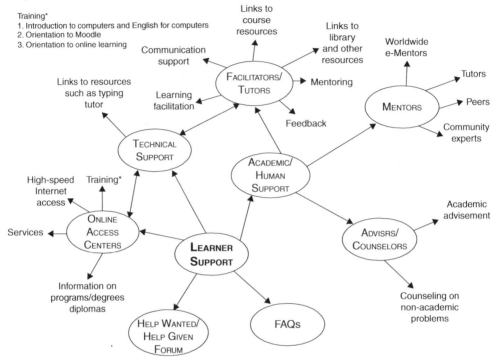

Figure 8.2 Learner support system for an online graduate-level course on culture and global e-learning. Created by Charlotte N. Gunawardena and Jane Erlandson and used with their permission.

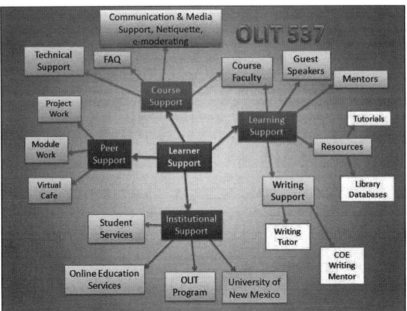

have access to the Internet in their homes and who will need to use the centers to access tutors and course-related resources. The support system for the U.S. course is designed based on the assumption that students have easy access to the Internet so that the course could be conducted entirely online.

When considering support for diverse learners in the online environment, it is best to design alternative activities to reach the same objective and give students the option to select activities that best meet their culturally adapted ways of learning.

Conclusions

This chapter pointed out the critical need to integrate learner support into online course design to assist diverse learners. To design a learner support system for online learning, we need to understand the online learner in context and in relation to the course, instructors, peer groups, workplace, family, culture, and society. As we look ahead, our challenge as online educators is to consider how diversity and context can become partners in the design of online learning and how online technologies can be employed to customize learner support for diverse learners.

Author's Note

Special thanks go to Ketaki Kekatpure for developing an annotated bibliography and refining graphics to support this chapter.

References

Crow, K. L. (2008). Four types of disabilities: Their impact on online learning. *Techtrends: Linking Research and Practice to Improve Learning, 52*(1), 51–55. doi:10.1007/s11528-008-0112-6

Dillon, C., & Blanchard, D. (1991, May). *Education for each: Learner driven distance education.* Paper presented at the Second American Symposium on Research in Distance Education, Pennsylvania State University, American Center for the Study of Distance Education, University Park, PA.

Glazatov, T. R. (2012). Inclusiveness in online programs: Disability issues and implications for higher education administrators. *Journal of Applied Learning Technology, 2*(1), 14–18.

Grabinger, S. (2010). A framework for supporting postsecondary learners with psychiatric disabilities in online environments. *Electronic Journal of E-Learning, 8*(2), 101–109.

Gursoy, H. (2005). A critical look at distance education in Turkey. In A. A. Carr-Chellman (Ed.), *Global perspectives on e-learning: Rhetoric and realities* (pp. 35–51). Thousand Oaks, CA: Sage.

Ke, F., & Kwak, D. (2013). Online learning across ethnicity and age: A study on learning interaction participation, perception, and learning satisfaction. *Computers and Education, 61*, 43–51. doi:10.1016/j.compedu.2012.09.003

Kelly, P., & Stevens, C. (2009). Narrowing the distance: Using e-learner support to enhance the student experience. *European Journal of Open, Distance and E-Learning,* no. 2. Retrieved from http://www.eurodl.org/?p=archives&year=2009&halfyear=2&article=380.

Kramsch, C., & Thorne, S. (2002). Foreign language learning as global communicative practice. In D. Block & D. Cameron (Eds.), *Globalization and language teaching* (pp. 83–100). London, UK: Routledge.

Li, J. (2012). *Cultural foundations of learning: East and West.* New York, NY: Cambridge University Press.

McIsaac, M. S. (1993). Economic, political, and social considerations in the use of global computer-based distance education. In R. Muffoletto & N. Knupfer (Eds.), *Computers in education: Social, political, and historical perspectives* (pp. 219–232). Cresskill, NJ: Hampton Press.

Murphy, K. L. (1991). Sociocultural context of interaction in Turkish distance learning: Implications for distance education teaching. In Dillon, C. L. (Ed.), *Proceedings of the First Forum on the Teaching of Distance Education* (pp. 164–184). Norman, OK: The Oklahoma Research Center for Continuing Professional and Higher Education, University of Oklahoma.

Nisbett, R. E. (2003). *The geography of thought: How Asians and Westerners think differently . . . and why.* New York, NY: Free Press.

Parrish, P., & Linder-VanBerschot, J. A. (2010). Cultural dimensions of learning: Addressing the challenges of multicultural instruction. *International Review of Research in Open and Distance Learning, 11*(2), 1–19.

Price, L. (2006). Gender differences and similarities in online courses: Challenging stereotypical views of women. *Journal of Computer Assisted Learning, 22*(5), 349–359.

Roberts, J. B., Crittenden, L. A., & Crittenden, J. C. (2011). Students with disabilities and online learning: A cross-institutional study of perceived satisfaction with accessibility compliance and services. *The Internet and Higher Education, 14,* 242–250. doi:10.1016/j.iheduc.2011.05.004.

Rourke, A., & Coleman, K. (2010). A learner support system: Scaffolding to enhance digital learning. *International Journal of Technology, Knowledge and Society, 6*(1), 55–70.

Sanchez, I., & Gunawardena, C. N. (1998). Understanding and supporting the culturally diverse distance learner. In C. Campbell Gibson (Ed.), *Distance learners in higher education: Institutional responses for quality outcomes* (pp. 47–64). Madison, WI: Atwood.

Smith, R. O. (2005). Working with difference in online collaborative groups. *Adult Education Quarterly, 55*(3), 182–199.

Uzuner, S. (2009). Questions of culture in distance learning: A research review. *International Review of Research in Open and Distance Learning, 10*(3), 1–19. Retrieved from http://www.irrodl.org/index.php/irrodl

Van Rosmalen, P. P., Sloep, P. B., Brouns, F. F., Kester, L. L., Berlanga, A. A., Bitter, M. M., & Koper, R. R. (2008). A model for online learner support based on selecting appropriate peer tutors. *Journal of Computer Assisted Learning, 24*(6), 483–493. doi:10.1111/j.1365-2729.2008.00283.x

Wu, B., & Teoh, A. (2008). The influence of national culture toward learners' interaction in the online learning environment: A comparative analysis of Shanghai TV University (China) and Wawasan Open University (Malaysia). *Quarterly Review of Distance Education, 9*(3), 327–339.

Yükseltürk, E., & Bulut, S. (2009). Gender differences in self-regulated online learning environment. *Journal of Educational Technology and Society, 12*(3), 12–22.

9

DIVERSITY IN EXPECTATIONS OF QUALITY AND ASSESSMENT

Albert Sangrà, Stella Porto, and Insung Jung

Quality of online learning is a complex and multidimensional issue (Jung, 2011). This is partly due to the extremely diverse range of definitions of *online learning* (Sangrà, Vlachopoulos, & Cabrera, 2012) and the various interpretations of *quality* in the context of online learning (Abdous, 2009; Dondi, Moretti, & Nascimbeni, 2006). If one considers quality as a means of achieving the aims of different participants in the teaching and learning process, then the three dimensions of online quality assessment, proposed by Harvey and Knight (1996), should be considered.

According to Harvey and Knight, the first dimension of quality assessment can be conducted at different levels within the organization. The institutional level relates to the mission and institutional objectives, whereas the program or course level evaluates learning objectives and online support programs. Another level of quality assessment can happen with the disaggregated elements of online learning such as content, learning materials, teaching strategies, support services, library system, and so on (Sangrà, Guàrdia, & González-Sanmamed, 2007).

The second dimension relates to stakeholders. Both Ehlers (2004) and Twigg (2001) examined quality in e-learning initiatives from various stakeholder perspectives, including that of students relevant to their progress, performance, and level of satisfaction and that of teachers, examining their degree of interest and effectiveness. Administrators may focus on cost-effectiveness and learning outcomes.

The third dimension is the approach to quality assessment. In this case, it may be difficult to talk about quality without focusing on a particular area or unit of analysis. Thus, four approaches can be taken: (a) a technological approach, which focuses on the whole set of technical requirements, devices, and software being used for online learning; (b) an economic approach, which looks into cost-benefit and financial results of online learning; (c) an educational approach, which values learning progress and the performance of online learners; and finally (d) a global approach, which aims at striking a balance between the aforementioned approaches.

Considering the complexity and value-laden nature of quality, this chapter will explore the diversity of expectations, experiences, and meanings of quality and assessment in online learning at different levels (institutional, program, and course levels) and from different perspectives (students, teachers, and administrators). It highlights similarities and differences in assessing the quality of online learning in three cultural contexts (Asia, Europe, and the United States) and offers implications of such concepts for online learning providers.

The Asian Context

Quality is a relative concept and may be viewed differently by different stakeholder groups. For example, in a study employing a mix of quantitative and qualitative methods, Cashion and Palmieri (2002) reported that 357 Australian learners who were in online vocational education and training programs rated flexibility as the number one factor in assessing the quality of online learning, whereas it was rated far lower by online instructors. On the other hand, factors such as induction, communication with teachers and other students, and a hybrid of face-to-face and online learning were deemed less important by learners while being cited as highly important by most instructors. Although the instructors believed that the learners would demand much training and support, learners did not indicate a need for a considerable amount of orientation or initial support to study online.

Differences in the view of quality in online education are also observed in various cultures. In the context of Asia, Jung (2012) surveyed over 1,600 Asian distance learners across 11 countries and 1 territory and identified several factors that learners considered important in assessing the quality of online education. Well-structured course materials that follow clear development guidelines and incorporate learners' needs were viewed as most critical (see chapter 16). Unlike Asian learners, European learners tend to perceive didactic and collaborative learning as a key quality factor in online learning, as discussed in the following section. A study conducted by Ehlers (2004) with experienced European online learners revealed that European learners focused on collaboration, online discussions, interactive tutor support, and didactics, which include provision for frequent feedback on individualized tasks. This may indicate that a majority of Asian learners, compared with their European and other counterparts, tend to perceive distance education as a form of independent study. As such, they value clearly organized course content with easy-to-follow directions, while taking little account of value-added elements of online learning, such as collaborative activities and interactions. This may explain why many online courses in Asia make relatively little use of interactive functions and collaborative learning (Latchem & Jung, 2009).

A 2-year action research, investigating the effects of scaffolding strategies for wiki-based online learning activity in a multicultural language class, found that students from different cultures held different beliefs and views of collaborative online learning (Jung & Suzuki, 2014). They observed intense debates in European groups, a fair division of labor in American groups, and no evidence of editing their paper together by the Korean groups. Although it was not possible to confirm that these variances were a consequence of cultural differences, it might be inferred that the cultural and perhaps educational differences influenced the different work patterns online. Literature (e.g., Eriksen & Fossum, 2000) generally supports that Europeans value public discussion of important social issues. This may explain the intensity of the European online learners' interactions.

Americans are known for their values of fairness for all and responsibilities from all, which may explain the more equal distribution of responsibilities among the American group members. Although these so-called Western groups focused on both the process and the product of wiki-based collaborative writing and editing, the Korean group failed to use the wiki editing function. Instead, the learners met in person, worked in a word processor, and copied their final report into the wiki. As argued by Park (2010) and Kim, Cho, and Kim (2010), Korean school culture tends to value outputs (e.g., scores in examinations and final school grades) and ignore the learning processes. This may help to explain the trends observed in the Korean groups.

The output-focused or examination-centered learning culture in Asia stems from Confucian philosophy. For centuries, examination has been the most important method of measuring people's abilities and virtues. The rationale is said to promote fairness, based on merit, rather than one's family background or political influence. Although many Asian schools and universities have introduced other ways of selecting their students, such as recommendations and family contributions, examinations and tests, in a variety of formats, still prevail when schools grant admission to new students. One could argue that these entrance examinations may have affected the teaching and learning culture, as well as learners' behaviors, in the Asian educational system. As Latchem and Jung (2009) reported, multiple-choice tests given at the end of each course is still a common way of assessment in many Asian distance universities. Online teaching is theory based, focusing primarily on memorization rather than developing higher order cognitive abilities or collaborative skills. Jung, Kudo, and Choi (2012) found that online collaboration presented psychological challenges for Japanese learners. One could argue that Asian learners, who focus on output rather than process, experience more stress in collaborative online learning environments. These students might consider learning processes such as building virtual relationships with other students, waiting for others' responses, and making group decisions unnecessary to acquire a good grade on the final examination.

Another important cultural dimension in education, highlighted by multiple studies, is that of plagiarism. Dryden (1999) found that Japanese students and faculty tended to view plagiarism as inappropriate but not a big deal. Rinnert and Kobayashi (2005) also confirmed that Japanese students did not perceive plagiarism as unacceptable. Compared with American students, they lacked understanding on how to properly cite their work. Possible reasons for the high rate of plagiarism among Asian students include external pressure to succeed (or getting a good grade), time limitation to complete their work, or simply a lack of knowledge about plagiarism (Bamford & Sergiou, 2005). With the sharp increase in plagiarism in an online environment, it is becoming more important to break old habits of Asian students and offer systematic training for properly citing sources.

The European Context

Online learning and the concept of quality are interpreted differently in the European context. Although one of the first universities to offer online learning was in Europe (Sangrà, 2001), higher education institutions in Europe are usually very suspicious and critical of innovative teaching and learning approaches. The discourse revolves primarily around the pros and cons of online learning, compared with face-to-face teaching.

From the learner's perspective, seven fields of quality in e-learning have been identified by Ehlers (2004): tutor support; collaboration; technology; cost expectations and benefits; information transparency of provider and course; course structure and presentation; and didactics, a method of systematic instruction. Cabrera (2008) examined graduate students' perceptions of an online educational process and pointed out several elements of the online learning process that were crucial for their learning experience: the teachers, the learning materials, the assessment, their peers, and the student services. Furthermore, Ralston-Berg (2009) highlighted organizational issues and the need for clarifying student expectations. He explained that interaction requirements, grading policy, logical navigation instructions, directions on how to access resources, timing, and the array of online activities are important considerations from the students' perspectives. Flexibility and accessibility of resources and information are the two most valued benefits of online learning according to Haywood, Macleod, Haywood, Mogey, and Alexander (2004). They argued that online learning fits better with their overloaded duties and helps them to save time. On the contrary, technology requirements are usually considered as a barrier to online learning from the students' point of view (Lao & Gonzales, 2005).

Introduced by Sharpe and Benfield (2005), emotionality and time management are two interesting aspects related to perceptions of the online learning experiences. Because both relate to students and teachers, they are considered in a permanent dialogic relationship. Emotionality is a concern given its link to isolation, alienation, and frustration. Sharpe and Benfield pointed out regarding the reaction of the students facing a changing pedagogy, "It is not easy to move students from traditional passive attitudes to interactions of socialization and information sharing or peer feedback" (p. 5). However, other studies, such as that of Cabrera (2008), have indicated that the e-learner experience enhanced self-esteem and developed the "joy of learning" (Cleveland-Innes, 2012).

Issues of time and time management can produce concerns: Students may feel under pressure because of time constraints, and they may also need to readapt their study patterns. Given the novelty of online learning, teachers are often uncertain about the amount of time that should be allocated for students to complete the online learning activities and achieve the desired learning outcomes.

Availability, accessibility of course materials, and flexible study at a time and pace suited to the student are the three main advantages of online learning identified in Voce's (2007b) survey at the University College London in the United Kingdom. Flexibility is of particular importance, as it allows students to balance their studies alongside other commitments, such as family and work. In challenging socioeconomic situations, this flexibility appears to be a trigger for development. It is worth noting that students were more in favor of asynchronous communication between student and teacher (72%) than of synchronous communication. On the other hand, Voce pointed out the drawbacks, which include lack of contact and interaction, technical issues, and Internet accessibility. Particularly, students complained about the fact that online learning reduces the amount of student-teacher interactions, and they were concerned about the wait time for responses. Interestingly, the same survey indicated the students' concern about the potential distractions of using the Internet to study. Despite the Net generation's multitasking characteristic, European students indicate a focused concentration while studying as an important factor affecting the success in online learning.

The perceptions of teachers are quite similar to those of students regarding the benefits of online learning: availability and accessibility of courses in terms of "anytime, anywhere" and ability to work at your own pace (Voce, 2007a). The perceived drawbacks are also similar. Both students and teachers consider technical issues as relevant; however, teachers are much more concerned about their own and students' technical skills. They contended that students and teachers are lacking the skills needed to foster an efficient and beneficial online learning environment. Other concerns relate to pedagogical reservations, regarding limited materials available both online and offline, and students' expectations of teacher availability. Regarding online learning activities, surveyed teachers gave more importance to the distribution of learning materials (84%) than any other activities. This reflects the traditional European teaching methodology that focuses less on multimedia and interactive materials (37%) and collaborative activities and group work (37%). In respect of communication, there is coincidence with the students' view, rating asynchronous higher than synchronous.

Given the novelty of online teaching and learning, the field of assessments offers many opportunities and much room for innovation. Currently, most online courses have either an online exam or a face-to-face exam at the end of the course. The search for computer-based solutions, addressing the concerns of plagiarism and cheating, is falling short of offering assessment systems that can solve the problem. Although unusual at this point, some online programs are using a continuous assessment system. The latest trend has been the use of e-portfolios (Barberà, Guàrdia, & Vall-llovera, 2009; Joint Information Systems Committee, 2008), helping to develop alternative assessment methods in online learning, which is likely to be the best way of assessing learning in the online learning environment. Some studies have suggested that few students (34%) consider online exams as beneficial (Voce, 2007b). New trends can encourage innovative online learning assessments, moving away from the replication of face-to-face structures and habits. The kinds of activities that students prefer are online revision and practice exercises (even if they are not contributing toward a final mark), online submission of course work, and the receipt of progress reports. Contrary to what has been said previously, peer assessment is not perceived as highly beneficial (37%). Although the assessment culture is moving to continuous assessment models, peer-to-peer assessment still has a long way to go in the European context.

The American Context

Online learning has grown considerably since its inception 20 years ago (Aslanian & Clinefelter, 2012), "to the point that in the fall of 2010, almost one-third of US postsecondary students were taking at least one course online" (Hill, 2012, p. 85). In a survey with over 3,000 online learners enrolled in 31 higher education institutions in the United States, Ralston-Berg (2012) found that the online learners focus on three main areas for overall quality assessment: interaction and facilitation, course materials, and learning activities. The degree of interaction among online learners is a major contributor to students' satisfaction, motivation, and performance. Students expect clearly stated requirements concerning interaction with the instructor and peers, as well as a prompt turnaround time for responses, grades, and feedback. "Learners appreciate faculty who help them think creatively; change opinions and sharpen analyses; and encourage them to take responsibility for their own learning by helping them plan and produce meaningful work" (Moore, 2002, p. 59). In addition, course materials that are current and relevant are absolutely important for the achievement of learning objectives (Palloff & Pratt, 2003). Students expect that knowledge and skills gained through studying well-designed course materials and meaningful learning experiences will be long lasting and preferably applicable in the near future. In particular, students expect learning activities to be meaningful to their own "personal and professional experiences, enhancing the value of prior learning, both formal and informal" (Sherry, 2003, p. 438).

For American students, student services and support are another key area in judging the quality of online learning, given its impact on their motivation and retention (Moore, 2011). Much like customers, American students expect easy and immediate access to "program information and institutional services—including feedback, tutorials, learning resources, advising, mentoring, testing, readiness and career placement, grade and transfer credit and transcript reporting, degree conferrals, and technologies" (Moore, 2002, p. 59). For the most part, American students are attempting to balance life, work, and study and thus expect accessible and efficient support toward successful program and course completion and value personalized attention and feedback.

Although faculty members are still somewhat skeptical when it comes to students' learning outcomes, there is evidence that beliefs are changing as to the potential of technology in providing students with rich learning experiences. Acquired experience with online teaching has had positive influences in changing perceptions of faculty members (Bolliger & Wasilik, 2009). Instructors who aspire to have meaningful interactions with students see the benefits of adopting technologies despite increased workload (Bolliger & Wasilik, 2009; Moore, 2011). However, large classes, unprepared students, poor course materials, and outdated technology tools often bring challenges to the instructors who wish to offer superior learning experiences online and lead them to develop skepticism toward the quality of online learning.

To ensure the quality of online learning, instructors need to be trained to use new technologies properly and effectively. In addition, they should be made aware of the best pedagogical practices involved in teaching with technologies (Moore, 2011). Because faculty success and satisfaction in online teaching often depends on the quality of the course design, competent instructors should be involved in the online course development and design phases. Whether provided with a template or fully involved in the creation of an online course, the instructors expect to be heard when it comes to feedback about the courses they are teaching. They wish to be able to actively participate in an academic community of practice, be recognized, and possibly be rewarded for excellence in online teaching. They should benefit from opportunities of professional development in their academic fields to enhance their online teaching practices (Moore, 2002).

Online instructors perceive high-quality support from institutions, including administrative, technological, and instructional services, as an important quality factor of online learning. They also see faculty evolution, which is a common practice in American institutions (Palloff & Pratt, 2008), as a fundamental component of overall course quality. Instructors typically expect to be evaluated by students through standardized instruments. However, given the high stakes associated with assessments and account-ability in American higher education, there is still an evident schism between policy makers and faculty with regard to common standards for course evaluation. Instructors often ask for other types of assessments that reach beyond the potentially biased student satisfaction surveys.

When examining institutional views on the quality of online education in the Amer-ican higher education context, one must consider issues of accreditation, funding, and regulations, which define a stricter set of alternatives when it comes to balancing the demands of cost, access, and quality. In the United States, accreditation is decentralized and self-regulatory, built on "a patchwork quilt, with varying standards" (Bates, 2012, p. 1). The growth of the for-profit providers in online education combined with the lack of official scrutiny has led to a pervasive distrust toward online education from the public. Many of the decisions made within institutions regarding online course offerings are based on requirements from accredited agencies, which in many cases are not suited for, or aligned with, best practices in online education. Such limitations are stifling consid-ering the potential of online learning to widen the spectrum of academic achievers and develop the innovative business models in higher education (Farmer, 2012; Flanagan, 2012; Hill, 2012).

According to the Sloan Consortium (n.d.), learning effectiveness and scale are two main institutional priorities in the United States. It is widely accepted in American higher education that the effectiveness of online learning should remain compatible with that of traditional classroom practices by integrating appropriate interactive and col-laborative online technologies, career-focused e-resources, well-prepared and engaging instructors, and authentic assessment methodologies. Scale, on the other hand, relates to cost-effectiveness and institutional commitment such as improving services while keep-ing costs in check, reasonable tuition and fees, and resource sharing through partnerships (Sloan Consortium, 2003).

Despite the ongoing efforts of institutions and policy makers regarding quality assurance in online education, major challenges still remain central in the higher edu-cation discourse. The lack of common standards in the American higher education system has led to a mushrooming of benchmarks and quality models. One such model is the rubric standards created by Quality Matters (QM), a nationally recognized, fac-ulty-centered, peer review process designed to certify the quality of online courses and online components in the United States. The rubric has eight general standards: course overview and introduction, learning objectives (competencies), assessment and meas-urement, instructional materials, learner interaction and engagement, course technol-ogy, learner support, and accessibility. Across these eight areas, 41 specific standards are used to evaluate the design of online and blended courses at the higher education level. Even though this kind of model offers useful quality guidelines, the issue of standards becomes more complex with the expanding diversity of online learning providers and formats.

For example, in the area of assessment, technology can provide a wide range of authen-tic assessments, but they may not applicable or reliable in all online learning contexts. When scalability is a necessity, assessment will probably require massive arrangements, where online exams and quizzes will play a central role in keeping costs low through the use of high-end technology for marking and preprogrammed feedback. However, in certain cultures such as the United States where issues of academic integrity and avoiding and detecting cheating and plagiarism are serious concerns, institutions are greatly challenged to undertake a multipronged approach, including the use of technology and instructional design practices, to develop policies and procedures that help avoid, detect, and sanction cheating and plagiarism.

Finding viable approaches to provide learning results analogous to those in conventional education while keeping costs down is still the main thread of all the debate concerning quality in online education in the United States, as Power and Morven-Gould (2011) noted.

Conclusion

As expected, perceptions of quality in online learning tend to differ according to the sociocultural context. Nevertheless, flexibility, the need for an appropriate and well-structured instructional design, and the delivery of good course materials are some of the common links that seem to be shared among all students as important for quality online learning experiences. American and European cultures have similar values regarding the work-life-study balance, whereas there are no related statements in the Asian context. The most striking difference emerged when researchers analyzed the learning preferences of the Asian students. Contrary to the current emphasis on interactive and collaborative designs in online learning environments, Asian learners give less value to these characteristics, focusing more on course content organization to enhance independent study. Their preference toward a more instructor-led approach to online learning is quite different from that of American and European students. In the Asian context, examinations are seen as a means to demonstrate virtue and merit. In the American and European contexts, students give more value to alternative and continuous assessment methods compared with traditional examinations. This suggests that different types of online learning assessments are necessary to respond to different teaching and learning methodologies and cultures. It is clear that further developments are needed in this field.

Skepticism of online teaching and learning is a common point shared by American and European teachers, as they consider a hybrid system blending online and face-to-face communications as a better form of online education. However, we should not disregard the fact that many students may face constraints in attending a traditional classroom setting. Rather than attempting to replicate traditional face-to-face teaching in an online format, online instructors need to be innovative in their methodologies. To help online educators devise appropriate online teaching strategies to meet the diverse needs of learners, training is necessary. Proper training and support for instructors to design effective online courses will increase levels of confidence in online teaching and thus lead to better perceptions of quality. Regardless of cultural and contextual differences, a pedagogical shift toward more interactive online teaching and learning approaches may help improve people's understanding of the benefits of online learning based on networked learning models and develop common quality standards in online learning.

References

Abdous, M. (2009). E-learning quality assurance: A process-oriented lifecycle model. *Quality Assurance in Education, 17*(3), 281–295.

Aslanian, C. B., & Clinefelter, D. (2012). *Online college students 2012: Comprehensive data on demands and preferences.* Learninghouse White Paper. Retrieved from http://www.learninghouse.com/resources/whitepapers/research-study

Bamford, J., & Sergiou, K. (2005). International students and plagiarism: An analysis of the reasons for plagiarism among international foundation students. *Investigations in University Teaching and Learning, 2*(2), 17–22.

Barberà, E., Guàrdia, L., & Vall-llovera, M. (2009, November). El e-Transfolio: Diseño tecno-pedagógico de un sistema de evaluación de las competencias transversales mediante un porta-folio electrónico. Paper presented at the Jornadas Internacionales de Docencia, Investigación e Innovación en la Universidad: Trabajar con e-portfolio, Santiago de Compostela, Spain.

Bates, T. (2012, October 31). Does the US accreditation system discriminate against online learning? [blog post]. Retrieved from http://www.tonybates.ca/2012/10/31/does-the-u-s-accreditation-system-discriminate-against-online-learning/

Bolliger, D. U., & Wasilik, O. (2009). Factors influencing faculty satisfaction with online teaching and learning in higher education. *Distance Education, 30*(1), 103–116.

Cabrera, N. (2008). *Las repercusiones de la Educación Superior, a distancia y virtual desde la perspectiva de los graduados. El caso de la UOC* (Unpublished doctoral disseration). Universitat de Barcelona, Barcelona.

Cashion, J., & Palmieri, P. (2002). *The secret is the teacher: The learners' view of online learning.* Leabrook, Australia: National Centre for Vocational Education Research. Retrieved from http://pre2005.flexiblelearning.net.au/research/nr0F03a.pdf

Cleveland-Innes, M. (2012). Emotional presence, learning, and the online learning environment. *The International Review of Research in Open and Distance Learning, 13*(4). Retrieved from http://www.irrodl.org/index.php/irrodl/article/view/1234/2333

Dondi, C., Moretti, M., & Nascimbeni, F. (2006). Quality of e-learning: Negotiating a strategy, implementing a policy. In U. D. Ehlers & J. Pawlowski (Eds.), *Handbook on quality and standardisation in e-learning* (pp. 31–50). Berlin, Germany: Springer.

Dryden, L. M. (1999). A distant mirror or through the looking glass? Plagiarism and intellectual property in Japanese education. In L. Buranen & A. M. Roy (Eds.), *Perspectives on plagiarism and intellectual property in a postmodern world* (pp. 75–85). New York: State University of New York Press.

Ehlers, U. D. (2004). Quality in e-learning from a learner's perspective. *European Journal of Open, Distance and E-Learning, 2004*(1). Retrieved from http://www.eurodl.org/index.php?article=101

Eriksen, E. O., & Fossum, J. E. (2000). *Democracy in the European Union: Integration through deliberation?* London, UK: Routledge.

Farmer, J. (2012, October 11). MOOCs: The new higher education? [blog post]. Retrieved from http://mfeldstein.com/moocs-the-new-higher-education/

Flanagan, C. (2012, November 1). Business model innovation: A blueprint for higher education. *Educase Review.* Retrieved from http://www.educause.edu/ero/article/business-model-innovation-blueprint-higher-education

Harvey, L., & Knight, P. (1996). *Transforming higher education.* Bristol, UK: The Society for Research into Higher Education and Open University Press.

Haywood, J., Macleod, H., Haywood, D., Mogey, N., & Alexander, W. (2004). *Student views of e-learning: A survey of University of Edinburgh WebCT Users 2004.* Edinburgh: Scottish Centre for Research into On-Line Learning and Assessment. Retrieved from http://www.homepages. ed.ac.uk/jhaywood/papers/surveyresults2004.pdf

Hill, P. (2012). Online educational delivery models: A descriptive view. *Educause Review.* Retrieved from http://www.educause.edu/ero/article/online-educational-delivery-models-descriptive-view

Joint Information Systems Committee. (2008). *Effective practice with e-portfolios: Supporting 21st century learning.* Retrieved from http://jisc.ac.uk/eportfolio

Jung, I. S. (2011). The dimensions of e-learning quality: From the learner's perspective. *Educational Technology Research and Development, 59*(4), 445–464.

Jung, I. S. (2012). Asian learners' perception of quality in distance education and gender differences. *The International Review of Research in Open and Distance Learning, 13*(2), 1–25. Retrieved from http://www.irrodl.org/index.php/irrodl/article/view/1159/2128

Jung, I. S., Kudo, M., & Choi, S. (2012). Stress in Japanese learners engaged in online collaborative learning in English. *British Journal of Educational Technology, 43*(6), 1016–1029. doi:10.1111/j.1467-8535.2011.01271.x

Jung, I. S., & Suzuki, Y. (2014). *Scaffolding wiki-based collaboration in a multicultural language learning context.* Manuscript submitted for publication.

Kim, H. W., Cho, S. Y., & Kim, M. (2010). Study and success on life satisfaction among adolescents, and the moderating effect of parent-adolescent communication. *Journal of Korea Home Economics, 48*(5), 49–60.

Lao, T., & Gonzales, C. (2005). Understanding online learning through a qualitative description of professors and students' experiences. *Journal of Technology and Teacher Education, 133*, 459–474.

Latchem, C., & Jung, I. S. (2009). *Distance and blended learning in Asia.* New York, NY, and London, UK: Routledge.

Moore, J. (2002). *Elements of quality: The Sloan-C Framework.* Needham, MA: Sloan Consortium.

Moore, J. (2011). A synthesis of Sloan-C effective practices. *Journal of Asynchronous Learning Networks.* Retrieved from http://sloanconsortium.org/publications/jaln_main

Palloff, R., & Pratt, K. (2003). *The virtual student: A profile and guide to working with online learners.* San Francisco, CA: Jossey-Bass.

Palloff, R., & Pratt, K. (2008). *Assessing of the online learner: Resources and strategies for faculty.* San Francisco, CA: Jossey-Bass.

Park, J. S. (2010). Effects of significance of study, pressure for the relationship among school adolescents' rights guarantee, self-esteem and subjective happiness. *Studies on Youth Welfare, 21*(1), 35–59.

Power, T., & Morven-Gould, A. (2011). Head of gold, feet of clay: The online learning paradox. *The International Review of Research in Open and Distance Learning, 12*(2), 19–39. Retrieved from http://www.irrodl.org/index.php/irrodl/article/view/916/1739

Ralston-Berg, P. (2009, August). *What makes a quality online course: The student perspective.* Paper presented at the Distance Teaching and Learning Conference, Madison, WI.

Ralston-Berg, P. (2012, March). *Student perspectives: Quality in online courses.* Paper presented at the UPCEA Annual Conference, Portland, OR. Retrieved from http://www.academia. edu/1497931/UPCEA_-_Student_Perspectives_of_Quality_PDF_

Rinnert, C., & Kobayashi, II. (2005). Borrowing words and ideas: Insights from Japanese L1 writers. *Journal of Asian Pacific Communications, 15*(1), 31–56.

Sangrà, A. (2001). The consolidation of a virtual university. *LLINE-Lifelong Learning in Europe, 2*, 76–84.

Sangrà, A., Guàrdia, L., & González-Sanmamed, M. (2007). Educational design as a key issue in planning for quality improvement. In M. Bullen & D. Janes (Eds.), *Making the transition to e-learning: Strategies and issues* (pp. 284–299). Hershey, PA: Idea Group.

Sangrà, A., Vlachopoulos, D., & Cabrera, N. (2012). Building an inclusive definition of e-learning: An approach to the conceptual framework. *International Review of Research in Open and Distance Learning, 13*(2), 145–159. Retrieved from http://www.irrodl.org/index.php/irrodl/article/view/1161/2185

Sharpe, R., & Benfield, G. (2005). The student experience of e-learning in higher education. *Journal of Learning and Technology, 1*(3), 1–7.

Sherry, A. C. (2003). Quality and its measurement in distance education. In M. G. Moore & W. G. Anderson (Eds.), *Handbook of distance education* (pp. 435–459). Mahwah, NJ: Lawrence Erlbaum.

Sloan Consortium. (n.d.). *The 5 pillars: The Sloan-C quality framework.* Retrieved from http://sloanconsortium.org/5pillars

Sloan Consortium. (2003). *Quality framework for online education.* Retrieved from http://www.adec.edu/earmyu/SLOANC-41.html

Twigg, C. A. (2001). *Quality assurance for whom? Providers and consumers in today's distributed learning environment.* Troy, NY: Center for the Academic Transformation, Rensselaer Polytechnic Institute.

Voce, J. (2007a). *E-learning at UCL: A staff perspective. Report on a survey.* London, UK: UCL. Retrieved from http://www.ucl.ac.uk/isd/staff/e-learning/tools/webct/migration/Staff-survey-report.pdf

Voce, J. (2007b). *E-learning at UCL: A student perspective. Report on a survey.* London, UK: UCL. Retrieved from http://www.ucl.ac.uk/isd/staff/e-learning/tools/webct/migration/Student-survey-report.pdf

10

DEVELOPING GLOBAL DIGITAL CITIZENS

A Professional Development Model

Chih-Hsiung Tu and Marina Stock McIsaac

Learners are bringing a variety of experiences to the digital learning space, and educators are faced with working with students from diverse social and cultural backgrounds. Strategies are needed to provide authentic meaningful learning experiences for digital learners. It is important, in this context, to develop global digital citizens (GDCs) who bring in a variety of social and cultural backgrounds and give them tools to succeed in a digital world. This chapter presents a model for online teaching and learning that can be used as a conceptual framework to identify strategies that would support educators to develop GDCs. Our GDC model promotes global citizenship through mutual understanding, respect for cultural diversity, and a process for creating a collaborative global knowledge network.

There are many challenges facing educators around the world. Information gathering, problem solving, collaboration, and networking require sophisticated digital communication skills that challenge educators as they become facilitators of knowledge building in the modern digital world. Educators are networked in many ways through the world of information and communication technologies, and they are challenged to use tools such as wikis, embedded in sociocultural contexts, to help the socially and culturally diverse students in their classes to become GDCs.

Learners need access to quality education, equal opportunity, knowledge, and skills to become fully participating members of today's global digital community. As members of this global community, we share in efforts to provide equal educational opportunities for all. Many in the international community have worked to resolve issues of social and cultural integration in society and the community (Eriksen, 2007) by funding initiatives that promote universal access to information and knowledge-building skills that will lead to global digital citizenship (Das, 2008). This chapter begins with challenges facing educators and describes two international projects that were designed to meet diversity challenges. Next, it presents a model for global digital citizenship for educators that suggests five dimensions or levels of digital citizenship development. These dimensions are enabled by six processes that increase the vertical progression of skills, facilitated by the horizontal expansion of sociocultural catalysts as tools for digital learners. This model is useful for educators and students alike, as it takes into account how learners from various backgrounds and cultures can engage in collaborative and constructivist learning activities by personalizing their learning, networking, and sharing in an expanding, diverse global digital society. By incorporating these processes and digital tools, educators can help learners progress from digital learners to GDCs.

Global Digital Citizens

In the United States, as in many countries, there are many disengaged students and high dropout rates. According to the population survey by the U.S. Bureau of Labor Statistics (2011), the cost of not having an education goes up as education decreases. Education has faced budget cutbacks and a reduction in academic, social, and cultural support for students who have integration problems in our high schools. But the problems go further than the classroom. The uneducated and undereducated continue to cost us, as a society, well beyond a student's high school years. The challenges that face education in the United States are magnified in the developing world where disease, poverty, and illiteracy must be overcome.

We must find ways to engage learners in a lifelong process of knowledge building and prepare them to become GDCs. A GDC is a learner who retains global learning perspectives in knowledge, skills, and disposition and exercises them during their life span by creating, sharing, and collaborating with other digital learners. If education can be made more participatory and relevant by taking into account the diverse social and cultural needs of students, we may be able to find a solution.

Projects With Diverse Populations

Two European Union (EU) projects—the twinning initiatives and the Mediterranean Migration Network (MMN)—illustrate how the needs of socially and culturally diverse learners are integrated in education. Both projects examine the issues of society and culture from the perspective of teaching in globally diverse settings.

EU Twinning

Communities of different social and cultural backgrounds within the EU come together for friendship, cooperation, and to better understand each other through twinning projects. Their aim is to pair communities or schools in a personal, grassroots exchange of ideas, viewpoints, and cultures in an effort to establish an atmosphere of mutual understanding and solidarity among European countries. For example, Twinning Tanzania pairs a class of European schoolchildren with a school in Tanzania. Students share their stories and get to know each other's environments and cultures. They collaborate, learn together, and help each other. Educators in these kinds of twinning projects are encouraged to work with students and other educators to expand awareness, cultivate understanding, and promote respect for diversity.

Mediterranean Migration Network

The MMN aims to promote collaboration and exchange of best practices between public and private organizations that are active in the fields of migration and integration. The project, supported by the European Commission's European Fund for the Integration of Third-Country Nationals, explores the establishment of databases for resources on migration, integration, and diversity. The project is led by the Centre for the Advancement of Research and Development in Educational Technology (CARDET) and has an international group of participating organizations (www.migrationnetwork.org/en). CARDET, as a nonprofit research and development organization with strategic partners worldwide, is well positioned to lead this project. Its mission is to inspire innovation and promote education, research, and development. In the MMN project, CARDET and partners are establishing a network of stakeholders in Mediterranean migration issues to exchange information and best practices on migration, integration, and diversity. The goals are to

- develop a collaborative framework among stakeholders;
- develop a database of resources on migration, integration, and diversity;
- build the professional capacity through educational material and activities; and
- promote collaboration among members of the MMN.

These projects have as their goals the preparation of citizens for a global society that respects diversity, provides for equality of educational opportunity, and prepares students for employment in the twenty-first century.

A Model of Global Digital Citizenship for Educators

Our model to prepare GDCs provides strategies for educators to facilitate global social networking skills of students. Educators and students are encouraged to utilize their own individual and customized set of social-cultural tools as they prepare themselves for the integrated, global knowledge-building environment. The model suggests five dimensions of learning identity grounded in sociocultural, constructivist, and connectivist pedagogies; six enabling processes; and three catalytic forces in the process of becoming a full GDC (see figure 10.1).

Five Dimensions of Culturally Diverse Online Education

The five dimensions are individual digital learner, social collaborator, cultural constructivist, community collaborator, and finally GDC. The student progresses from being a digital learner and moves upward through social, cultural, and environmental levels, developing the skills required to move through each level of the five dimensions, finally arriving at the level of GDC.

This learning environment is part of a digital world that is organic and evolving. The role of educators is to facilitate student progress from an individual digital learner to a GDC. Effective educators model and engage digital learners in the use of social and cultural tools in the framework of those enabling processes such as personalizing,

Figure 10.1 Dimensions, enablers, and catalysts for global digital citizens.

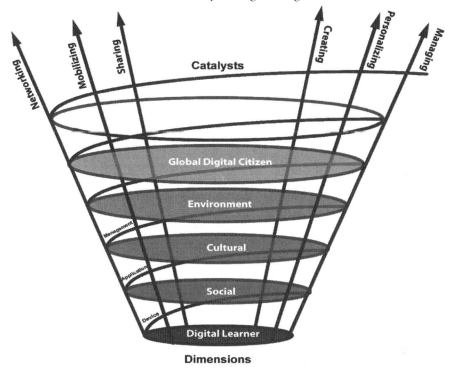

networking, creating, and sharing. The model builds learning environmental sustainability to ensure that students acquire learning skills, knowledge, and dispositions with global perspectives.

Individual Digital Learner
A competent digital learner should posses the knowledge of global digital citizenship. The strategies for educators to prepare digital learners to become competent GDCs are those that help learners to obtain knowledge of global learning elements (i.e., digital access/divides, communication, digital literacy, digital etiquette/law, digital rights/responsibilities, digital health/wellness, and security) (Ribble, Bailey, & Ross, 2004).

In addition, educators should assist individual digital learners to build and customize their personal learning environments (PLEs) by connecting and networking people, resources, and tools. Individual digital learning is a connectivist activity. PLEs provide support for students to set their own learning goals, manage their learning, and communicate with others (van Harmelen, 2006). Siemens (2007) argued that a PLE is a collection and connections of tools, resources, and people, brought together under the conceptual notion of openness, interoperability, and learner control. Students should be engaged in activities creating PLEs by connecting different tools to individualize their human networks and learning resource on customized personal portals, such as iGoogle, Netvibes, My Yahoo, Windows Live Personalized Experience, and mobile portals. Educators can help students make these connections through the use of new digital social learning tools. Connectivism is based on the notion that knowledge is distributed across a network of connections, and learning consists of how well people are able to build and navigate those networks (Downes, 2011). The key guidelines to nurturing individual digital learners include the instruction of global learning elements that allow the personalization of digital learning environments.

Suggested strategies for online educators are to

- create, present, and manage appropriate digital profiles with photos, avatars, and/or multimedia as digital social, global identities; and
- engage individual learners in building their own PLEs by allowing them to select their own digital tools (e.g., iGoogle, mobile apps) rather than use preassigned tools.

Social Collaborator

Vygotsky (1978) determined that full cognitive development requires social interaction. The degree to which a person masters life skills is dependent on how much the person engages in social behaviors. Social and collaborative activities have become essential for knowledge building. The web provides a mechanism for connecting individuals around the globe. Collaborative instructional methods require learners to engage in joint interactive practices to enrich their skills and share their enriched knowledge.

The key guideline to nurturing social collaboration is the integration of Web 2.0 tools into group and community work. Web 2.0 is frequently referred to as a collaboration web (Educause, 2008). Web learners and collaborators engage in meaningful and authentic web activities.

Suggested strategies are to

- connect social collaborators in digital meeting, information, and exchanging ideas; and
- engage social collaborators in the content cocreating and editing and social content and resource sharing.

Web 2.0 tools for collaborative work are simple, flexible, and free and offer a familiar web interface. With web browsers, collaborators are able to edit group documents, hold online meetings, exchange information, and collaborate in any number of ways to use authoring tools to meet, to tailor their needs, and then to share them with others. Collaborators consistently "weave" their web threads into learning activities.

Cultural Constructivist

Constructivism is a learner-centered theory that focuses on the multiple perspectives of a learner's environment. Individuals construct meaning based on their experiences, their environment, and their own perspectives. Constructivist learning environments support multiple perspectives and people from diverse social and cultural backgrounds who can construct knowledge from their various experiences and activities. To be meaningful, knowledge must be constructed by each learner and not transferred by educators. The activities that lead to knowledge acquisition should be authentic, experience-based objects and events that have meaning for the learner, as learning is individual and unique to each person. Because of its emphasis on the individual, constructivism is ideally suited to incorporate cultural learning differences (Piaget, 1926).

The critical guideline to nurture cultural constructivists is to value each individual cultural collaborator's perspectives, strengths, and talents to diversify communities.

Suggested strategies are to

- invite cultural constructivists to share their views based on their own experiences, strengths, talents, and diversified social and cultural backgrounds;
- design authentic and experience-based learning activities to enrich and honor cultural differences among collaborators; and
- facilitate multiple learning communities and go beyond the classroom community to reach global levels.

Working in a culturally diverse, constructivist online learning environment may present a challenge to both instructor and student. Instructors need a thorough understanding of the cultural and educational backgrounds of online students to help guide them along their quest to become a GDC (Goodfellow & Lamy, 2009). Instructors should engage students in active learning community activities so students can learn and reflect based on their own needs, intentions, and goals. To reflect constructivist cultural learning, a learning community goes beyond learners getting together to learn. Educators can draw on their learners' social contexts to design and facilitate different learning communities, such as communities of interest, communities of purpose, communities of passion, and communities of practice.

Community Collaborator

The community learning aspect represents a GDC's ability to facilitate community learning through building and sharing dispositions of learners and engaging them in forming a self-organized digital community where they can support one another in global learning environments. Massive open online courses are emerging learning environments aimed at large-scale participation and open access, such as Corsera and Udacity. Students' learning and educators' teaching should go beyond the communities and advance them to lifelong learning environments.

A learning community is decidedly different from "community learning." Both learners and instructors reflect multicultural aspects as they build community learning environments. A learning community focuses on learners acquiring knowledge as a community, whereas community learning focuses on the learning of both learners and the community itself; therefore, community learning results in "environments" that grow with learners as an organic process.

By comparison, in community learning, learning is gained both horizontally and vertically. Community members learn, and the community learns. Both types of learning are critical because community growth and development and the learning of community members enhance each other. Therefore, the model that stretches learning from a school learning community to lifelong learning is a good example of the relationship between learning community and community learning. Zhao (2012) argued that educators should move from project-based learning to product-oriented learning to solve real-world problems and to help solve community challenges. He asked, "What can I make that is meaningful to me and useful to others?" (p. 207).

One example of focusing on long-term learning is the Global Textbook Project that applies wiki-based technology to compose textbooks at the University of Georgia (http://globaltext.org). This is evidence of online community learning work that facilitates the generation of collective knowledge to share with others who may have or may not have the budget or opportunity to access textbooks.

Suggested strategies are to

- design instruction that focuses on community learning that generates both individual and community learning as shown in the Global Textbook Project, and
- embed global learning elements into online instruction to fulfill inclusive practices. Students create learning products not just for their own learning but also for the benefit other digital learners by sharing.

Global Digital Citizenship

The goal of the digital learner is to become a GDC who is able to create, share, and network knowledge with the use of digital tools. These tools may be devices, communication applications, or management environments that function as digital change agents. The educator's aim is to transform digital learners into competent GDCs by helping them to become individual digital learners, social collaborators, cultural constructivists, community collaborators, and GDCs. One example focusing on benefiting network learners is the Global Network Technology Training Project where students create network technology training sessions for education professional development at Northern Arizona University (see Chapter Resources on p. 113, this chapter).

The suggested strategies for online educators are to

- support learners to demonstrate knowledge, skill, and use of global digital elements; and
- encourage learners to engage community collaborators in global learning environments to become true lifelong learners and share their knowledge to make the global environments better, such as with class projects engaging learners from different of parts of the world.

Six Enablers for Online Educators

The five dimensions in the model require six different enabling processes to advance learners from active individual digital learners to competent GDCs. These enabling processes that impact the dimensions of learning are personalizing, networking, creating, sharing, mobilizing, and managing. Online educators should empower learners and engage them with these impetuses to make their learning more dynamic.

Personalizing

Personalizing learning allows learners to control and manage their own learning processes based on their strengths and needs. The key guideline for personalizing an enabling process is to empower learners to recognize their own strengths and to apply a personalized portal to organize multiple tools, resources, and people in one central location to create more open network learning.

The suggested strategies are to

- encourage learners to select their own tools and scaffold them to build human networks to share personalized network learning resources, and
- personalize learning environments to establish goals, manage content, and communicate.

Networking

The key guideline is to connect tools, resources, and people to create social learning networks. The networking force should go beyond human networking. Networking multiple learning tools to support human networking and learning resources is critical. The strategy to enhance the networking force is to encourage learners to select and to apply multiple preferred tools to support their learning networks. Rather than employing each tool separately, networking with multiple tools to fulfill individual learning goals is critical because integrating multiple tools simultaneously is the best strategy for learning (Dede, 2008). Educators are advised to integrate multiple tools, such as a wiki, a blog, Twitter, and so on, to support instruction.

The suggested strategies are to

- engage learners in connecting their human learning networks by using social networking tools such as Twitter to connect teaching, learning, and personal networks; and
- share and aggregate resources to build a network learning community. An example is educators' devising social tagging architecture to engage learners to use tagging schemes to share resources (see Chapter Resources, p. 113) through RSS (really simple syndication) feeds.

Creating

The key guideline is to engage learners in content creating and cocreating. Learners are engaged in contribution-oriented pedagogy environments. This participatory environment requires a deeper level of social interaction that engages learners so they can experience design strategies (Baird & Fisher, 2005) that keep learners' experiences in mind so they are able to determine and craft their own learning experiences.

The suggested strategies are to

- engage learners in self-publishing activities such as blogging, tweeting, or using wikis; and
- integrate participatory web and user-generated content to develop content and to guide collaboration, promoting learners to express their diversified viewpoints through collaborative development of wiki content (see Chapter Resources, p. 113).

Sharing

The key guideline is to use social networking tools that engage learners in the processes of sharing, exchanging, and modifying their mental models with other learners to craft and obtain their learning identities. Their shared thinking processes are unveiled as learners employ each other as resources by providing information and sharing experiences. For example, applying social tagging architecture can facilitate sharing of community-created content and resources, and therefore current community learners can interact with previous community learners' shared social content and resources. Social sharing is one attempt to understand the mental models of the other parties through mutual explanations by projecting different identities. A more effective explanation refers to sharing, self-reflecting, negotiating, and self-explanation, called elaborated explanation (Dillenbourg, Baker, Blaye, & O'Malley, 1996).

The suggested strategies are to

- engage learners in social content sharing to deepen their learning by the way of content creating, sharing, reviewing, reflecting, editing and shaping, reediting, and organizing with their own and others' mental perspectives to transform social content sharing from the local classroom or community to the global community level; and
- devise the community-community sharing interaction to intensify learning impetus and transcend the spatial and temporal constraints, allowing different communities to interact as seen in the aforementioned Global Network Technology Training Project.

Mobilizing

Mobilizing would enhance learning and make it ubiquitous learning. With or without mobile devices, learning is always mobile. With mobile devices, learning can be more meaningful. The key guidelines for enhancing mobilizing learning are to promote social context awareness, location-based communication, and personalized multilayered interactivity or augmented learning and to optimize digital and social identities through mobile technologies. Mobile technology affords learners the building of social relationships by constantly observing social interaction on their mobile technologies. Mobile learners are aware of and are connected to social interaction and can determine and control how and when and in what way to interact with others. Location-based technology makes communication and interaction more meaningful because both real and virtual realities overlap. Mobile interactivity becomes more personalized and more multilayered because mobile learners can determine when and in what way they would like to interact with others via multiple channels, such as texting, liking, retweeting, e-mailing, and recreating, remixing, and sharing multimedia content. In addition, mobile learners can optimize digital and social identities by sharing and managing their social and cognition footprint.

The suggested strategies are to

- mobilize educators, learners, devices, instructional activities, and content; and
- create activities and content that can be accessed ubiquitously, pushing interaction beyond physical boundaries.

Managing

Constantly managing the open network learning environment (ONLE) to facilitate learners' PLEs is the sustainable force for the GDC model. The key guideline is that educators should build ONLE to allow digital learners to develop and manage their PLEs. ONLE is a digital environment that empowers learners to participate in creative endeavors, conduct social networking, organize and reorganize social contents, and manage social acts by connecting people, resources, and tools. In ONLE, Web 2.0 tools are integrated into design environments that are totally transparent or open to public view. The same architecture can be used to design the degree of openness that users perceive is vital for each individual situation. ONLE permits learners to build their own PLE through open, social, and network learning architectures (Tu, Sujo-Montes, Yen, & Chan, 2012).

The suggested strategies are to

- design network-learning architecture that is open, flexible, and cloud based;
- update ONLE regularly, strategically, efficiently, and effectively to reflect current learning and teaching needs; and
- encourage learners to manage and update their PLEs constantly to reflect their current learning goals, such as lifelong learning.

Three Catalysts for Digital Sociocultural Teaching and Learning

The catalysts are visualized as spiraling forces, or change agents, that can be activated to increase the momentum of the individual's progress. The spiraling sociocultural catalysts are tools that are the individualized, personalized connecting strands weaving the processes of becoming a GDC. The objects that are associated with social practices and acts should be considered cultural tools in digital sociocultural learning environments. Sociocultural tools can be categorized into three sets: instrumental tools, semiotic tools, and premeditated tools (Robbins, 2001). Individuals utilize tools differently; their perceptions and use of tools could influence their participation in meaningful activities while they are engaged in digital social interaction.

Digital Devices

Digital devices as instrumental tools, such as computers, tablets, and smartphones, extend digital learners' capability to learn. Learners apply the same or similar instrumental tools to engage in social interaction as semiotic tools. From the aspect of digital management practices as premeditated tools, although the digital devices are the same, the learners' perceptions of the functions of the tools could be very different in the social learning environment because of embedded individual cultures as premeditated tools.

Learners can use digital devices to

- enrich social learning context and awareness,
- enhance location-based communication,

- personalize multilayered or augmented interactivity, and
- optimize their digital and social identities with Facebook, Twitter, blog statuses, profiles, social content sharing, and so on.

Digital Communication Applications

Ranging from text based and audio/visual to information visualization (infoviz), digital communication applications are used to reveal the participant's intentions and relationships in social activities, in addition to delivering information. For example, *infoviz*, defined as the information design that "uses picture, symbols, colors, and words to communicate ideas, illustrate information, or express relationships visually" (Emerson, 2008, p. 4), uses tag clouds and establishes a visual timeline or visual social network and circle to visually promote shared social activities.

Digital Management Practices

Simply applying digital devices and digital communication applications may not result in effective digital sociocultural learning. Digital management practices need to be designed, created, and developed by learners to improve social interaction and enhance the distribution between humans and technologies. The examples of digital management tools are PLEs and mobile applications (apps) that make the learning more individualized, ubiquitous, and collective. Both students and educators should carefully evaluate, select, employ, and manage them in an interactive and collaborative fashion.

Digital management tools should be used to create ONLE where participatory web and user-generated content, aggregations, mash-ups, remixes, RSS, community-community interactions, social networking, social tagging, infoviz, mobile learning, and augmented reality are promoted. While evaluating and selecting the tools, educators should scrutinize and evaluate these ONLE instructional strategies. One tool may not pertain in all these ONLE instructional strategies. Tools embedded into ONLE instructional strategies empower students and educators to connect their resources to make their learning network more dynamic.

Conclusion

Global digital citizenship is an ultimate learning identity. Competent GDCs need to obtain the essential knowledge in collaborative instructions and digital citizenship and be proficient in social networking technology skills and open learning. They also need to reach advanced practices in a community of practice and in instructional practices. A competent GDC would retain global learning perspectives in knowledge, skills, and disposition and exercise them during their life span.

Proficient GDCs should be capable of generalizing their global digital knowledge and skills from local to global communities to build their ideal global social identities, obtain knowledge from effective global learning curriculum, and apply effective social network technologies. With the fundamental knowledge and skills in place, GDCs can practice open learning by sharing learning content and resources in an open network environment; therefore, their learning is meaningful and of value to the global community.

Our model is proposed for online educators to empower students with the abilities and skills to solve global problems and build knowledge collaboratively while respecting each other's strengths through cultural and social differences and to be better prepared to meet the challenges of our changing world. To meet the sociocultural challenges in developing GDCs, online educators should acquire a thorough understanding of global digital learning, ascertain the true value of collaborative cultural learning tools, and employ the applications of open network learning strategies.

Chapter Resources

Resources for this chapter can be found at www.delicious.com/chihtu/GDCPD. To share related resources on this site with other readers, please tag your resources with the tag #GDCPD. View the readers' shared resources at https://delicious.com/search?p=GDCPD.

References

Baird, D. E., & Fisher, M. (2005). Social media and digital learning styles. *Journal of Educational Technology Systems, 34*(1), 5–32.

Das, A. K. (2008). *Open access to knowledge and information: Scholarly literature and digital library initiatives—The South Asian Scenario*. New Delhi, India: UNESCO House.

Dede, C. (2008). Theoretical perspectives influencing the use of information technology in teaching and learning. In J. Voogt & G. Knezek (Eds.), *International handbook of information technology in primary and secondary education* (pp. 43–62). New York, NY: Springer.

Dillenbourg, P., Baker, M., Blaye, A., & O'Malley, C. (1996). The evolution of research on collaborative learning. In E. Spada & P. Reiman (Eds.), *Learning in humans and machine: Towards an interdisciplinary learning science* (pp. 189–211). Oxford, UK: Elsevier.

Downes, S. (2011). *Connectivism and connective knowledge*. Retrieved from http://www.downes.ca/post/54540

Educause. (2008). *2008 horizon report*. Retrieved from http://www.nmc.org/pdf/2008-Horizon-Report.pdf

Emerson, J. (2008). *Visualization information for advocacy: An introduction to information design*. Retrieved from http://backspace.com/infodesign.pdf

Eriksen, T. H. (2007). Complexity in social and cultural integration: Some analytical dimensions. *Ethnic and Racial Studies, 30*(6), 1055–1069.

Goodfellow, R., & Lamy, M. N. (2009). *Learning cultures in online education*. New York, NY: Continuum Studies in Education.

Piaget, J. (1926). *The language and thought of the child*. London, UK: Routledge & Kegan.

Ribble, M., Bailey, G. D., & Ross, T. W. (2004). Digital citizenship: Addressing appropriate technology behavior. *Learning and Leading With Technology, 32*(1), 6–12.

Robbins, D. (2001). *Vygotsky's psychology-philosophy: A metaphor for language theory and learning*. New York, NY: Springer.

Siemens, G. (2007). *PLEs: I acronym, therefore I exist*. Retrieved from http://www.elearnspace.org/blog/2007/04/15/ples-i-acronym-therefore-i-exist/

Tu, C. H., Sujo-Montes, L., Yen, C. J., & Chan, J. Y. (2012). The integrations of personal learning environments and open network learning environments. *TechTrends, 56*(3), 13–19.

U.S. Bureau of Labor Statistics. (2011). *Current population survey.* Retrieved from http://www.bls
.gov/emp/ep_chart_001.htm

Van Harmelen, M. (2006). Personal learning environments. *Proceedings of the Sixth International Conference on Advanced Learning Technologies.* Retrieved from http://octette.cs.man
.ac.uk/~mark/docs/MvH_PLEs_ICALT.pdf

Vygotsky, L. S. (1978). *Mind in society.* Cambridge, MA: Harvard University Press.

Zhao, Y. (2012). *World class learners: Educating creative and entrepreneurial students.* Thousand
Oaks, CA: Corwin Press.

11

LEADERSHIP CHALLENGES IN TRANSCULTURAL ONLINE EDUCATION

Michael F. Beaudoin

To make worldwide online learning education portable, compatible, and successful, cultural sensitivity is required to recontextualize online products and services that identify and address differences and similarities. In global online learning, there are formidable barriers to access (e.g., cost, technology, language, gender, literacy), and a lack of cultural awareness exacerbates the potential for failure of both individuals and organizations involved. Taking into account the various "locales" of the global e-learning community is an essential prerequisite for online planners, managers, and instructors. Technology has facilitated cross-cultural exchanges, but has this phenomenon truly blurred the distinctions and differences between nations, races, or cultures? Although it is true that people of diverse orientations have become more exposed to the cultures and norms of others, does this necessarily simplify the teaching-learning process (Johnson, 2007)?

It is perhaps naive to think that faculty reaching diverse learners via online instruction will become a mediating force that mitigates cross-cultural barriers in educational settings. Instructors are not immune to cultural biases that influence self-perceptions of their role, authority, and relationship to students. And even in those instances where faculty adopt a student-centered approach, it may be that students' own cultural norms inhibit a more open and flexible predisposition to learning. Despite the presence of enabling technology, it can still be difficult for students enrolled in online courses to relate to fellow classmates, representing stark cultural differences. Many accessing online learning for the first time have to adapt not only to the medium but also to the culture shock of academia, requiring that learners become rapidly "encultured" to new practices, relationships, expectations, and rituals to succeed.

This chapter discusses and analyzes these issues and dilemmas, arguing that they should be considered by those who enter into the online education arena, especially where diverse cultures are involved and affected. Specifically, the chapter examines, from both practical and philosophical perspectives, challenges that online education leaders face in diffusing innovation, establishing collaborative organizational arrangements, addressing differing teaching-learning styles in cross-cultural settings, and maintaining ethical behavior in these activities. Viable models and suggested strategies are offered that online education leaders might employ in launching and sustaining programs to ensure the integrity of providers and the welfare of consumers.

In this discussion, *leadership* is defined as creating the conditions within programs and institutions that are conducive to fostering, designing, implementing, and managing academic offerings and services that are of high quality, innovative, and culturally, politically, and economically sensitive to the environments in which they are introduced. *Transcultural online education* is defined as the design and delivery of instruction, support services, and infrastructure to launch and sustain such enterprises provided across national, ethnic, and linguistic boundaries that separate diverse sociocultural entities.

Challenges and Solutions: What Research and Practice Tell Us

Diffusion of Innovation

Rogers and Shoemaker's classic work *Communication of Innovations: A Cross-Cultural Approach* (1971), primarily intended to inform practitioners introducing change into traditional settings, provides keen insights to those currently engaged in the implementation of online education, especially within conventional academic systems. Indeed, much of their work is no less applicable today to online educators attempting to diffuse e-learning in sub-Saharan Africa than it was to agricultural workers trying to introduce new crops in Asia some 40 years ago.

The diffusion of new ideas inevitably impacts existing social structures, including educational systems, and those systems, even if they ultimately benefit from change, often resist the implementation of such innovations. Rogers and Shoemaker noted that any innovation typically involves a process of invention, diffusion, and consequences. This process is smoothest when both parties share common meanings, language, culture, and so on. When we consider how challenging it can be to introduce alternative education into familiar settings (e.g., online courses into an institution offering classroom instruction where all parties share a common culture), to engage in this endeavor between entities that possess differing cultural values, the communication and acceptance of innovation can be far more daunting.

Also complicating the change process is the phenomenon of "uncertainty avoidance"—the value placed on risk and ambiguity in a culture. Where this element is strong, a society's members are less likely to be receptive to unfamiliar ways of doing things if these present unclear and unpredictable situations (Gunawardena, Wilson, & Nolla, 2003). If receivers of an innovation perceive it to be better than what they have or at least compatible, to be not too complex to deal with, can be tried with relatively little risk, and presents obvious benefits, its adoption is more likely to happen. The "early adopter" typically represents an individual within a social system who is generally more open and receptive to innovation. If also considered an "opinion leader," he or she can influence others within that system to modify their attitude to be more accepting of change. But if the rate of change is too sudden and too rapid, even when there appears to be some receptivity, then disequilibrium occurs. Leaders who plan to introduce online education into a setting in which most transactions occur face-to-face, or where conventional ways of teaching prevail, should anticipate some resistance and develop a careful plan for the diffusion of such innovations. In this regard, Rogers and Shoemaker's seminal work on change has obvious implications for online education leaders today.

Cross-Cultural Partnerships

In an era of rapidly increasing globalization, particularly in the information and education sectors, new alliances between educational entities, especially those representing both developed and developing nations, can be useful in comingling resources and expertise to offer new educational opportunities to underserved areas. A common organizational arrangement for developing and delivering online offerings, especially in the international arena, is a partnership between two or more entities (often called a consortium) that comingles their respective expertise to complement one another. Consortia represent a way for organizations to extend their activities without incurring added costs to expand their operations unilaterally by pooling resources and cooperating more cost-effectively. This form of partnership is a promising means to address the disparity between institutions representing well-endowed nations and those in poorer countries. In addition to regional consortia, others represent collaborations of multiple institutions from across an entire country. There are also international alliances, representing both developed and developing countries, designed to overcome barriers imposed by differing language, culture, accreditation, articulation, and student support.

A common approach utilized in joint programs is a shared division of labor, through which one organization might lead the academic aspects and another is responsible for nonacademics (e.g., marketing, logistics). Despite the advantages to such an arrangement, there can also be difficulties; there is often not equity between the two partners, especially if one has greater expertise or more prestige than the other. Joint programs that engage in programming together, each contributing more or less equal resources, create the prospect for more equal benefits, as each partner is likely to have some advantage to leverage and safeguard its own interests.

International online education partnerships have the potential to be both especially satisfying, as well as particularly challenging. Despite careful stewardship from each party, a seemingly stable partnership can be disrupted and even sabotaged by seemingly small but subtle differences, whether influenced by personal style or organizational culture. Once educational programs transcend national borders, any number of social and cultural issues may arise, along with all the same issues that can plague partnership programs offered within a homogeneous setting.

Every organization has a culture with values and expectations that may be implicit but are not always explicit between partners aspiring to work collaboratively. Goodwill may erode if each party defines the desire for success differently. One side may see the priority as ensuring students receive satisfactory services, whereas the other sees the highest possible number of recruits converted to registrations as the overarching goal. A more entrepreneurial partner will typically value tangible results; the other, perhaps with a more service-oriented focus, values meaningfulness of purpose. Neither side is more inherently professional than the other; rather, each has a particular perspective on what it values most. Each is anchored in its respective core values and cultural context so that a situation may constitute a dilemma for one party, yet the other remains oblivious to an issue needing resolution. As Kidder (1995) pointed out, one's moral imperative could be another's moral dilemma. Yet, partners do not always agree in advance to a set of principles for problem solving and decision making.

Sergiovanni (1992) suggested that promised cooperation cannot be substituted for true commitment. Collegiality relies on norms and values agreed to by like-minded people who have a common commitment with shared identity and goals and who feel obligated to work together for the common good. But if cultural determinants influence what constitutes common good, then agreement by all parties may not come easily. One player may be immersed in a progressive, change-oriented environment, whereas another is bound to traditional mores that see change as a threat. Leadership within collaborating organizational bodies is guided by a moral authority and culturally defined values that influence each group; these are not likely to be easily changed within any group to accommodate another. If such differences are not expressed and negotiated with cultural sensitivity, relationships can deteriorate and perhaps be plagued by tension and mistrust, even as both parties pretend their working relationship remains civil and productive.

At another level, one partner may advocate a teaching-learning philosophy that its partner finds inappropriate for the population it serves. For example, a Western institution will likely promote discussion, critical thinking, and group work as essential to learning, whereas a partner from a more traditional society finds the notion of students discoursing with peers or challenging the teacher's views to be culturally and socially inappropriate. And what about educational partners with differing notions regarding the appropriate language of instruction? Should the Western institution insist that all instruction be in English, even if students have limited ability in English, while the partner expects all instruction be in the native language?

Perhaps the greatest weakness of partnership arrangements is not any inherent flaw that plagues their existence but rather that their agendas tend to be overly ambitious, especially those within settings that have significant educational need yet lack adequate resources to address their goals. The educational challenges facing developing countries are formidable, especially efforts to expand access, via instructional technology, to the underserved in remote regions. Organizations dependent on inadequate infrastructure, lacking a culture that promotes innovation and reform, and entrenched in educational systems that are incompatible with the concept of open education may insist that they and the region are simply not ready to launch ambitious efforts at online education, even with a willing partner. There is ample evidence that many attempts in this direction have not realized much genuine success in the short term and that conditions receptive to innovative educational change will remain elusive for some time to come.

There are many in academe that hold conflicting positions on complex educational issues, especially if these perspectives involve considerations across cultural boundaries and connections between multiple institutions. Even seemingly small differences can easily grow in magnitude and significance. For instance, most academics are determined that programs or courses they are associated with remain true to their intellectual origins and not be altered to accommodate other motives, especially if these appear to have monetary goals or if they are perceived as being adverse to students' interests. Both individual and organizational values may become embroiled in an organizational culture clash exacerbated by differing ethical perspectives that dissolve into disagreement and discord, ultimately compromising the good intentions that precipitated the relationship.

Despite these challenges, Konrad and Small (1989) argued that institutional collaboration is essential to achieve complex online education programs. There is evidence that partnerships, including those in developing areas with resource-challenged institutions, can introduce and infuse new educational opportunity, energy, and excitement into a setting, especially if those involved are allied for the purpose of diffusing e-learning to better meet the needs of underserved populations. This author's own experience in several educational partnerships might be instructive, so selected examples of potential cultural clashes that were eventually reconciled into collaborative arrangements are offered. In this regard, it is useful to first distinguish between various types of cultural differences that can contribute to clashes. One of these differences can be described as organizational culture, another as educational culture, and a third as ethnically based cultural differences.

When initially launching the first distance education program at his home institution, the author recognized that the lack of prior experience in this arena would likely compromise the efficiency and effectiveness of such an initiative and so convinced his university to contract with a for-profit company specializing in marketing online courses and programs. Although a division of labor involving one partner responsible for academics and the other for marketing seemed like a convenient arrangement, it involved a good deal of negotiation to arrive at a clear understanding of how each party could satisfy the primary needs of its respective organizational culture (e.g., one's goal to preserve its reputation, and the other to keep its desire for generating profits).

In another case, two higher education institutions, one American and the other European, seemed initially to share very compatible goals in cosponsoring an online doctoral program. But as joint planning ensued, it quickly became apparent that the respective educational cultures of the two parties were sufficiently disparate, in terms of such critical matters as decision making, faculty control, and curriculum, that the early optimism devolved into irreconcilable differences that led to the project's abandonment. In this instance, no amount of goodwill could overcome stubborn institutional barriers.

And in a third instance, the author advocated the establishment of his institution's first major international program, one that would provide an academic degree to complement the professional credential of health providers in the host country. A highly collaborative planning effort put every detail in place that augured well for a joint instructional team composed of U.S. and host-country faculty. But almost immediately, the stark differences in how these two instructor cadres managed their classrooms, and the different expectations each had regarding student workload and academic performance, threatened to unravel the program. In this situation, despite good intentions, ethnic differences in teacher-student dynamics caused a cultural clash in the classroom. Ultimately, careful intervention led to more adequate cross-cultural training of both faculty groups.

Addressing Differing Teaching-Learning Styles in Cross-Cultural Settings

Those who design and deliver global online learning can wield significant power and influence, and their decisions can affect a wide range of practices (e.g., curriculum, learning and teaching styles, online interaction, assignments, assessment, and privacy). So, how best to develop, implement, and sustain technology-based education for diverse global populations is a critical issue. Bates (1999) offered valuable insights into why ambitious and well-intended online initiatives do and do not work, especially when they cross international borders where social, cultural, political, and economic issues arise. In an era largely driven by the quest to generate revenues, differing sets of values and motives can complicate the process of implementing and sustaining viable programs. Bates raised several pertinent questions (paraphrased next) that every online education planner and provider ought to consider:

- Why engage in international online education? Should institutions in richer countries deliver educational courses and services in poorer countries?
- If students in countries with limited resources want access to higher education not available in their own country, why not? Should institutions in less developed countries with less expertise offer educational opportunities on their own to build capacity and expertise?
- Is there altruism or profit or both involved in marketing and delivering online courses internationally? Does this matter if this provides new knowledge and skills otherwise not available in recipient countries? Does this improve the quality of education and provide new economic and social development?
- If courses offered internationally are available to only the most affluent with access to technology, does this widen the socioeconomic-digital divide? Does taking tuition money from students from a poor country make it harder for them to invest in their own educational infrastructure?
- Can we ensure that students learning via international programs will receive the same quality of instruction and services as those in a sponsoring institution? Who is responsible for ensuring program integrity for both providers and consumers?
- Do joint international programs enable a poorer or less experienced institution to acquire online education expertise, or does the arrangement benefit the dominant organization at the expense of its partner?
- How much latitude should be allowed to accommodate cultural differences that could make a program relevant and beneficial for diverse learners, even if doing so threatens to "lower standards"?

Regardless of how such issues are resolved, they highlight the complexity and potential ethical conundrums of transcultural online education. Planning involves more than simply choosing appropriate technology, yet technical issues often overshadow far more important questions that, if overlooked, can scuttle any endeavor. Political realities can also threaten success. Western institutions now engaged in opening branch campuses in collaboration with Ministries of Education in the Middle East must contend with unknown variables such as governmental intrusion, contract changes, and so on. When difficult organizational, political, fiscal, pedagogical, and technical questions are compounded by cultural and ethical dilemmas, no wonder so many promising initiatives ultimately fail to realize their potential.

Boubsil and Carabajal (2011), in an insightful perspective on the implications of globalization, highlighted the growing trend among U.S. institutions to assess how distance education can meet the demand for transnational or "borderless" education. They suggested this expansion is driven not by any moral imperative to improve education in developing countries but rather now by the increasingly urgent need to generate additional revenues. And although most of these providers typically are equipped with a mission statement, sound educational programs, well-qualified faculty, solid infrastructure, and ample resources, this does not necessarily ensure that their offerings will always be compatible with the needs and interests of recipient nations or regions.

Demiray and Sharma (2009) identified strategies for promoting cultural sensitivities in global e-learning, based on principles relating to what they termed as "localization" (e.g., making cultural issues visible, promoting high interactivity, empowering global learners, and creating a high-trust learning ecology). These goals sound convincing and have merit, but it takes an exceptionally talented and sensitive individual or team to design and execute a comprehensive strategy that addresses the complex interplay of culturally driven issues that typically confront even the most well-intentioned online program planners.

Hai-Jew (2009) referred to those engaged in cross-cultural initiatives as "global boundary crossers" (p. 184). This seems an appropriate moniker to associate with those who move beyond the familiar confines of their own cultural milieu and cross over into new territory, where there is always some inherent risk in the unfamiliar. The field of online education, now more than ever, demands a cadre of bold and culturally sensitive leaders and educators eager and able to lead the way to new destinations.

The Ethics of Educational Innovation

Humankind shares a long and tragic history of cross-cultural intrusion, more often motivated by aggression than altruism. Yet, we also can chronicle many benign examples of transnational contact that has resulted in beneficial societal outcomes, including positive impacts on education. The United States, for example, sent teachers to the Philippines more than 100 years ago and, in more recent times, has sent thousands of Peace Corps volunteers to those same islands to teach in schools and colleges. It has also provided education and training resources through various agencies, including hundreds of professors serving as Fulbright scholars in institutions in many developing countries. And many institutions in the United States have developed successful partnerships with counterparts in other countries to offer student and faculty exchanges, implement new academic programs, and develop education infrastructure.

We have emphasized that launching and sustaining new academic programs is a complex enterprise, especially online education projects attempted by institutions that aspire to design and deliver academic offerings and services across cultural boundaries, often doing so with little or no prior experience. Inherently parochial, colleges and universities usually experiment with online courses on their own, seldom doing so with the benefit of other providers' experience and insight, even when attempting ambitious efforts to bring new programs of study to new markets via alternative delivery modes. This lack of prior experience in online education, coupled with unfamiliarity with different cultural milieu, is frequently exacerbated by the lack of any training in how to address ethical issues that inevitably present themselves with subtle yet potentially powerful consequences (Beck & Murphy, 1994).

Effective and ethical administrative practice in international online education settings encompass a wide variety of beliefs and behaviors including, for example, what is or is not taught, how it is taught, and what constitutes effective teaching and satisfactory learning. In this regard, online education providers, whether individuals or institutions, bear great responsibility for exhibiting appropriate professional practice. Leaders must reflect on differing perspectives, constantly examining their own cultural, social, and ethical assumptions, and thus develop the capacity to find and build on common ground. Sensitive decision makers recognize that cultural differences are manifested not only in language and social contexts but also in pedagogical practices (e.g., learning modes range from rote to reasoning; memorization to application and analysis; lecture to discourse; empirical to anecdotal) (see also chapter 2).

An especially challenging conundrum for educational leaders overseeing cross-cultural instruction is how to responsibly address different student learning styles, language barriers, attitudes toward instructors, and other dynamics that can profoundly affect learning outcomes and, ultimately, the overall success of a transnational online education effort.

There is a danger that some program leaders, eager to demonstrate their cultural sensitivity, may accommodate students by instituting certain practices to satisfy student preferences that could dilute the quality of education provided. A quite different response could be that instructors insist that any deviation from the norms they are accustomed to is unacceptable to maintain academic quality. Neither approach necessarily resolves such issues satisfactorily, and a response at either extreme could compromise the integrity of a program and the ethics of those leading it.

How can decision makers deal with these complex scenarios to best satisfy educational, cultural, qualitative, and ethical considerations? Faculty training that helps instructors devise alternative teaching styles; creatively modify assignments, readings, and tests that are more manageable yet still achieve desired learning objectives; allow certain discussions in the local language; and adopt more learner-centered policies can establish a more supportive learning environment, make teaching more satisfying for faculty, and give students a greater sense of achievement while maintaining sufficient quality in an ethical and culturally sensitive manner.

Are there viable models for culturally sensitive leadership in transnational online education initiatives? Space limitations do not allow for a detailed presentation of case studies to illustrate the concepts and characteristics discussed in this chapter, but perhaps even more useful here is a summary of various models that have proven effective in efforts for collaboration in distance education between the United States and developing countries, reported by the Association Liaison Office for University Cooperation in Development (2002) from proceedings of a 2002 roundtable.

- *Enabling model:* This is a multifaceted approach, involving technology transfer, infrastructure development, training, multicultural and language content, communication networks, creating digital libraries and open-source materials, and modeling best practices to improve local capacity. It encourages institutions to redesign instruction and resources and has best impact with high enrollments.
- *Contractual model:* This model involves multiple players guided by agreed-on means of conducting business that collaboratively identify appropriate technology,

focus on specific curricula, train and reward a committed staff, and have adequate institutional support.

- *Brokering model:* This model is complex and requires effective communication protocols and established processes; sponsoring institution and local broker must possess technical, financial, and political capacity to perform respective roles.
- *Multiple alliance model:* In this case, different types of partners comingle resources for mutual benefit. One acts as the coordinating unit, and partners bring differing expertise, contribute funding, and strengthen each other's capacity.
- *Commissioning model.* This model is a systems approach managed by a qualified central team. It features specialized division of labor, hierarchy of expertise, use of selective technology, and emphasis on quality instructional design.

Conclusions: Moving Toward Culturally Sensitive Leadership in Online Education

No facile formula is readily available for guiding appropriate action in multicultural educational situations, whether in online education or in other fields. Making and executing sound decisions depends on many variables, and challenging dilemmas are not easily resolved, even among compatible partners. Kidder (1995) argued that "noble compromise" is necessary, often requiring that a third option be reached that is not the first choice but nonetheless an acceptable one. Kidder suggested that by successfully making a tough choice on one issue, online educators can clarify their respective positions and thus guide them toward satisfactory resolutions on difficult issues in the future.

Those engaged in the design and delivery of online education need to identify and articulate their assumptions and values to determine how compatible or disparate these may be relative to the situation they impact and acknowledge and resolve issues likely to compromise effective outcomes. Whether providers or consumers, participants must respect one another's differing attitudes, values, and beliefs and be sensitive to cultural nuances, which can be best achieved by sharing their respective positions on all issues and options, realistically assessing consequences of each choice, exploring possible compromise positions, and, finally, coming to clear and explicit agreement on the most suitable set of arrangements to guide their work together.

The following are some useful guidelines for individuals and organizations engaged in transnational online education might benefit from:

- Decision makers should articulate and agree to "rules of engagement" and identify parameters of mutually acceptable behavior.
- All parties must be clear regarding their respective motivation for moving into any joint international online education arrangement. Each should acknowledge the benefits it envisions for itself and its constituents.
- Letters of agreement are important to clearly define goals, expectations, responsibilities, time frames for planning, deliverables, financial arrangements, and so on before any actual activities are launched.
- Key administrators, planners, course developers, and instructors should be sensitized to any potentially volatile issues before any products or services are offered.

- Cultural nuances must be recognized and potential "culture clashes" identified in order to anticipate and overcome issues that could easily sabotage a well-intended plan.
- Faculty and others interacting across cultural lines should receive cross-cultural training.

How might further research in this area provide useful information and insight to ensure that these and other strategies are implemented before online courses and programs are offered across national boundaries? How might participants benefit from lessons previously learned and documented by others who have succeeded (or failed) in similar prior efforts? Here we take a cue from Cookson (2000), who referred to "Travelers' Tales," noting that most chronicles of past programs and practices have been largely descriptive and not generalizable to comparable situations. There are too many examples of educational providers that moved aggressively into unfamiliar territory to launch online programs without establishing any prior protocols for systematic analysis of what worked and what did not work and why. What is needed at this point is not more scholarly studies with elaborate hypotheses tracking numerous variables operant in cross-cultural settings but rather practitioners planning and managing programs who give more thoughtful attention to formative assessment methods so that they may more reliably document program activities and learning outcomes that inform and influence future practice.

Despite the absence of any single definitive model for designing, delivering, and sustaining online education across cultural boundaries, there remains a compelling argument for continued and increased initiatives to advance educational objectives, whether achieved unilaterally or through collaborative processes. Ultimately, progress is likely to be realized only with the presence and perseverance of effective institutional leadership that recognizes the potential of online education, is willing to take risks, and engages in transformative roles that not only change leaders' respective institutions but also reform education practice and enhance access to education for more citizens. The difference between success and failure in these enterprises depends on adequate attention and commitment to maintaining the highest ethical standards and the greatest cultural sensitivity that both individuals and organizations can achieve. Certainly, this effort and its potential benefits are far too important not to succeed!

References

Association Liaison Office for University Cooperation in Development. (2002, October). *Strategies for US–developing countries collaboration in distance education.* Policy Roundtable Series, Washington, DC. Retrieved from http://www.hedprogram.org/resources/loader.cfm?csModule=security/getfile&pageid=3310

Bates, T. (1999, September). *Cultural and ethical issues in international distance education.* Paper presented at the Engaging Partnerships Collaboration and Partnership in Distance Education, UBC/CREAD Conference, Vancouver, Canada.

Beck, L. G., & Murphy, J. (1994). *Ethics in educational leadership programs: An expanding role.* Thousand Oaks, CA: Corwin Press.

Boubsil, O., & Carabajal, K. (2011). Implications of globalization for distance education in the United States. *The American Journal of Distance Education, 25*(1), 5–20.

Cookson, P. (2000, June). *A framework for comparative distance education research: Cross-national, cross-cultural, interdisciplinary and cross-institutional perspectives.* Paper presented at the conference on Research in Distance and Adult Learning in Asia, Open University of Hong Kong, Hong Kong SAR. Retrieved from http://www.ouhk.edu.hk/cridal/cridala/conf/messages/13/cookson.pdf

Demiray, U., & Sharma, R. (Eds.). (2009). *Ethical practices and implications in distance education.* Hershey, PA: Information Science Reference.

Gunawardena, C. N., Wilson, P., & Nolla, A. (2003). Culture and online education. In M. Moore & W. Anderson (Eds.), *Handbook of distance education* (pp. 753–775). Mahwah, NJ: Lawrence Erlbaum.

Hai-Jew, S. (2009). Why "cultural sensitivities" and "localizations" in global e-learning? In U. Demiray & R. C. Sharma (Eds.), *Ethical practices and implications in distance learning* (pp. 155–198). Hershey, PA: Information Science Reference.

Johnson, R. (2007). Foreword. In Y. Inoue (Ed.), *Technology and diversity in higher education* (p. viii). Hershey, PA: Information Science Publishing.

Kidder, R. (1995). *How good people make tough choices.* New York, NY: Fireside.

Konrad, A., & Small, J. (1989). Collaboration in distance education. In R. Sweet (Ed.), *Post-secondary distance education in Canada: Policies, practices and priorities* (pp. 197–203). Athabasca, Canada: Athabasca University Press.

Rogers, E., & Shoemaker, F. (1971). *Communication of innovations: A cross-cultural approach.* New York, NY: Free Press.

Sergiovanni, T. (1992). *Moral leadership: Getting the most of school improvement.* San Francisco, CA: Jossey-Bass.

12

GENDER ISSUES IN ONLINE LEARNING

Colin Latchem

Kanwar (2013) observes that *gender* refers to both men and women, and in open, distance, and online learning, the focus must be on promoting equality, whichever sex is disadvantaged. There is clearly a need for more understanding of the gender dimensions of online learning to ensure equality in online course design and provision (e.g., Bidjerano, 2005; Price, 2006; Rovai, 2001; Rovai & Baker, 2005).

This chapter examines gender considerations in online learning. As indicated elsewhere in this book (see chapters 2 and 4), there are inconsistent or contrary findings in regard to gender differences in online study. Some studies have concluded that gender is irrelevant because online learning systems are nongendered. Others have concluded that online study can actually favor women. Although these findings do not provide definitive answers to the questions of gender and cross-gender communication in cyberspace, they do help to make the issues clearer and alert readers to the fact that females and males may have distinct learning needs and there is need to ensure gender equality and flexibility in the online learning environment. This chapter also shows the ways in which women can not only gain from but contribute to online learning.

Gender Considerations in Online Learning

In many countries over the past 10 years, mature (over age 40 years), single-parent, minority, and low-income women have become the largest group among adult learners. Increasing numbers of these women are studying online, and in some countries females constitute the majority of online learners. In the United States at the turn of this century, 60% of the students studying online degree courses were women (Kramarae, 2001), most of whom were over age 25 years. Curiously, despite the fact that students' main reasons for taking a massive open online course (MOOC) are advancing in their current job and satisfying curiosity, a number of studies (e.g., Christensen et al., 2013) have shown that significantly fewer females than males are currently signing up for MOOCs, especially in the developing countries. Martin and Walter (2013) said that U.S. universities are missing a great opportunity to export gender equality, powerful female role models, and classes taught by women that could profoundly influence how young people around the world think about the roles women play in society.

Gender Neutrality and Gender Predisposition

Margolis and Fisher (2002) suggested that online learning environments are gender neutral and provide a democratic and equal environment. On the other hand, B. Anderson (2006) observed that simply moving a learning community online does not mean that it automatically becomes democratic, less aggressive, or free of the gender-related problems that plague traditional classrooms. Gunn, McSporran, Macleod, and French (2003) suggested that online learning may have the same asymmetrical gender and power dynamics as traditional face-to-face learning environments, with male students displaying dominant, controlling, arrogant, and other deviant behavior.

Kramarae (2001) pointed out that for many women, online learning is "a third shift" in which they grapple individually and often in isolation with time constraints that hinder them in fitting distance learning into their already packed work and family lives. Müller (2008) found that female online students have to cope with the multiple responsibilities of being an income provider, parent, and student; insufficient interaction with faculty; and problems or frustrations with the technology. Given that researchers such as Cooper and Weaver (2003) have suggested that women tend to avoid technology, their extensive involvement in online learning seems surprising. However, according to cyberfeminist Sadie Plant (1996), the Internet is a quintessentially "female technology," allowing the free exchange of information, the lessening of hierarchy, the nurturing aspects of virtual communities, and the ending of patriarchy. At the same time, women may well find that this mode of study demands more motivation, determination, and time-management skills than traditional classes, and their ability to cope will depend largely on how connected they feel with their tutors and fellow students.

Discussion forums, chat rooms, blogs, and tweets provide female online learners with opportunities to share their concerns, experiences, and learning with their fellow learners and join self-help groups. Asynchronous text-based online discussion may well suit women who are shy or reticent or who prefer to have more time to digest a variety of viewpoints and express themselves without verbal interruption (Gunn et al., 2003). However, the 24/7 stream of messages adds considerably to the amount of required reading time and may be daunting for students who are unused to writing, are self-conscious about their writing skills, or prefer face-to-face contact. And the relative anonymity of online study may encourage some other students to post remarks that they would not make in person, which can upset or alienate.

"Voice" and Online Communication

Although it is important to avoid gender stereotyping and acknowledge that there can be considerable variations within each gender and particular context, there is a considerable amount of research on psychological gender differences in communications. In general, men are held to construct and maintain an independent self-construal, whereas women are thought to construct and maintain an interdependent self-construal (Cross & Madson, 1997). As a consequence, men tend to be more independent and assertive, use language to establish and maintain status and dominate in relationships, and transmit information and offer advice in order to achieve tangible outcomes. By contrast, women tend to be more expressive, tentative, and polite in conversation, valuing cooperation and using dialogue in order to create and foster intimate bonds with others by talking about issues they communally face (Basow & Rubenfeld, 2003). Confirmation of these gender-related differences in online course communication patterns was found by Rovai (2001), with the majority of men (and some women) exhibiting an "independent voice" and the majority of women (but also some men) using a "connected voice" in their written messages, indicating a higher sense of "belonging."

Women are also less likely to swear or interrupt than men and more likely to be uncertain and give the impression of being subordinate to men. Men cope with stress by withdrawing from conversations or situations, whereas women cope by reaching out and talking about the causes of their stress (Gray, 1992). In online discussions, males are more likely to post longer messages, begin and close discussions in mixed-sex groups, assert opinions as facts, use insults and even profanity to get their way, and in general manifest an adversarial orientation toward their interlocutors. Females, by contrast, tend to post relatively short messages and are more likely to qualify and justify their assertions and express support for others (Herring, 1996). All of these socially constructed behaviors have the potential to cause misunderstandings between males and females engaged in online learning.

Gladys We (1993) observed that there are as many ways of communicating online as there are individuals and that online communication has the potential both to be liberating and to duplicate all of the misunderstandings and confusion that arise in interactions between women and men in everyday life. She did find that when the contact is professional, communication tends to be relatively free of gender cues, whereas when the contact is social, for example, in a newsgroup, women may be more aware of gender differences, be more guarded with men than women, and feel freer about expressing their feelings and talking about own life experiences. Some men felt that it was easier to get to know women online; others distrusted the shifting nature of online personas.

D. M. Anderson and Haddad (2005) found that female voices that might not be heard in face-to-face teaching and learning because of gender-based role socialization, cultural differences, or individual personality traits can be more commonly heard in online courses. They also found that female students in online courses were more willing to reach out to their professors than they would be in face-to-face environments where again role socialization inhibited them from speaking out or even seeking help. As a consequence, they concluded that these females experienced deeper perceived learning in online courses than in face-to-face courses.

Female users can attempt to minimize discrimination and conflict in online exchanges by adopting gender-neutral usernames, but their message style and content may still display features of culturally learned gender styles (Bruckman, 1993). It might be thought that in countries where gender relations are highly regulated and cross-gender communication is strictly limited, online forums where there is no call to reveal name, age, marital status, and so on might provide opportunities for dialogue with fewer prejudices and misunderstandings. However, Madini and De Nooy (2013) found that in the case of a public discussion forum involving expatriate Saudi students, clues to gender were considered essential to all but the briefest exchanges, and the communication still remained largely gender segregated. Another study into online education involving Arab Gulf students in the United States by Al-Harthi (2005) also confirmed the persistence of gender segregation in online interaction. The female students tended to be very careful of what they said with the men, particularly those who knew them and their families, and even log off a chat with an instructor and other American students when any Muslim man joined in the group discussion.

So, Does Online Learning Favor Women?

As shown, current research reveals a mixed account of whether women fare better or worse in online learning. Yükseltürk and Bulut (2009) found no gender differences in motivational beliefs, learning variables, and achievement in online learning. Hyde (2005) found more significant learner differences *within* a female or male group than *between* groups of female or male learners. Gunn et al. (2003) found that women often perform better than men in online learning, suggesting that some aspects of an online learning environment are beneficial to female students. Fisher, Cox, and Gray (2008) suggested that the decreased opportunity for intrasexual competition, to which younger women are more sensitive, provides an explanation for their high participation rates in online courses. Rovai and Baker (2005) found that female students in online graduate education courses in which they outnumbered males felt more connected to their fellow students, that their online learning experiences were more aligned to their educational values and goals, and that they learned more than their male peers. It should be noted that all such studies relate to learners from different age groups or backgrounds and working within different instructional design and online environments, so it is impossible to draw overall conclusions.

Access and Culture

Internet access is fast becoming indispensable in a hyper-connected world, and Price (2006) reported that the numbers of women with online access in high-income countries often equal or exceed male levels of access. On the other hand, Burke (2001) suggested that different domestic arrangements of space and time in regard to home computers can be crucial factors in women's access to online learning.

When it comes to the developing world, the World Bank (2011) reported that many girls and women are unable to benefit from the opportunities offered by the new technologies because they lack the access, funds, education, and technical skills to participate equally in the knowledge economy. A recent Intel study (Kakar, Hausman, Thomas, & Denny-Brown, 2013) found that nearly 45% fewer women than men have access to the Internet in sub-Saharan Africa; 35% in South Asia, the Middle East, and North Africa; and 30% in Eastern Europe and Central Asia. Interviewing women in Mexico, India, Egypt, and Uganda, the researchers found that the other major factors contributing to women's lack of online presence are long-held cultural attitudes and expectations that exclude them from the Internet and women simply not knowing what the Internet is or how it might benefit them. In India, for example, they found that technology is still regarded as the exclusive province of men, women are concerned that their families wouldn't approve of them being online, and there are concerns within families, not without cause, about young inexperienced girls and women accessing undesirable material on the Internet or being contacted through chat rooms and Facebook by sexual predators, kidnappers, and traffickers.

One in five women in India and Egypt interviewed in this Intel study felt that the Internet was inappropriate for them and had no information of any use to them. However, 75% to 80% of all the women surveyed regarded the Internet as "liberating." The greatest use of the Internet by the majority of these women was educational: studying and researching online and helping with their children's homework. The second highest use was learning about health issues and services, which obviated the problems of limited access to medical professionals and embarrassment over discussing sensitive topics with men.

Infrastructure is expanding, there are almost as many mobile-cellular subscriptions as people on earth, fixed broadband prices dropped by 82% between 2008 and 2012, and 3G technology provides a means of serving rural subscribers in both developing and developed countries (International Telecommunications Union, 2013). All of these developments, together with growing awareness among women that the Internet is a gateway to development opportunities augur well for increased women's learning online.

As shown in the following section, women are not only gaining from but also contributing to online learning.

Women Contributing to Online Learning

In his Hole-in-the-Wall (www.hole-in-the-wall.com) computer experiment exposing children to basic PCs in poor parts of India, Professor Sugata Mitra found that children did best with adults offering advice and encouragement. He reasoned that no one was as willing and able to do this as grandmothers. This gave him the idea of the "Granny Cloud" or, to give it its official name, Self Organized Learning Environments (SOLE). Supported by the School of Education, Communication, and Language Sciences at Newcastle University, grandmothers in the United Kingdom and other countries, many of whom are retired teachers (there are also some male retirees involved), act as voluntary "e-mediators" for schoolchildren thousands of miles away in India. These "grannies" help the children with their reading and learning about different cultural traditions. Suneeta Kulkarni, who coordinates the scheme across India, says that she has seen big differences in the children's learning, and the scheme has now been extended to schools in Colombia, South America, and most recently the United Kingdom to help children in the early stages of reading (Wakefield, 2012).

Being more inclined to demonstrate communal characteristics, nurturance, and concern for others, women would appear to have exactly the qualities required for initiating and leading online educational and community development programs where there are no preexisting hierarchies or traditions of leadership and where the aim is social mobilization through awareness building, empowerment, capacity building, and creating participatory environments. Kanwar, Ferreira, and Latchem (2013) provided examples of women creating and leading online learning communities to counter ignorance, maltreatment, gender bias, and discrimination within their societies and to spread beliefs, ideas, behaviors, and practices from one community to another and from one generation to another.

Jensine Larsen, the founder of World Pulse (http://worldpulse.com), a nonprofit social media enterprise headquartered in Portland, Oregon, found that grassroots women in far-flung places who are denied a voice, devalued, or facing extreme discrimination in their communities and families can find encouragement and develop courage through online conversations with other women. They in turn can become change agents in indigenous movements, unleashing the creative human potential of women across the globe. Today, nearly 60,000 women in more than 190 countries connect through World Pulse. They are speaking out on their most pressing issues, and their stories are being picked up by the BBC, CNN, TED, the Canadian Broadcasting Corporation, the United Nations, the *Huffington Post*, and other media outlets. This networking is also helping these women to find jobs, start new programs and enterprises, and discover other means of changing their lives and lifting their communities.

Female information technology specialists Yasmine El-Mehairy and Zeinab Samir wanted to establish a start-up that added value rather than being yet another commercial online product. Realizing that Middle Eastern and North African parents required different knowledge than Western parents on such matters as what babies should weigh, vaccination schedules, and how to handle teenagers and lacked the money and time to obtain such information, they created a bilingual Arabic and English website SuperMama (http://supermama.me/ar). The content is designed specifically for mothers and mothers-to-be in the Arab world. For example, European mothers are advised to give their children Vitamin D for bone development; in the Arab region, Vitamin D is naturally formed in the body as a result of the stronger sunlight. Surveys and focus groups establish which topics and common problems are to be addressed. The main writers are women working from home, and Arab and Egyptian volunteer specialists ranging from doctors and teachers to nutritionists and exercise experts confirm or dispel the indigenous child-raising knowledge that has been communicated between the generations. Around 15% of the site's visitors are men, so one section is designed to help men better understand parenthood and child care issues. SuperMama is nonpolitical and nonreligious. In its first month, the website had 2,000 registered users and over 20,000 unique visits. SuperMama's revenue comes from advertisement banners, sponsorships, and product placements within the articles and videos, and the winning of a considerable number of national and international prizes ensures further investment (Beslui, 2013).

Core4women (www.core4women.org) was founded in 2009 by Gail Weatherly, distance education coordinator at Stephen F. Austin State University, Nacogdoches, Texas. She launched this free website after receiving many phone calls from women, some almost in tears, about the problems they were experiencing in studying while caring for their children. The project began with a small group of female mentors familiar with online learning trialing the free Ning social networking site to assist a small group of female students who were victims of abuse or poverty. It was found that these women were far more willing to share their inner and intimate thoughts with other women than they would be with men. Core4women now uses Google Apps, and women in all U.S. states and 28 other countries use this website to share their concerns, experiences, ideas, and information and to seek guidance from voluntary mentors on such matters as how to locate online degree programs, how to seek funding, how to register, how to engage with others in online environments, and how to juggle family or work responsibilities and study.

The Global Entrepreneurship Monitor (2013) reported that 126 million women across the world are operating new businesses, and another 98 million are running established businesses. But Burch (2013) posited that companies, communities, and countries recognize the need to invest even more in women's entrepreneurship because such investment is investment in the world's collective future. Women who are would-be entrepreneurs also need training in business skills, help in balancing work and family commitments, and advice on securing financing because they often lack capital or collateral and face discriminatory regulations and ingrained gender bias.

Women On the Web (WOW) (www.womenentrepreneursontheweb.com) aims to increase women's participation in the Google Business Groups (GBG), provide technology-enabled entrepreneurship opportunities for women by leveraging the power of the Internet at the early stage of their start-ups, and create an online community for sharing their experiences and supporting each other. Begun in India, the program will be available in Latin America, South East Asia, India, sub-Saharan Africa, and the Middle East. WOW was conceived by some female googlers in Hyderabad in 2011. One of these women, Keerthana Mohan, recalled, "When we spoke to women entrepreneurs, we quickly gauged two things: an entrepreneurial appetite and the need for a lot more exposure online." The business leaders at Google were receptive to the idea, and the initiative was launched in January 2012 (Bhattacharya, 2013).

Goldman Sachs's 10,000 Women program provides underserved women around the world with training in business planning, marketing, finance, accounting, and management. In September 2013, Goldman Sachs launched a public Twitter presence for this program using the handle @GS10KWomen. Within 1 month the account had over 20,000 followers.

The Cherie Blair Foundation for Women's Mentoring Women in Business Program (www.cherieblairfoundation.org) enables successful male and female mentors around the world to provide online mentoring and support for women who are establishing small to medium enterprises in Malaysia, Kenya, South Africa, Rwanda, China, Pakistan, and the Philippines. During the yearlong courses, the mentors Skype or use smart phones or tablets for fortnightly 1-hour sessions to help these female neophytes develop knowledge and skills in business and technology. The process is shown to be having a positive impact on these aspiring entrepreneurs' English and ability to use technology and access and succeed in new markets.

In India, Chetna Sinha is an economist, farmer, activist, and founding president of the Mann Deshi Mahila Bank Ltd., a microenterprise cooperative development bank whose clients are women earning an average of INR 40 (US$1) a day. She also founded the Mann Deshi Foundation to empower and train women and self-help groups in business, entrepreneurism, property rights, and technology. An FM community radio station, information kiosks equipped with information and communications technologies (ICTs), and a Mobile Business School for Rural Women (two custom-designed buses taking ICT-based training into the remote areas) enable thousands of women to learn about financial and business matters, receive vocational training, and become knowledgeable and skilled in computer and mobile phone operations. This prepares them for establishing small enterprises such as making photo frames, making paper cups, running tea shops, and selling takeout foods, farm and garden produce, and cell phone recharge coupons (Sinha, 2013).

Conclusion

Technological advances and more enlightened policies and practice in education are putting the Internet in the hands of more and more women who can gain from the knowledge, networks, and learning communities on offer. For those keen to expand the personal, social, and economic benefits of formal education, nonformal education, and informal learning across the globe, there has never been a better time to help girls and women realize their potential and improve the circumstances of their families, communities, and the world at large.

Green and Trevor-Deutsch (2002) found that in Africa, Asia, the Caribbean, and the South Pacific, the barriers faced by women in accessing online learning are the same as those they face in accessing education of any kind: illiteracy, shortage of time, and sociocultural factors. So to help women advance educationally, socially, and economically; provide social and political advocacy; and fight against injustice, discrimination, and violence against women, new kinds of online network are needed to link "connected" women with "unconnected" women's groups.

In applying online learning to development in developing countries, it is important to appreciate that the uses of the technology are socially constructed and may have different impacts on women and men. So care is needed to ensure that the new tools, networking capabilities, and approaches accord with women's needs, priorities, and circumstances. Outside formal Western education or academic contexts where women may initiate and author online programs, females are virtually absent as substantive producers of content. It is therefore important that they are given training and support in producing content that is relevant to their needs and truly reflects their particular viewpoints, experiences, and concerns.

Von Prümmer and Rossié (2001) stressed that in developed and developing countries alike, any educational institution or development agency striving for gender equity must be committed to presenting itself in a nonsexist and gender-inclusive way, have an explicit policy regarding the design and content of websites, institute monitoring procedures with sanctions for offences, and take measures to educate users in netiquette.

As shown in this chapter, online learning environments may well inherit some of the culture, acquired behaviors, perspectives, and values of the traditional classroom and the groups or communities from which the teachers and learners are drawn. So as Moore (2006) observed, for online learning to successfully address gender issues, teachers and learners need to step out of their own cultures and temporarily enter into the cultures of others.

It is always advisable to be alert to the fact that females and males may have distinct learning needs and ensure gender equality and flexibility in the online learning environment by doing the following:

- Ensure that all learners, male or female, enjoy the same degree and freedom of online access and comment.
- Never make assumptions based on gender regarding behaviors, abilities, or preferences of learners.
- Be aware that gender bias in education and wider society is a series of microinequities whose impact is cumulative and often unrecognized or ignored.

- Avoid treating males and females differently on the basis of sex, but recognize that learners are diverse and have different learning characteristics and needs.
- Make sure that expectations in subjects such as math and science are the same for all learners. Both sexes can succeed in these subject areas.
- Check all content, examples, activities, and language metaphors that create or perpetuate gender bias.
- Be alert to gendered expectations and use of praise and other feedback.
- Provide for cross-sex collaboration in learning activities and project work.
- Encourage both male and female learners to undertake the technical aspects of the work, perform in leadership roles, and provide role models.
- Be alert to the possibility of gender bias in peer ratings by learners.
- Be alert to any uneven ratio of learner-learner and learner-teacher interactions.
- Monitor and obtain feedback on learner-interaction styles.
- Be sensitive to how learners of both sexes feel about the cultural climate of the online environment.
- Avoid any form of online harassment or sexist behavior.

References

Al-Harthi, A. (2005). Distance higher education experiences of Arab Gulf students in the United States: A cultural perspective. *The International Review of Research in Open and Distance Learning, 6*(3). Retrieved from http://www.irrodl.org/index.php/irrodl/article/view/263/406

Anderson, B. (2006). Writing power into online discussion. *Computers and Composition, 23*(1), 108–124.

Anderson, D. M., & Haddad, C. J. (2005). Gender, voice and learning in online course environments. *Journal of Asynchronous Learning Networks, 9*(1), 3–14.

Basow, S. A., & Rubenfeld, K. (2003). "Troubles talk": Effects of gender and gender-typing. *Sex Roles, 48*, 183–187.

Beslui, R. (2013, April 8). *Taking on the giant.* Retrieved from http://www.takingonthegiant.com/2013/04/08/yasmine-el-mehairys-supermama-website-expert-tips-for-supermoms/#respond

Bhattacharya, S. (2013, July 12). Google India to launch WeOW initiative to help women's start-ups connect online. *The Economic Times.* Retrieved from http://articles.economictimes.indiatimes.com/2013-07-12/news/40536802_1_google-india-women-entrepreneurs-rajan-anandan

Bidjerano, T. (2005, October). *Gender differences in self-regulated learning.* Paper presented at the Annual Meeting of the Northeastern Educational Research Association, Kerhonkson, NY.

Bruckman, A. S. (1993). Gender swapping on the Internet. In *Proceedings of INET '93.* Reston, VA: The Internet Society. Retrieved from http://www.cc.gatech.edu/~asb/papers/conference/gender-swapping.txt

Burch, T. (2013, November 18). Why the world needs women entrepreneurs. *The Economist.* Retrieved from http://www.economist.com/news/21589133-investing-businesswomen-will-boost-economy-everyone-says-tory-burch-chief-executive-and

Burke, C. (2001). Women, guilt, and home computers. *Cyberpsychology, Behavior, and Social Networking, 4*(5), 609–615.

Christensen, G., Steinmetz, A., Alcorn, B., Bennett, A., Woods, D., & Emanuel, E. J. (2013). *The MOOC phenomenon: Who takes massive open online courses and why?* (Working Paper).

Philadelphia: Office of the Provost, University of Pennsylvania. Retrieved from http://www.meducationalliance.org/sites/default/files/the_mooc_phenomenon.pdf

Cooper, J., & Weaver, K. D. (2003). *Gender and computers: Understanding the digital divide.* Mahwah, NJ: Lawrence Erlbaum.

Cross, S. E., & Madson, L. (1997). Models of the self: Self-construals and gender. *Psychological Bulletin, 122*(1), 5–37.

Fisher, M., Cox, C., & Gray, M. (2008, January). Gender, intrasexual competition, and online learning. *European Journal of Open, Distance and E-learning, 1.* Retrieved from http://www.eurodl.org/?p=archives&year=2008&halfyear=1&article=327

Global Entrepreneurship Monitor. (2013). *Global Entrepreneurship Monitor 2012 women's report.* London: Global Entrepreneurship Research Association, London Business School. Retrieved from http://gemconsortium.org/docs/download/2825

Gray, J. (1992). *Men are from Mars, women are from Venus: A practical guide for improving communication and getting what you want in a relationship.* New York, NY: HarperCollins.

Green, L., & Trevor-Deutsch, L. (2002). *UNESCO meta-survey on the use of technologies in education in Asia and the Pacific.* Retrieved from http://unesdoc.unesco.org/images/0013/001349/134960e.pdf

Gunn, C., McSporran, M., Macleod, H., & French, S. (2003). Dominant or different? Gender issues in computer supported learning. *Journal of Asynchronous Learning Networks, 7,* 14–30. Retrieved from http://www.cs.lamar.edu/faculty/osborne/COSC1172/v7n1_gunn.pdf

Herring, S. C. (1996). Gender and democracy in computer-mediated communication. In R. Kling (Ed.), *Computerization and controversy* (2nd ed., pp. 476–489). New York, NY: Academic Press.

Hyde, J. (2005). The gender similarity hypothesis. *American Psychologist, 60,* 581–592.

International Telecommunications Union. (2013). *The World in 2013: ICT facts and figures.* Geneva, Switzerland: Author. Retrieved from http://www.itu.int/en/ITU-D/Statistics/Documents/facts/ICTFactsFigures2013-e.pdf

Kakar, Y. W., Hausman, V., Thomas, A., & Denny-Brown, C. (2013). *Women and the web: Bridging the Internet gap and creating new global opportunities in low and middle-income countries.* Santa Clara, CA: Intel. Retrieved from http://www.intel.com.au/content/dam/www/public/us/en/documents/pdf/women-and-the-web.pdf

Kanwar, A. S. (2013). Preface. In A. S. Kanwar, F. Ferreira, & C. Latchem (Eds.), *Women and leadership in open and distance learning and development* (pp. vii–ix). Vancouver, Canada: Commonwealth of Learning. Retrieved from http://www.col.org/PublicationDocuments/pub_ps_WomenLeadership.pdf

Kanwar, A. S., Ferreira, F., & Latchem, C. (Eds.). (2013). *Women and leadership in open and distance learning and development.* Vancouver, Canada: Commonwealth of Learning. Retrieved from http://www.col.org/PublicationDocuments/pub_ps_WomenLeadership.pdf

Kramarae, C. (2001). *The third shift: Women learning online.* Washington, DC: American Association of University Women Educational Foundation.

Madini, A. A., & De Nooy, J. (2013). Disclosure of gender identity in Internet forums: A case study of Saudi Arabian forum communication. *Gender, Technology and Development, 17*(3), 233–257.

Margolis, J., & Fisher, A. (2002). *Unlocking the clubhouse: Women in computing.* Cambridge, MA: MIT Press.

Martin, L. L., & Walter, B. F. (2013, January 25). Setting an online example in educating women. *Los Angeles Times.* Retrieved from http://articles.latimes.com/2013/jan/25/opinion/la-oe-martin-online-gender-equality-20130125

Moore, M. (2006). Editorial. *The American Journal of Distance Education, 20*(1), 1–5.

Müller, T. (2008). Persistence of women in online degree-completion programs. *International Review of Research in Open and Distance Learning, 9*(2). Retrieved from http://www.irrodl.org/index.php/irrodl/issue/view/31

Plant, S. (1996). The future looms: Weaving women and cybernetics. In L. H. Leeson (Ed.), *Clicking in: Hot links to a digital culture* (pp. 123–135). Washington, DC: Bay Press.

Price, L. (2006). Gender differences and similarities in online courses: Challenging stereotypical views of women. *Journal of Computer Assisted Learning, 22*(5), 349–359.

Rovai, A. P. (2001). Building classroom community at a distance: A case study. *Educational Technology Research and Development Journal, 49*(4), 33–48.

Rovai, A. P., & Baker, J. D. (2005). Gender differences in online learning: Sense of community, perceived learning, and interpersonal interactions. *The Quarterly Review of Distance Education, 6*(1), 31–44.

Sinha, C. G. (2013). Helping other women through non-formal education and community development. In A. S. Kanwar, F. Ferreira, & C. Latchem (Eds.), *Women and leadership in open and distance learning and development* (pp. 137–148). Vancouver, Canada: Commonwealth of Learning. Retrieved from http://www.col.org/PublicationDocuments/pub_ps_WomenLeadership.pdf

Von Prümmer, C., & Rossié, U. (2001). Gender-sensitive evaluation research. In E. J. Burge & M. Haughey (Eds.), *Using learning technologies: International perspectives on practice* (pp. 135–144). London, UK, and New York, NY: RoutledgeFalmer.

Wakefield, J. (2012, April 30). Granny army helps India's school children via the cloud. *BBC News Technology.* Retrieved from http://www.bbc.co.uk/news/technology-17114718

We, G. (1993). Cross-gender communication in cyberspace. *The Arachnet Journal on Virtual Culture, 2*(3). Retrieved from http://mith.umd.edu//WomensStudies/Computing/Articles+ResearchPapers/cross-gender-communication

World Bank. (2011). *Engendering ICT toolkit.* Washington, DC: Author. Retrieved from http://web.worldbank.org/WBSITE/EXTERNAL/TOPICS/EXTGENDER/EXTICTTOOLKIT/0,,contentMDK:20272989~menuPK:562602~pagePK:64168445~piPK:64168309~theSitePK:542820,00.html

Yükseltürk, E., & Bulut, S. (2009). Gender differences in self-regulated online learning environment. *Educational Technology and Society, 12*(3), 12–22.

13

TRANSFORMATIVE LEARNING THROUGH CULTURAL EXCHANGES IN ONLINE FOREIGN LANGUAGE TEACHING

Kerrin Ann Barrett

Increasingly, distance education programs are reaching out beyond the traditional purview of brick-and-mortar institutions to provide access to education for students in other countries. The technology revolution that has taken place over the past 15 years has led to new innovations in education. Among these innovations is the use of web-enabled technology to teach foreign languages. Using Voice over Internet Protocol (VoIP) to converse with native speakers over distance in real time is one promising approach to language development. One of the first experiments in using synchronous methods to teach language in the online environment was Global Digital's EnglishNow program.

This chapter is based on a study conducted in 2007 that explored the lived experiences of teachers and learners in a VoIP-enabled online language learning classroom over distance and across cultures (Barrett, 2008). Specifically, this study explored the lived experiences of U.S. teachers and Taiwanese teaching assistants (TAs) teaching English as a foreign language (EFL) to Chinese and Taiwanese students using an online multimedia platform. The synchronous VoIP enhancement to the virtual classroom created new dynamics in distance education across culture that provided fertile ground for exploration.

The research question of the study was, "How do participants in a cross-cultural synchronous online English as a foreign language environment supported by Voice over Internet Protocol perceive the teaching and learning context and their lived experience?"

The eight themes that emerged from the data analysis to describe this unique program and online cross-cultural language learning environment are summarized as follows: technology affordances and use, characteristics of teachers, characteristics of learners, interactions and their dynamics, administration, language development, conflict, and transformation. This chapter focuses on the final theme, transformational learning.

Theoretical Background

Sociocultural theory provides the overarching framework for the other perspectives included in this study. Tangential, yet nonetheless supportive, are the fields of foreign language learning, intercultural communication, and transformational learning. Each of these fields offers its respective theories pertaining to teachers and students from different cultures interacting through the Internet while learning English. For this chapter, the viewpoints presented will center on strategies for creating and sustaining synchronous online language learning environments and Glaser's grounded theory, as it served as a theoretical basis of this qualitative study.

Sociocultural theory informs the field of distance education by providing a framework for understanding the social dynamics that underlie computer-mediated communication (CMC) as it applies to teaching and learning. Several learning theories rely, in part, on social interaction to explain how learning occurs (Bee & Gardner, 2012). Beginning in the late 1990s, technology afforded the opportunity for implementing sociocultural theory into online teaching and learning. Significant for this study, Gunawardena and Zittle (1997) found that social presence is a predictor of satisfaction within a CMC environment.

A fundamental principle in sociocultural theory as it relates to language learning is the notion that learners' communicative resources are formed and re-formed in the very activity in which they are used, in other words, linguistically mediated social and intellectual activity (Lantolf & Thorne, 2006). The literature is replete with studies demonstrating the importance of sociocultural approaches to language development (John-Steiner, Panofsky, & Smith, 1994; Ochs, 1986) and online teaching and learning (Brandl, 2012; Garrison, Anderson, & Archer, 1999; Gunawardena, 2003).

Foreign language teaching through online education has grown tremendously over the past 10 years, taking advantage of the growth in social networking and the availability worldwide of the Internet. Virtual learning environments have diversified the opportunities for teachers, instructional designers, and learners by varying and broadening the alternatives for the learning and teaching of languages (Tuncer, 2009). For example, online environments that include the capability to speak in real time have afforded the possibility of instant feedback on pronunciation and grammar and promoted interactions between learners from different cultural backgrounds to support each other's language development.

To take advantage of such online environments, researchers and educators need to consider what is added to the experience that could not be obtained in the traditional classroom through online education (Liang & Bonk, 2009) and look for ways of making online intercultural exchanges a more seamless and fluid process (O'Dowd, 2010). It is not enough to be able to speak together online; careful instructional design must be applied to online course environments that maximizes technology affordances in the areas of cultural exchanges and language development.

With an effective online course design in place, learners and teachers alike will be able to interact and share knowledge and ideas. The adult learning theory of transformational learning posits that sharing ideas can transform individuals through stimulating cognitive and affective changes in perception and habits of mind (Mezirow, 1990). Central to this research is Mezirow's concept of *perspective transformation*, which he defined as the process of becoming aware of how and why our assumptions have come to constrain the way we perceive our world, then changing these structures to a new, more inclusive and expanded perspective, and then acting on these new understandings.

Taylor (1994) extended Mezirow's theory in his study on intercultural competency and transformational learning, finding that becoming interculturally competent results in perspective transformation. In particular, Taylor's study confirmed that cultural disequilibrium acts as a catalyst in becoming interculturally competent. Of import to the findings presented in this chapter is a key conclusion of Taylor's research—that the outcome of the process of becoming interculturally competent is an evolving intercultural identity.

Because of the nature and novelty of the online environment that was studied, Glaser's grounded theory was chosen as a research methodology. Grounded theory is an inductive process whereby hypotheses and concepts arise from the data, and theory generation is systematically worked out in relation to the data during the course of the research (Glaser & Strauss, 1967). To illustrate the rationale for using grounded theory in this study, Glaser (1999), in a speech on the future of grounded theory, remarked, "Answers that work are wanted. Grounded theory tells us what is going on and how to account for the participants' main concerns, and reveals access variables that allow for incremental change. Grounded theory is what is, not what should, could, or ought to be" (Glaser, 1999, p. 840). Thus, grounded theory offers a way to delve deeply into what is "going on" in cross-cultural online environments supported by VoIP.

Study Approach

This study used a qualitative approach to explore in detail the phenomena of the lived experiences of participants in a VoIP-enabled online cross-cultural language learning environment. Phenomenology was combined with a grounded theory approach, drawing on the ethnographic tradition. This discovery process used the emic voice of the participants, as well as the artifacts that supported the program.

Learning Community Members

The participants were teachers, students, TAs, and administrative staff in the EnglishNow-Advanced program. All were located in Taiwan and throughout the United States. Native speakers of English were recruited from the United States as teachers for EnglishNow-Advanced, many who had experience in Teaching English as a Foreign Language (TEFL) or in Teachers of English to Speakers of Other Languages (TESOL). Teachers ranged in age from mid-20s to early 50s. Gender was mixed, with approximately equal numbers of male and female teachers. All had basic computer skills but had to master the synchronous VoIP-enabled online environment.

In the EnglishNow-Advanced program, the students ranged in age from 8 to 55 years. Students lived primarily in Taiwan and China, although the program had several students from Singapore, Indonesia, and Korea. The students in this study ranged in age from 13 to early 40s. The administrative staff of EnglishNow was the smallest group of participants. They were American and Taiwanese, ranging in age from late 20s to early 40s.

Gathering the Data

Online course design and instructional setting: The primary instructional setting for this program was an online learning environment that used a ShowNet software platform. The program website used text, multimedia, and graphics to teach EFL at the low and high intermediate levels and at the advanced level and for different audiences (e.g., secondary school children, business people, university students). English was the primary means of communication, though for low intermediate classes, Chinese was also used to scaffold the learning process. Once the learners made a choice on their level of course, they were led to a learning space that showed a brief article on a current event, the primary artifact used to teach English.

Before the online class began, the teacher uploaded these prepared articles about current topics or events into the whiteboard area. The article was accompanied by a set of open-ended discussion questions, vocabulary, a set of questions about the article, and a workspace. The platform provided the capability of uploading Internet pages as supplementary material to the article present, as well as provided a set of drawing tools to illustrate key points in the text. The teacher also could upload objects, application screenshots, and media files. The instructional material was based on American culture and idioms. An example of one of these articles is titled "Hotel Stars," which was used to teach vocabulary within the context of a common rating system for hotels in the United States. Students and teachers used the toolbars at the top and side of the screen to enhance the learning experience by highlighting words and launching web pages, among other teaching tools.

Interactions between teachers and students were supported by the synchronous interface, which had a text chat box at the bottom of the screen and VoIP-enabled communication. Because the primary objective of the program was to improve speaking ability in the target language (English), oral communication rather than written was encouraged.

High bandwidth capability, such as that afforded by cable modem, DSL, or T1/T2 lines, was required because of the necessity for clear and reliable synchronous voice communication by teachers, TAs, and students. One constant challenge was ensuring that students' software settings for sound were working properly. To address this issue, administrative staff created an online frequently asked questions menu to provide detailed instructions for troubleshooting the sound feature.

Interviews: Twenty-one participants were interviewed for this study, including the researcher, who was interviewed by a colleague in the same manner as the other 20 participants who were interviewed. Native speaker teachers, TAs, students, and administrative staff who were interviewed in the previous studies conducted by the author between 2003 and 2006 were contacted again, in addition to recently joined students who were recommended by John, a teacher in the program.

With the program ended, the interview questions focused on enabling the participants' lived experiences to emerge through stories and remembrances of critical incidents.

Making Sense of the Data

The emic voice of the participants—teachers, TAs, administrators, and students—were interwoven throughout the analysis to tell the story of this unique program. The data were analyzed using grounded theory methodology, which is an inductive process. Common properties that appeared to contribute to an understanding of the teaching and learning experience in a VoIP-enabled environment were identified.

The data analysis process began during data collection, in keeping with grounded theory methodology. Because data collection and analysis are co-occurring in grounded theory, free and focused coding of the interview and archival data was conducted during interview transcription. ATLAS.ti, together with hand-drawn concept maps, was used to code and assist in analyzing the data. The free codes were collapsed into focused codes (categories) as the codes became saturated. For example, it became evident that a number of codes related to "teacher characteristics," as reported by all four participant groups.

Theoretical sampling was conducted to further understand the relationship of teacher characteristics to participants' perception of the teaching and learning environment and their lived experiences. This analytical procedure enabled the derivation of the eight themes that support the framework.

Emergent Interrelated Themes

Eight interrelated themes emerged from the data analysis to answer the research question, with Glaser's grounded theory methodology forming the basis for their development. Thus, the themes are grounded in the data, echoing the emic voice of the participants in the study. These eight themes are as follows:

1. Technology meets online language learning: The central role of synchronous VoIP combined with multimedia enriches online language learning.
2. Teachers as learners, teachers as community builders: Teacher characteristics form the basis of a thriving online language learning community.
3. Students as learners, students as teachers: Overcoming innate shyness helps people to become full participants in the online community.
4. Interactive, dynamic sessions encourage participation and enhance the quality of the teaching and learning experience in the online synchronous VoIP-enabled environment.
5. Innovative technology delivering TEFL classes and material needs constant support and a dedicated staff to support an online learning environment.
6. The positive impact of synchronous VoIP on language development resulted in improvement in communicative competency in both Taiwanese and American participants.
7. Conflict stemming from behavior issues, cultural differences, and disagreements based on nationality are disruptive to the online class environment and must be dealt with in a culturally appropriate manner.

8. Transformational learning can occur in a cross-cultural VoIP-enabled environment as the result of human connectedness brought about by participants' sharing lived experiences that in turn builds a tightly knit community of practice. Participants reported that their perspectives and worldviews were changed as the result of sharing their lived experiences with one another, building the human connection as it strengthened participants' transnational community of practice.

The major theme focused on in this chapter is the final theme, transformational learning, supported by three other themes that relate to the technology-enhanced environment found in a media-rich synchronous online learning environment.

The results of this study showed that transformational learning at some level occurred for all of the participants as a consequence of the cross-cultural interactions that took place in the online classroom. Many responded that their worldview changed as a result of being a part of this online EFL program. A series of small, disorienting dilemmas, primarily technology based at first and evolving into cultural dilemmas later, was the source for this perspective shift. Culture, in particular cultural exchanges, played a primary role in the social dimension of learning to speak English online. The community of practice that was established across two very different cultures, American and Taiwanese, in this rich multimedia synchronous environment provided abundant opportunities for transformational learning to occur.

Creative Use of Online Multimedia Tools

The central role of synchronous VoIP combined with multimedia enriches online language learning. The creative use of the tools in this multimedia online language learning environment, in particular the VoIP tool, became the building block for the teaching and learning space of EnglishNow. The program director explained the difficulties and frustrations inherent in implementing this new technology, articulating the need for constant talk in a real-time environment with VoIP, as follows: "When there's dead air everybody gets confused. Is it a technical problem? Is teacher passed out? Is teacher mad? Or frustrated? So, we needed somebody with patter."

Despite problems with bandwidth and the VoIP technology itself, the Taiwanese TAs/teachers and American teachers creatively used every facet of the multimedia interface to create a vibrant online classroom environment. As one Taiwanese TA/teacher put it, "You don't have the means of body language or facial expression or gestures to help you, so everything has to come through your voice. Now it's important about the things you say and the content. Also it's important how you say it." Added an American native speaker (NS) teacher, "You could hear in their voice when they didn't understand something or you knew when there was tension over the line, you know, you knew when there was something that was, like, really well done or something that was confusing or something that didn't quite fit right." In addition to speaking, teachers drew explanatory figures and posted additional content to enrich the teaching and learning space.

Two other interesting findings emerged from the data analysis regarding the use of voice-enhanced real-time technology: the role of singing and laughter in easing students' fears and making the online environment comfortable. One American NS teacher commented,

> Stick out in your mind? All those experiences where there were classes when students would sing. All they would do is sing songs. I'm getting all choked up. It was just so touching even then to see the community that songs and music bring and how in these classes people loved them! They couldn't wait until it was their turn to sing a song.

Aside from singing, laughter also emerged as another way to break the ice, making students and teachers less apprehensive and nervous. An American NS teacher who was new to online teaching talked about her experience as follows: "I think someone would almost always laugh. . . . Then I would relax."

Singing is inherently social. A natural extension of this atavistic tendency in human beings is to extend singing into group settings in the online environment. Laughter, too, should be encouraged in the VoIP-enabled environment to create a welcoming learning environment for both students and teachers.

The importance of engaging and creative teaching methodologies in the online classroom was a supporting theme for transformational learning, whereby interactive and dynamic sessions encourage participation and enhance the quality of the teaching and learning experience. As one Taiwanese TA/teacher remarked, "I turn on the happy power." A Taiwanese student added, "It was exciting and fancy learning."

Improvement in Communicative Competency Through Speaking in Real Time

Another theme that emerged from this study and supported the occurrence of transformational learning was the positive impact of synchronous VoIP on language development, that is, improvement in communicative competency in both Taiwanese and American participants. As one Taiwanese TA/teacher summed it up, "Because the most important thing is to communicate with each other." Anecdotal evidence from this study suggests that participants' language ability improved through the use of synchronous VoIP because they could both speak and hear in real time. All 5 Taiwanese students reported that language use shifted from what Habermas (1984) termed "instrumental learning," or learning that is used to control and manipulate the environment, to "communicative learning," or learning what others mean when they communicate.

Transformational Learning in a Cross-Cultural Online Community

This study revealed that transformational learning can occur in a cross-cultural VoIP-enabled environment as the result of human connectedness brought about by participants' sharing lived experiences that in turn builds a tightly knit community of practice. One of the Taiwanese students described his experience in the online learning community thus: "It was a special program and attracted special people to the class."

At the outset of this study, it was anticipated that from the data would emerge findings centering on language development in an online synchronous VoIP-enabled environment. Instead, it became apparent very early on in the study that the human connection was central to the participants' lived experiences. One American NS teacher said, "It wasn't the language. That was just the excuse."

As the analysis progressed, it came to light that something far deeper and powerful had occurred in participants' lives. Even in the retelling of their experiences respondents were overtaken emotionally, with some crying outwardly. One Taiwanese student expressed herself thus when asked about what the program experience meant to her: "Since they stopped the program, many of us has [sic] been so sad and even got sick, because we lost the focus in our life."

The findings revealed another phenomenon that stretched beyond the desire to communicate and connect. Participants were transformed by their experiences in this unique online environment. EFL teachers who had never been abroad became culturally aware, and Taiwanese shopkeepers became global citizens. In the words of one student, who owned a beetle nut stand, "I am different." This transformation occurred as a series of small disorienting dilemmas that began with making a decision to go online to learn a language in a synchronous VoIP-enabled cross-cultural community. It is argued that every step along that journey is disorienting, beginning with overcoming the technology barrier.

According to Mezirow (2000), a "disorienting dilemma" occurs in an adult learner's life to cause her or him to reflect critically, with the end result that the individual's conception of himself or herself and worldview are inexorably changed. In EnglishNow, there were a number of these disorienting dilemmas faced by all participants. Yet emotions also were a critical component of these dilemmas, a facet of transformative learning brought out by Dirkx (2006) in his research on teaching for change.

As the interview data were analyzed using constant comparison, the data revealed that transformational learning depended on one key factor: the sharing of personal experiences in the safe environment purposefully created by the teachers, both American and Taiwanese. Teachers spoke of using their voice as a tool, encouraging students in a way that was both insistent and subtle.

Students who described themselves as nervous and shy over time became active participants in the virtual classroom, assisting their peers and their teachers with meaning making. American and Taiwanese teachers who described themselves as "apprehensive," "feeling my way," and even "bored" became, in the words of one American teacher, "addicted" to this new way of teaching a foreign language across culture and distance. Normally shy Taiwanese students became outgoing and full participants online, developing friendships with other students and the TAs and teachers. "I'm not feel [sic] shy anymore," said one Taiwanese student, while another remarked, "Everyone is like a friend." With the necessary ingredients—teaching characteristics combined with student motivation—cultural shyness can be overcome to more fully engage students who would not otherwise participate. As the program director summed it up, "So it wasn't about language learning. It was really about forging a connection."

Feedback was central to fostering a vibrant online learning environment. This feedback was immediate because of the synchronous environment and occurred between teacher and student and from student to teacher. As John commented, "Also another big reason I like teaching at EnglishNow is that, well, you get the instant feedback even though we don't see each other." John also spoke of how much it meant to him to have his students say how much they appreciated him and how they benefited from his class.

One Taiwanese TA/teacher described this transformation thus: "Since EnglishNow creates a safe semi-chatroom and discussions require personal experience, involved, transformation[al] learning happens where people seek solutions to their life problems." The implication for teachers in this type of online environment is that they must be comfortable with both expressing themselves and allowing students to share their feelings and personal experiences in order to foster a safe online environment and build and sustain community online if transformational learning is to occur.

Sharing Cultural Information and Experience: Language Learning, Intercultural Competency, and Perspective Transformation

Another central finding of this study was the impact of culture on teaching and learning in a synchronous VoIP-enabled online environment through the sharing of cultural information and experiences. This study showed that culture is not only transmitted through language but integral to learning a language and another way of thinking and being in the world. Language learning is not only the process of improving linguistic and communicative competency but also a process of learning the culture of the target language.

Transformational learning was a significant finding in this study particularly in regard to achieving intercultural competency. Supporting this finding is Taylor (1994), whose study on intercultural competency and transformational learning found that becoming interculturally competent results in perspective transformation. Through synchronous online cultural exchanges, both informational and interactional, participants in this study experienced perspective transformations that resulted in their becoming more interculturally competent, as well as confident of those abilities.

In transformative learning theory, the educator plays a significant role in the student's perspective transformation. Certainly, "fostering transformative learning in the classroom depends to a large extent on establishing meaningful, genuine relationships with students" (Cranton, 2006, p. 5). The analysis of the interview data shows that teachers in EnglishNow had meaningful and genuine relationships with their students.

Recommendations for Online EFL Educators

The EnglishNow online language learning program was unique in many ways. The findings that emerged from this grounded theory study challenge us to take a closer look at the affordances of technology in education and the role of culture in learning and teaching over distance. The study disclosed the importance of teaching characteristics, methods, and strategies that are appropriate for a cross-cultural synchronous VoIP-enabled classroom. It also supported the importance of interactivity in online language learning classrooms, especially online environments that support synchronous voice communication.

Following is a list of practical guidelines for educators and/or administrators to meet cultural challenges in online learning based on the research findings presented in this chapter:

Tips for Instructors

- Acknowledge the additional time that nonnative learners need to listen and respond to questions in a synchronous environment. Repeating silently to yourself "one spaghetti, two spaghetti, three spaghetti" and remembering to breathe will provide learners with the time they need to formulate answers and participate in discussions.
- Offer the service of e-mentors in online classes. TAs and instructors can play the role of e-mentor to new faculty, easing the process of entry into this new way of teaching and simultaneously increasing teaching effectiveness.
- Offer a private chat feature within online courses for informal conversations and community building. Shy students who may not wish to ask questions in front of the class can have an opportunity to reach out to a trusted peer or the teacher without feeling embarrassed during class time.
- Design online instruction to allow peers to teach one another when appropriate. Allowing students to teach other students and support the teacher builds confidence and improves speaking ability.
- Become familiar with the students' culture(s) and be sensitive to cultural differences. Students feel a sense of inclusion when their culture is appreciated and respected in the online environment, strengthening ties in the learning community.
- Use social presence to create a bond with students and lessen transactional distance by exuding warmth and compassion (affective traits) to students by
  - using voice modulation (synchronous) and positive superlatives (asynchronous and synchronous),
  - bringing to the online environment a good sense of humor,
  - conveying a sense of caring about students' responses,
  - building trust, and
  - making learning fun!

Tips for Learners

- Use affect, creativity, and curiosity in responding to instruction and peers.
- Participate as you feel comfortable by laughing, singing (synchronous), and showing your creative side in activities (asynchronous and synchronous).
- Help peers in your class to build their confidence and to form an online community of learners.

Tips for Support Staff

- Immediate, online support (synchronous and asynchronous) for teachers and learners will keep the class running smoothly and lessen obstacles to access that could impact quality of instruction and student retention.

- Provide dedicated teacher support in order to maintain teachers' effectiveness.
- Leave open communication channels, "backdoors," to enable faculty and TAs to quickly troubleshoot problems if the primary online learning environment is not working.
- Plans should be in place for substitute coverage if faculty are unable to attend a synchronous session.
- Show teachers how to use the technology available in new ways to make learning dynamic and fun. Students' participation and the overall quality of the course are enhanced when technology is used creatively.
- Provide culturally sensitive conflict resolution for issues that may arise between students due to a lack of cultural awareness in order to maintain harmony in the virtual classroom.

In addition to these tips that arose out of the study, the finding that transformational learning took place, primarily as a result of cross-cultural exchanges between teachers and learners, demonstrates the importance of recognizing and appreciating cultural differences in the online environment. Enriching the online classroom with purposive activities that draw out similarities and differences between cultures serves both to engage students and to make them feel more comfortable in what is for many a new way of learning. With online education programs expanding rapidly around the globe, the intersection of culture, language, and synchronous CMC provides a rich palette for creative ideas in sharing cultures and promoting intercultural understanding.

References

Barrett, K. A. (2008). *An exploration of EFL teachers' and learners' lived experiences in a synchronous online VoIP-enabled cross cultural language learning environment* (Doctoral dissertation). Available from ProQuest and PQDT. (3318114)

Bee, S. B., & Gardner, D. (2012). Crossing the borders in language learning through the use of webA-conferencing as an eA-learning tool. *International Journal of Web Based Communities, 8*(1), 120–132.

Brandl, K. (2012). Effects of required and optional exchange tasks in online language learning environments. *ReCALL, 24*(1), 85–107.

Cranton, P. (2006, Spring). Fostering authentic relationships in the transformational classroom. *New Directions for Adult and Continuing Education, 109,* 5–13.

Dirkx, J. M. (2006, Spring). Engaging emotions in adult learning: A Jungian perspective on emotion and transformative learning. *New Directions for Adult and Continuing Education, 109,* 15–26.

Garrison, D. R., Anderson, T., & Archer, W. (1999). Critical inquiry in a text-based environment: Computer conferencing in higher education. *The Internet and Higher Education, 2*(2), 87–105.

Glaser, B. (1999). Keynote address from the fourth annual Qualitative Health Research Conference: The future of grounded theory. *Qualitative Health Research, 9*(6), 836–845.

Glaser, B., & Strauss, A. (1967). *The discovery of grounded theory: Strategies for qualitative research.* New York, NY: Aldine de Gruyter.

Gunawardena, C. N. (2003). Researching online learning and group dynamics. In Y. Fritze, G. Haugsbakk, & Y. T. Nordkvelle (Eds.), *Dialog og naerhet.* Kristiansand, Norway: Norwegian Academic Press.

Gunawardena, C. N., & Zittle, F. N. (1997). Social presence as a predictor of satisfaction within a computer-mediated conferencing environment. *The American Journal of Distance Education, 11*(3), 8–26.

Habermas, J. (1984). *The theory of communicative action, Volume 1: Reason and the rationalization of society* (T. McCarthy, Trans.). Boston, MA: Beacon Press.

John-Steiner, V., Panofsky, C. P., & Smith, L. W. (1994). *Sociocultural approaches to language and literacy: An interactionist perspective.* New York, NY: Cambridge University Press.

Lantolf, J. P., & Thorne, S. L. (2006). *Sociocultural theory and the genesis of second language development.* Oxford, UK: Oxford University Press.

Liang, M. Y., & Bonk, C. J. (2009). Interaction in blended EFL learning: Principles and practice. *International Journal of Instructional Technology and Distance Learning, 6*(1), 3–15.

Mezirow, J. (1990). *Fostering critical reflection in adulthood.* San Francisco, CA: Jossey-Bass.

Mezirow, J. (2000). *Learning as transformation: Critical perspectives on a theory in progress.* San Francisco, CA: Jossey-Bass.

Ochs, E. (1986). Introduction. In B. Schieffelin & E. Ochs (Eds.), *Language socialization across cultures* (pp. 1–13). New York, NY: Cambridge University Press.

O'Dowd, R. (2010). Online foreign language interaction: Moving from the periphery to the core of foreign language education? *Language Teaching, 44*(3), 368–380.

Taylor, E. W. (1994). Intercultural competency: A transformative learning process. *Adult Education Quarterly, 44*(3), 154.

Tuncer, C. (2009). Learning and teaching languages online: A constructivist approach. *Novitas-ROYAL, 3*(1), 60–74.

14

INTERNATIONAL INTERPRETATIONS OF ICONS AND IMAGES USED IN NORTH AMERICAN ACADEMIC WEBSITES

Eliot Knight, Charlotte Nirmalani Gunawardena, Elena Barberà, and Cengiz Hakan Aydın

According to Hall (1973), culture hides itself most effectively from its own participants who have acquired their native culture over time through contextual, social, and cognitive processes of which they are largely unaware. Research suggests that instructors and designers are frequently unaware of the cultural biases and implicit messages about culture that their learning materials and environments convey to learners (Bodycott, 2006). Many of the images and icons used in online environments depend on meanings, concepts, metaphors, objects, and so on that are bound to the particular cultural context in which they were designed (Chu & Martinson, 2003; Duncker, 2002). When designing icons and images for online learners, educators and designers must become aware of their own cultural biases and those of the learners who are participating at a distance. There is a dearth of research that investigates how perceptions of icons and images used within North American academic websites may differ across cultures. This chapter presents the findings of a research study that examined international cultural perspectives of the visual meanings of icons and images on North American academic websites to determine whether the meanings designed from an American cultural perspective were understood in other cultural contexts. The study evolved a great deal since the time of the authors' earlier publication on a cross-cultural analysis of icons and images used in North American web design (Knight et al., 2006). It added a new content analysis with two additional groups of participants, developed new interpretations as a result of the additional participants, and offered a different conceptual framework for this chapter.

Conceptual Framework

How an icon conveys information graphically is an important factor in how accurately its intended meaning is interpreted by the viewer. The graphic form of a message may be representational, abstract, or symbolic, and these three ways of communicating may be conceptualized as points along a continuum rather than discrete categories (Jonesson, Maurer, & Goldman-Segall, 1996).

Representational icons convey meaning by describing what is depicted visually and may vary in the degree of realism incorporated. Representational icons may be more easily interpreted and less likely to elicit unintended interpretations. However, when poorly designed, representational icons may contain visual features that are unrelated to the icon's intended meaning or unfamiliar to audiences from diverse cultural contexts. Recognition of abstract icons may depend on the icon's degree of resemblance to the object depicted. Icons that communicate symbolically may bear no resemblance to what is represented. Because symbolic icons typically reference culturally agreed-on meanings that must be learned, these icons may be difficult to use across cultural contexts.

Classifications of icons may be based on the icon's graphic form and the object or concept to which the icon relates. Two broad categories of icons include Information Type Icons that provide access to a specific kind of information, such as a Campus Map or Instructional Guide, and Function Type Icons that provide access to a distinct function, such as Search. Information Type Icons may elicit a broad range of unintended meanings and can be more difficult to interpret across cultural contexts than Function Type Icons. Metaphors commonly used in interface design include verbal metaphors, virtual interface metaphors, and composite metaphors (Preece, 1994). Verbal metaphors use an analogy based on the user's existing knowledge to present an idea using a known referent. Virtual interface metaphors, such as the familiar desktop metaphor, rely on the user's existing knowledge and represent familiar physical objects in the form of icons and graphic images. The composite metaphor combines objects used in two or more metaphors to represent new, more complex functions and is thought to be helpful in conveying more explicit meanings (Preece, 1994). Metaphors that are embedded in a specific cultural context may be irrelevant when used across cultures.

Comprehension of metaphors such as the desktop metaphor depends on the degree to which significant aspects of the metaphor match the user's mental model of the related physical object (Duncker, 2002). Understanding culturally sensitive aspects of computer metaphors requires experience in the cultural context of the real-world objects that a given metaphor references, as well as consideration of the usability of the computing metaphor in general (Duncker, 2002).

Marcus and Gould (2000) applied Hofstede's (1980, 1997) classification of cultural variability to explain cultural differences in the design of user interfaces and websites and provided useful insight into how culture influences design, but they indicated the weakness of Hofstede's classification, which lies in the assumption of a single dominant culture within each country. Hofstede's classification does not support the analysis of characteristics among individuals within the same national culture.

Johnston and Johal (1999) applied Hofstede's classification to the analysis of the Internet as a virtual cultural region and suggested that the Internet has a culture of its own. Although findings consistent with Hofstede's classification indicate that culture influences web design, studies reveal similarities in design between countries in apparent contradiction with the dimensions of Hofstede's classification, which may indicate that culture does not influence web design in a manner compatible with Hofstede's classification (Burgmann, Kitchen, & Williams, 2006; Singh, Zhao, & Hu, 2003).

It is more prudent to examine the Internet as a culture in its own right. Internet culture is a participatory media culture in which capturing, manipulating, and sharing visual and textual forms of content within private and public spheres are valued as important means of individual expression. In the online environment, visual attention is the most significant commodity, and the visual mode is the predominant mode in communication. Graphic designers know that the visual form of a message will always surpass the textual content in both immediacy and emotional impact. (See chapter 5 for detailed discussions of online visual culture.)

As the Internet has become more integrated into daily life, the relationship between offline and online worlds has expanded considerably. Given the emphasis on the cognitive and social aspects of online interaction in shaping Internet culture and the absence of visible distinctions or physical interaction online, there is a need to understand how attributes not immediately evident through interaction online, such as age, gender, and ethnic origin, influence cultural perceptions. And, there is a need to understand how individual attributes such as education or expectations, which are less related to visible distinctions, influence cultural perceptions in the online environment. The Shaw and Barrett-Power (1998) model provides a relevant framework for understanding these various types of readily detectable and underlying attributes and their impact on cognitive paradigm dissimilarity.

Shaw and Barrett-Power (1998) identified sources of cultural differences, including readily detectable attributes and underlying attributes. Readily detectable attributes are immediately evident in the individual such as age, gender, and national or ethnic origin. Underlying attributes are classified into two categories: those closely related to attributes that are readily detectable and that represent cultural values, perspectives, attitudes, and beliefs (Type I) and those underlying attributes that are less strongly correlated with readily detectable attributes, which are of a personal nature, including socioeconomic and personal status, education, past work experiences, personal expectations, and so on (Type II). According to the model, underlying attributes impact cognitive paradigm dissimilarity (Shaw & Barrett-Power, 1998). This research applies the cultural model developed by Shaw and Barrett-Power (1998) to the analysis of international cultural perspectives of the meanings of icons and images drawn from North American academic websites to determine whether the participants' interpretations were culturally related.

Study Approach

Questions

The study asked the following questions:

- What meanings did participants assign to the icons, and why did they assign them?
- What factors in the different cultural contexts influenced participants' interpretations of icons and images?
- How did the gender, age, and educational attainment of the participants influence the cultural interpretations?

- How did the visual form of icons and images influence the interpretations that were assigned?
- How were the interpretations that were assigned to the icons and images influenced by the context of the Internet?

Participants

Sixty-nine participants from Turkey, 68 from Sri Lanka, 59 from Spain, and 58 from the United States participated in this study. Participants were drawn from university computer labs and Internet cafés. Participants from Turkey were drawn from Anadolu University, where Turkish is spoken by 90% of the population. The population in Turkey is composed mainly of Turks, who constitute approximately 70% of the population. Kurds and other minority groups compose around 30% of the population. The country's official language is Turkish, and the majority of the population is Muslim. Sri Lankan participants were drawn from computer labs at the Open University of Sri Lanka in Nawala and Nugegoda in Colombo and from Internet cafés in the hill country and the southern and east coasts of Sri Lanka. Sri Lanka is a multiethnic society composed predominantly of Sinhalese people, a majority of whom are Buddhists, Tamils, Muslims, and Burghers. The main languages are Sinhala and Tamil. English is taught as a second language in Sri Lankan schools and is widely spoken by educated Sri Lankans who have access to and frequently use the Internet. Spanish participants were drawn from the Open University of Catalonia and from Internet cafés in Barcelona and spoke Catalan and Spanish. U.S. participants were drawn from the University of New Mexico and spoke predominantly English. The cultural sites chosen represent the ethnic and cultural diversity in the population within the countries. Data from Morocco are not reported in this study. Table 14.1 shows the demographic characteristics of participants from the four countries, including the age range, gender, and daily Internet usage.

Feedback From Participants

A website including 18 icons and images from 26 U.S. academic websites was created. The data were collected using HTML web forms in the participants' native languages, including Turkish, Spanish, and English. U.S. icons and images were selected based on research suggesting that comprehension of the intended meanings of icons may be

TABLE 14.1
Demographics

Country	Age Range (Years)	Male (%)	Female (%)	Daily Internet Usage (%)
Sri Lanka	18–59	57	43	35
Spain	23–60	32	66	88
Turkey	18–24	49	51	79
United States	18–65	24	76	88

Figure 14.1 Icons selected for the study. Icons #4 and #5 used with permission by Blackboard, and Icons #1, #3, #6, #7, #8, #10, #13, and #18 used with permission by WIT Press. Icons #1, #6, #8, #10, and #13 used with permission by Illinois State University Library, and Icons #3, #7, and #18 used with permission by Ohio State University.

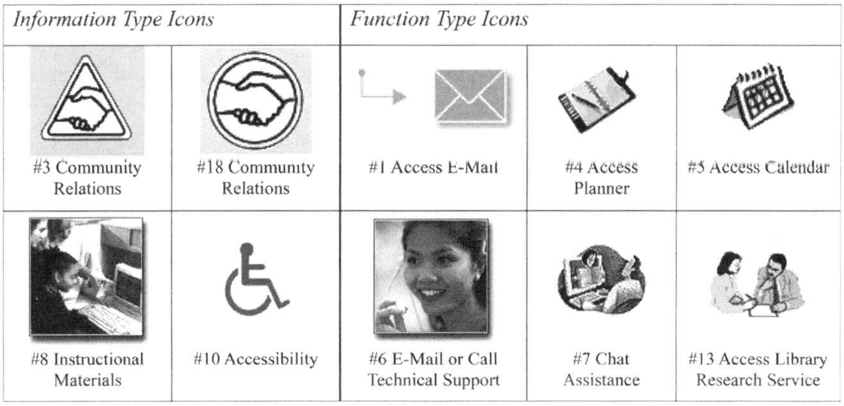

Information Type Icons		Function Type Icons		
#3 Community Relations	#18 Community Relations	#1 Access E-Mail	#4 Access Planner	#5 Access Calendar
#8 Instructional Materials	#10 Accessibility	#6 E-Mail or Call Technical Support	#7 Chat Assistance	#13 Access Library Research Service

influenced by cultural differences between the mental models of U.S. graphic designers and those of cross-cultural users. Other criteria for the selection of the icons were the concept of the icons (Information and Function Type Icons as shown in figure14.1) and the icons' visual form (three line drawings: #3, #10, #18; three photographic images: #4, #6, #8; and four illustrations: #1, #5, #7, #13). Information Type Icons represent the type of information or topic the user will access by clicking the icon. Function Type Icons represent an online function or activity that can be accessed by clicking the icon.

The instrument was pilot tested with U.S. participants twice, revised based on feedback, and distributed to the researchers in the various cultural contexts to translate. The web pages requested demographic information and asked participants to provide meanings for 12 icons representing online functions and for 6 icons representing online information types.

Educational attainment refers to the participant's highest level of school completed or the highest degree received. As reported in table 14.2, a majority of the participants reported completing a general certificate of education (GCE), certificate, or diploma or studying for a bachelor's or master's degree or PhD.

Procedure

The web pages were distributed over the Internet in the United States during the fall term of 2004, in Turkey during the fall term of 2006, and in Spain during the fall of 2008. A majority of participants who were comfortable with computers submitted their interpretations online; other participants completed the printed version in their preferred language while looking at the online version. Qualitative analysis of the cultural interpretations was conducted with the assistance of researchers in the respective countries who

TABLE 14.2
Educational Attainment of the Participants

Education Completed	Sri Lanka (%)	United States (%)	Turkey (%)	Spain (%)
Completed less than 8th grade	0	0	0	5
Completed 8th grade	0	0	7	3
Completed general certificate of education	12	0	0	0
Completed high school	9	3.1	3	15
Completed certificate or diploma	1	0	0	0
Studying for bachelor's	43	15.6	39	10
Completed bachelor's	13	12.5	15	36
Studying for master's	4	18.8	17	2
Completed master's	9	25.0	1	6
Studying for doctorate	0	15.6	13	8
Completed doctorate	1	9.4	3	15

were fluent in the participants' languages and who analyzed the interpretations and provided guidance regarding sociocultural contexts. A structured and open-ended content analysis was used to examine the cultural interpretations of the icons in relation to the icons' meaning as functional or informational representations within the U.S. academic websites (Miles & Huberman, 1994).

Two categories of interpretations are used for reporting the data. Interpretations closely related to the icon's intended meaning from a North American perspective that were conceptually related to the icon's online function are reported as "Closely Related." For example, interpretations of the Technical Support Icon such as "Technical Assistance" are reported as "Closely Related." Interpretations that were not related to the Internet and would not be helpful to the user in the online context, that were less related to the icon's intended meaning, or that referred to less related functions, information types, and so on are reported as "Less Related." For example, the interpretation of the Technical Support Icon "A Smiling Girl" is reported as a "Less Related" interpretation.

Cultural Perspectives of Icons and Images

Community Relations Icon

Icon #3 is a line drawing of a handshake enclosed within a triangular border to represent community relations information. Icon #18 uses the same graphic enclosed within a circular border. These icons are presented together to compare the influence of the figure-border relationship of the two icons on the participants' interpretations.

A majority of interpretations of Icon #3 by Spanish, Sri Lankan, Turkish, and American participants were less related to the intended meaning of the icon in the American context and were interpretive rather than literal. Turkish interpretations of Icon #3 referenced traffic-related meanings. Spanish interpretations of Icon #18, with the circular border, frequently mentioned traffic signs. Within the European contexts, circular traffic signs have many different meanings depending on the color, width, and internal symbol and may indicate prohibition, restrictions, and so on. One Spanish participant, who referred to the triangular border of Icon #3 in the interpretation as "a dangerous relationship," mentioned that Icons #3 and #18 are similar graphically but have opposing meanings.

Interpretations of the graphic may be influenced by business protocols and customs in which a handshake represents agreement, acceptance, and trust. Spanish participants who were male associated the icon with communication. In Spain, a handshake is an everyday greeting between men, whereas women kiss each other twice. Older Turkish participants associated the icon with an agreement or formal relationship between two companies, whereas younger Turkish participants focused on social meanings.

In Sri Lanka, traffic signs are less visible and less important, and fewer Sri Lankans related Icon #3 to traffic signs. Sri Lankan interpretations of Icon #3, which are of interest, are "help" and "peace." Both interpretations were from male participants from Batticaloa on the east coast of Sri Lanka, which was ravaged by a separatist war when the data were collected. These participants interpreted the icons the same way, which could indicate that the sociocultural context in which they live influenced their interpretations of the icon in representing their desire for peace. It is also possible that these participants had seen posters with a similar image advocating peace between the warring ethnic groups. More Sri Lankan participants assigned the handshake the meaning of friendship when it was enclosed in a circle as opposed to a triangle. In Sri Lanka, the circle represents unity, the universe, the Sun, heaven, eternity, and perfection and has more calm and peaceful connotations than the triangle. In Buddhism and Hinduism, prominent religions of Sri Lanka, the circle has significance as the circle of life in spiritual and ritual practices. Respondents in Sri Lanka who did not assign the meaning of "friendship" to the handshake when it was enclosed within a triangle gave it the meaning of "friendship" when it was enclosed within a circle.

Instructional Materials Icon

Icon #8 uses a photograph of three people gathered around a computer to represent the concept of instructional materials. All interpretations were closely related to the icon's intended meaning, but none referred specifically to instructional materials. Interpretations less related to the intended meaning mentioned "technology in education," "teamwork," "group work," and "computers and education." When data were collected in Spain in 2008, primary and secondary students in information and computer technology classes worked in pairs because of the reduced number of computers, which may account for the interpretations "teaching," "learning," "teamwork," and "ICT [integrated coteaching] classrooms." Meanings such as "computer-based education" and "distance education" provided by Turkish participants may be associated with the high percentage of working students in distance education classes at Anadolu University. Sri Lankan participants with more education provided more interpretive meanings related to the Internet context.

Accessibility Icon

Icon #10 is used internationally to indicate accessibility for individuals with limited mobility, including users in wheelchairs. The fact that most interpretations of the icon were closely related can be attributed to the symbol's widespread use in public contexts: public transportation, public buildings, and so on. The symbol's use in public contexts may have interfered with interpretation of the intended meaning within the specific context of the Internet, because many participants provided the literal interpretation "handicapped." Sri Lankan participants provided less related interpretations such as "cycling" and "transportation" more frequently than other participants, possibly because the symbol is less visible within the Sri Lankan cultural context.

E-Mail Icon

Icon #1 uses a stylized arrow pointing at an envelope to represent accessing e-mail. A majority of interpretations were closely related and emphasized the function of sending or receiving e-mail. In Spain, the national mail company logo uses a similar image, which may account for Spanish interpretations such as "post office service." Closely related Spanish interpretations referred to the icon's function as "e-mail," whereas less related interpretations associated the icon with an activity such as "send," "mail received," and so on. The arrow incorporated in the icon may suggest the action mentioned in Spanish interpretations.

One unique interpretation of Icon #1 was "Buddhism," from a 32-year-old female Buddhist from Colombo who speaks Sinhala. Sri Lankan monks typically wear saffron robes. The saffron color is prominent in the Buddhist flag and the pennant-shaped Hindu flag of Sri Lanka and India (see figure 14.2). The participant may have holistically perceived the icon's saffron color and the rectangular shape of a flag. Within collectivist cultures, the use of a holistic, field-dependent cognitive style has been attributed to interdependence in social orientation (Nisbett, Peng, Choi, & Norenzayan, 2001).

Planner Icon

Icon #4 uses a photograph of a planner with the function of accessing an online planner. The icon was interpreted with a high degree of accuracy by all participants. The

Figure 14.2 E-mail icon (left) and Hindu flag (right). E-mail icon used with permission by WIT Press and Illinois State University Library. Hindu flag created by the first author.

photographic form of the icon may have promoted a literal interpretation, because the majority of meanings described the icon as a diary. Spanish people are very accustomed to using diaries similar to the one represented by the icon, although electronic tools are quickly replacing them. Spanish interpretations such as "write a text" may have been associated with the presence of the pencil in the photograph, a detail unrelated to the function represented. Younger Spanish participants, who frequently use electronic organizers, provided closely related interpretations of meaning. Although many Turkish interpretations were closely related, the majority of participants' interpretations were less related, such as "a notebook," "notepad," or "record." Sri Lankan participants who identified the icon as a "planner" had a higher level of education.

Calendar Icon

A majority of interpretations of Icon #5, an illustration of a calendar that represents the function of accessing an online calendar, were closely related. In the Spanish language the terms for *calendar*, *diary*, and *agenda* are sometimes used interchangeably, which may explain why one participant, a 52-year-old woman with a PhD, understood the icon to represent an annotation book. Most interpretations by daily Internet users were related to the Internet. However, one interpretation by a 21-year-old Sri Lankan from Piliyandala, a suburb of Colombo on the west coast of Sri Lanka, provided the interpretation "temporary house" (Knight et al., 2006). After the tsunami in 2005, which destroyed thousands of homes and displaced half a million people in Sri Lanka, different types of tents and temporary shelters were visible along the island's coastal areas. This may have influenced the interpretation of this icon as a tent.

Technical Support Icon

Icon #6 uses a close-up photograph of a smiling Asian woman wearing a headset to signify the technical support function. The icon reflects U.S. business trends of outsourcing technical support services to lower cost, English-speaking South Asian countries. Spanish and Turkish participants who used the Internet infrequently provided less related interpretations. American and Sri Lankan participants provided more closely related interpretations such as "assistance" and "technical support." Less related Spanish interpretations included references to the woman's gender and expression and to various online communication technologies. In Spain it is common for telephone assistants and receptionists to wear headsets, which may account for the Spanish interpretations that include telephone references. Turkish interpretations that emphasized gender rather than the work role could be attributed to the fact that not many people work as telephone operators in Turkey.

Chat Assistance Icon

Icon #7 uses an illustration of a man in front of a computer with a woman emerging from the screen to represent the function of chat assistance. Spanish and American participants provided less related interpretations. Spanish participants who assigned the closely related meaning "chat" were younger. Sri Lankan participants provided more closely related meanings such as "chat through the Internet to check references" and "Internet chat." Many Turkish participants provided interpretations related to distance education. One Turkish interpretation of interest was "alienation." Distance education is a necessity for dealing with large enrollments at Anadolu University. Many students at Anadolu perceived the large online classes as impersonal and alienating.

Research on Demand Icon

Icon #13 represents the concept of accessing research-related assistance with an illustration of a man and woman at a table. The woman is holding a pen, and the man is looking at the paper on the table and touching his chin. Interpretations by Spanish, Turkish, and Sri Lankan participants were less related to the concept of accessing research-related help. Sri Lankan interpretations that were less related stressed meetings and discussion and meanings such as "interaction between two people." Turkish interpretations that were closely related emphasized work and the workplace, and closely related Spanish interpretations focused on meanings such as "help or consultation in teaching" but did not convey the idea of accessing research-related help.

Discussion and Conclusions

This analysis identified cultural differences that influenced participants' perceptions of the images and icons using the following attributes of the Shaw and Barrett-Power (1998) model: readily detectable attributes (such as national origin, age, and gender), underlying attributes I (cultural values, perspectives, and attitudes), and underlying attributes II (socioeconomic and personal status, and education), which are less strongly connected to the readily detectable attributes. The influence of the Internet's context on participants' interpretations and the influence of the icon's visual form were examined. Recommendations for design of effective icons for cross-cultural distance learners are presented.

Age is a Readily Detectable Attribute that influenced participants' perceptions of meaning. Younger Spanish and Turkish participants associated the Community Relations Icon #3 with entertainment or social meanings, whereas older participants provided meanings related to business etiquette. Younger participants' greater frequency of Internet use and Internet-related technologies were associated with interpretations that were more relevant to the online context and closely related to the icon's intended meaning. For instance, most of the Spanish participants who provided closely related interpretations of the Chat Assistance Icon were younger. Spanish participants who associated the Planner Icon with an "electronic organizer" were younger.

The significance of the participants' native languages and different ways of thinking was important in the participants' perception of the icons' meanings. The participants' language, a readily detectable attribute, was closely related to the participants' national origin and influenced interpretations of the Planner and Calendar Icons. Within the participant's native language, words for objects depicted by the icons that were visually and functionally similar were used interchangeably. For example, Spanish participants used the words *diary* and *planner* interchangeably.

Visual interpretations of the icons were influenced by underlying attributes I, which represented cultural attitudes and perspectives regarding gender and appropriate behavior strongly related to the participants' national origin. Turkish participants' interpretations reflected cultural attitudes regarding participation by women in the workforce related to the participants' national origin. Sri Lankan participants' cultural attitudes and beliefs associated with the circular form of the icon may have influenced interpretations such as "friendship" that were assigned to the circular version of the Community Relations Icon. Underlying Attributes II (socioeconomic status and education) influenced the participants' ability to provide interpretive meanings relevant to the online context. The participants' frequency of Internet use was associated with their awareness of the icon in relation to its online function and with the ability to provide interpretations that would be useful in the online context. For instance, Sri Lankans who interpreted the Planner Icon as a "planner" had a higher level of education and were more likely to be business people or managers rather than people from rural areas.

Frequency of Internet use determined participants' ability to interpret the intended meanings of the icons and images, even among U.S. participants who shared the designer's cultural biases. Interpretations less related to the context of the Internet and to the icon's intended meaning were from infrequent Internet users. Less related interpretations reflected the different cultural contexts. For example, Sri Lankan participants provided meanings for the community relations icon related to the significance of the circle of life in spiritual and ritual practices within the Sri Lankan cultural context. Information type icons such as the instructional materials icon elicited less related interpretations than function type icons such as the e-mail icon.

The graphic form of the icon or image influenced how participants interpreted the meaning. For instance, photographic icons were more frequently interpreted in literal terms by participants, who identified what the icon represented rather than provided an interpretive meaning. Drawbacks associated with photographic icons relate to the lack of conceptual focus and the tendency for features that were unrelated to the conceptual meaning to be included in the representation. Details in the photographic icons that had no bearing on the meaning were sometimes emphasized in interpretations. For instance, the pen depicted in the woman's hand in the research on demand icon, which was not related to the icon's meaning, elicited interpretations that emphasized the pen.

Recommendations for Designers and Further Research

The interpretation of visual meanings may reflect the distance between the cultural values of the viewer and those of the designer. The viewer's values and sociocultural context are as important as the function or concept to be conveyed by the icon's visual form and should be explicitly known by the designer. Designers should incorporate research in the early stages of the design process to investigate the online learners' distinct sociocultural contexts and perspectives to determine how learners will interpret the icons and images. Political and economic issues that may impact learners' perspectives should be considered. Many culturally specific meanings existing in one culture do not exist in other cultures, and designers should focus on adaptation of culturally appropriate visual elements that will reflect learners' values, attitudes, and beliefs.

This research suggests the following:

- Photographs may be difficult to use across cultural contexts because they are information dense and may contain details that carry distinct cultural meanings.
- Icons and images that are representational and require literal interpretations, such as the e-mail icon, planner icon, and calendar icon, may be most reliable for use in multicultural online environments.
- Icons that are conceptually focused and contain little detail, such as the accessibility icon and calendar icon, are less likely to elicit unintended interpretations.

References

Bodycott, P. (2006). Cultural cross-currents in second language literacy education. *Intercultural Education, 17*(2), 207–219.

Burgmann, I., Kitchen, P., & Williams, R. (2006). Does culture matter on the web? *Marketing Intelligence and Planning, 24*(1), 62–76.

Chu, S., & Martinson, B. (2003). Cross-cultural comparison of the perception of symbols. *Journal of Visual Literacy, 23*(1), 69–80.

Duncker, E. (2002). Cross-cultural usability of the library metaphor. *Proceedings of the Second ACM/IEEE-CS Joint Conference on Digital Libraries 2002* (pp. 223–230). Portland, OR: ACM Press.

Hall, E. T. (1973). *The silent language.* New York, NY: Anchor Book Editions.

Hofstede, G. (1980). *Culture's consequences: International differences in work-related values.* Beverly Hills, CA: Sage.

Hofstede, G. (1997). *Cultures and organizations: Software of the mind.* New York, NY: McGraw-Hill.

Johnston, K., & Johal, P. (1999). The Internet as a virtual cultural region: Are extant cultural classification schemes appropriate? *Internet Research, 9*(3), 178–186.

Jonesson, D., Maurer, H., & Goldman-Segall, R. (1996). DynamIcons as dynamic graphic interfaces: Interpreting the meaning of visual representation. *Intelligent Tutoring Systems, 12*(1), 35–48.

Knight, E., Gunawardena, C., Bouachrine, F., Dassanayake, N., Kulasuriya, C., & Gnanakumar, T. (2006). A cross-cultural analysis of icons and images used in North American web design. In K. Morgan, C. A. Brebbia, & J. M. Spector (Eds.), *The Internet and society II: Advances in education, commerce and governance* (pp. 135–144). Southampton, UK: WIT Press.

Marcus, A., & Gould, E. W. (2000, July–August). Cultural dimensions and global web user-interface design. *ACM Interactions*, pp. 32–46.

Miles, M. B., & Huberman, A. M. (1994). *Qualitative data analysis: An expanded sourcebook* (2nd ed.). Thousand Oakes, CA: Sage.

Nisbett, R. E., Peng, K., Choi, I., & Norenzayan, A. (2001). Culture and systems of thought: Holistic vs. analytic cognition. *Psychological Review, 108*(2), 291–310.

Preece, J. (1994). *Human computer interaction.* Wokingham, UK: Addison-Wesley.

Shaw, J. B., & Barrett-Power, E. (1998). The effects of diversity on small work group processes and performances. *Human Relations, 51*(10), 1307–1325.

Singh, N., Zhao, H., & Hu, X. (2003). Cultural adaptation on the web: A study of American companies' domestic and Chinese websites. *Journal of Global Information Management, 11*(3), 63–80.

15

AN ANALYSIS OF CULTURE-FOCUSED ARTICLES IN OPEN, DISTANCE, AND ONLINE EDUCATION JOURNALS

Aisha S. Al-Harthi

As Moore and Kearsley (2005) suggested, learner success in distance education systems is associated with one's ability to overcome "distractions" from one's environment to find a "quiet time" for learning at work and home. This is a characteristic of industrialized people, as Peters (2007) hypothesized. He assumed they need to be individualistic and inner directed to achieve personal success. They have the ability to break from their cultural conditions to pursue their own initiatives and professional aspirations to achieve a better life for themselves. This general societal atmosphere as Peters (2007) suggested is an enabling factor for distance education. This assumption is consistent with the shift in distance education as learners assume more responsibility for their learning and, therefore, need to be more self-directed and self-regulated. However, research in the field about groups from different cultures shows variability in the ability and preference of individuals from these cultures to do so (Al-Harthi, 2010; Gunawardena et al., 2001; Smith & Smith, 1999; Tu, 2001). Practitioners respond to this dilemma, as summarized by Gibbs (2003), by either "adjusting [their] pedagogy to align with locally dominant cultural norms and beliefs or developing [their] students so that they can learn in ways appropriate to pedagogies of demonstrable effectiveness" (pp. 220–221). Studies of culture in open, distance, and online education provide a research base for practice by understanding, explaining, interpreting, and inferring appropriate pedagogy for learners from different cultural backgrounds.

Despite the importance of understanding culture in the context of open, distance, and online education in order to offer appropriate pedagogies, cultural issues have not been adequately investigated by researchers in the field, as pointed out by Lee, Driscoll, and Nelson (2004). Therefore, this study attempts to examine how much, to what extent, by whom, and in what aspects research on cultural issues has been conducted in the field of open, distance, and online education based on a content analysis of three international journals over the past decade, from 2001 to 2011. Identifying the representation of the concept of culture, researchers' cultural background, and specific issues explored in the major publications can help researchers draw a clearer picture for relevant research directions related to cultural issues and avoid random and repetitive studies. The purpose of this study is to examine contextual features of cultural studies carried out in the field of open, distance, and online education and make inferences from available research papers to provide the basis of future cultural studies in the field. In doing so, the study is guided by theory, previous research, and expertise in the field of research (White & Marsh, 2006) and adopts the method of the content analysis of the sample of culture-focused articles in three international journals. Specific questions asked in the content analysis include the following:

- To what extent is culture represented in the open, distance, and online education journals?
- What type of research is conducted to investigate culture?
- Who are the writers of culture-focused articles? What is their gender and work-country affiliation?
- What aspects of culture are researched in open, distance, and online education?

This chapter discusses the findings from the content analysis of culture-focused articles selected from three open, distance, and online education journals and suggests implications of such findings. It also explains how those articles were selected and how the content analysis was conducted.

Methodology

To answer these questions, this study conducted a content analysis following three phases of the culture-focused articles published in three major international journals in the field of open, distance, and online education. First, a literature search was conducted to find out how well culture is represented in open, distance, and online education publications. Second, a detailed content analysis of selected culture-focused articles was administered to determine the extent to which these articles represent culture. Third, various cultural issues of the articles were analyzed and categorized.

Phase 1: Journal Selection

Three major international journals in the field of open, distance, and online education were identified for the content analysis: *The American Journal of Distance Education* (AJDE), *Distance Education* (DE), and *Open Learning: The Journal of Open, Distance and e-Learning* (OL). As table 15.1 shows, these journals are associated with three internationally recognized distance education entities in three different countries. All three journals are available through the Taylor and Francis Online database, and they are classified under the subject of "Open & Distance Education and eLearning."

Phase 2: Culture-Focused Article Selection

In selecting the culture-focused articles from these three journals, I took the following steps. First, the total number of published articles in the three journals was calculated. An estimated 819 items were published in the three journals between 2001 and 2011. This is a rough estimate that I calculated by randomly choosing one of the issues and

TABLE 15.1
Publication Information of the Journals Included in the Study

Journal	Country	Affiliation	Year of Establishment	Number of Issues per Year
AJDE	United States	Pennsylvania State University	1987	3 (1978–2001) 4 (2002–date)
DE	Australia	Open and Distance Learning Association of Australia Inc.	1980	2 (1980–2004) 3 (2005–date)
OL	United Kingdom	Open University	1986	3

Note. AJDE = *The American Journal of Distance Education*, DE = *Distance Education*, and
OL = *Open Learning: The Journal of Open, Distance and e-Learning.*

counting the number of items (editorials, articles, book reviews, etc.) in the issue. Then, I multiplied this number by the number of issues per year and then multiplied the new number by the number of years (10 years in this study). This rough estimate was used to identify the extent of publications and accordingly the extent of cultural publications.

Second, an electronic search was conducted through the Taylor and Francis Online database. Through this database, I searched the word *culture* within each journal. As explained previously, a time frame was applied to include only articles published in the past 10 years, from 2001 to 2011. The articles published during these years tended to focus on online education. Publications from 2012 were excluded because at the time of the study, not all issues had been published in the selected journals. As a result, 273 articles were found to include the word *culture*.

Third, additional refining criteria were applied in selecting culture-focused articles. To be included in the content analysis, the articles needed to (a) mention the noun *culture* or the adjective *cultural* more than once, (b) extensively and directly address cultural issues, and (c) address a specific culture or more than one culture (e.g., Western or non-Western culture, culture of two countries, cultural issues within one country). After reviewing the content of articles based on these criteria, I reduced the number of articles that had a real focus on culture to 125 articles (46% of the identified 273 articles that used the word *culture*). As shown in table 15.2, 125 articles or 15% of all the published articles in the three journals between 2001 and 2011 focused on culture in open, distance, and online education.

Phase 3: Open Coding of Cultural Issues

Open coding, as suggested by Strauss and Corbin (1998), was used to explore the cultural issues presented in the 125 journal articles. This was conducted by labeling the key cultural issues discussed in the articles. Then these labels were grouped into four categories: cultural types, cultural aspects, cultural impact, and cultural approaches. This categorization was guided by two literature perspectives on culture. The first perspective is associated with what is referred to as the essentialist view of culture (Anderson &

TABLE 15.2
Number of Articles According to Article Selection Criteria From 2001 to 2011

Journal	Published Articles	Articles With the Word Culture	Articles With a Culture Focus
AJDE	274	51	11
DE	273	109	56
OL	272	113	58
Total	*819*	*273*	*125*
%	*100*	*33*	*15*

Note. AJDE = *The American Journal of Distance Education,* DE = *Distance Education,* and
OL = *Open Learning: The Journal of Open, Distance and e-Learning.*

Simpson, 2007; Goodfellow & Hewling, 2005). This view perceives culture as dispositions of individuals brought into the educational environment and includes characteristics of individuals like their nationality, gender, and location. These different dispositions of individuals are grouped as either the "types" category or the "aspects" category. The first category reflects contrasts of different types of culture based on the previous dispositions, whereas the second category presents components or elements of culture that are addressed in these articles based on these dispositions.

The second perspective on culture views culture as the product of individual interaction with the classroom environment (Anderson & Simpson, 2007). This is also referred to as "small cultures." It focuses on the emergence of a classroom-specific culture that is influenced by students' and tutors' interactions, content, pedagogic orientation of materials and media, and program and institution culture (Fay & Hill, 2003). This perspective allowed us to go beyond simply describing cultural types and components within the educational environment and to actively investigate the impact of culture on the teaching and learning environment for the purpose of finding approaches to deal with that impact. In the present study, articles were examined to see if they presented any cultural impact or suggested a cultural approach.

Findings and Discussions

In this section, the findings are first presented and discussed regarding the four questions on representation of culture that appeared in the three open, distance, and online publications: research type, authors' gender and work-country affiliation, and cultural issues examined in the publications. These findings are then discussed within the context of the field and sometimes compared to similar analyses in other fields.

Representation of Culture

Regarding the first question of the study, the analysis revealed that about a third (33% or 273 articles) of a total number of 819 articles published in the three journals between

2001 and 2011 mentioned the word *culture*. After a careful content analysis of those 273 articles, it was revealed that in many articles the word *culture* was minimally addressed. That is to say, in many articles, *culture* was mentioned only once and used as an abstract term such as *research culture, organizational culture, teaching and learning culture*, and *evaluation culture*, without further exploring cultural issues related to those subcultures. Forty-six percent of those articles that used the word *culture* actually addressed culture intentionally and extensively.

As illustrated in table 15.2, 15% of the total number of articles published in the three international journals during the past decade focused on cultural issues. A topic review in many family therapy journals reveals that articles that addressed ethnic, minority, and cross-cultural issues make up around 5.9% of the total number of articles published in those journals in a 12-year period (Feinauer, Pistorius, Erwin, & Alonzo, 2006). So, in comparison with our case, this is almost one third of the 15% representation of cultural issues in the open and distance education journals. Another content analysis of four international journals in vocational and career development over 34 years reports the representation of topics related to careers in a specific culture or country to be 30.9%, which is double the percentage in our case. Surprisingly, culture-related topics were most common in those journals (Nilsson et al., 2007). In conclusion, I believe that the representation of cultural issues discussed in the context of open and online education is adequate.

Research Type and Method of Culture Studies

Categorization of article types in the study followed the six categories suggested by the publication manual of the American Psychological Association (APA, 2010): empirical studies, literature reviews, theoretical articles, methodological articles, case studies, and other types of publications. Empirical studies present a clear sequence of introduction, method, results, and discussion. Literature reviews present, summarize, and comment on a clear problem from published research studies. Theoretical articles present advances in a theoretical issue by either refining theoretical constructs or building a new theory. Methodological articles present new methodological approaches in research. Case studies present case-specific material on individuals, groups, or organizations following a case study approach. Other types of publications include brief reports, editorials, monographs, obituaries, and book reviews. Table 15.3 shows the distribution of article type per journal.

In the articles with a culture focus, culture was mostly present in empirical research studies (36.8%) followed by theoretical articles (26.4%) and other types of publications such as editorials and book reviews (24.8%). None of the articles were found to be methodological articles. Case studies (11.2%) and literature reviews (0.8%) were at the bottom of the list. It is worth noting here that most case studies in this analysis were simply reporting an application and/or practice in an institution or a country without employing a rigorous case study methodology. The three journals are scholarly peer-reviewed research-based journals, yet empirical research studies constitute only a little more than a third of the culture-focused articles. This implies that the culture-focused articles published in these journals are mostly descriptive, anecdotal, and opinion-based articles.

Empirical studies were further classified into qualitative, quantitative, and mixed-methods studies following the categorization of Creswell (2003). Of the 46 empirical

TABLE 15.3
Distribution of Articles by Type of Research

| Journal | Articles With the Word Culture | | | | | | |
	Empirical Studies	Literature Reviews	Theoretical Articles	Methodological Articles	Case Studies	Other	Total
AJDE	19	4	2	0	3	23	51
DE	42	1	22	1	28	15	109
OL	27	0	36	0	20	30	113
Total	*88*	*5*	*60*	*1*	*51*	*68*	*273*
Journal	Articles With a Culture Focus						
	Empirical Studies	Literature Reviews	Theoretical Articles	Methodological Articles	Case Studies	Other	Total
AJDE	5	1	1	0	0	4	11
DE	25	0	14	0	7	10	56
OL	16	0	18	0	7	17	58
Total	*46*	*1*	*33*	*0*	*14*	*31*	*125*
%	36.8	0.8	26.4	0	11.2	24.8	100

Note. AJDE = *The American Journal of Distance Education*, DE = *Distance Education*, and OL = *Open Learning: The Journal of Open, Distance and e-Learning.*

studies, more than half of the studies (56.5%) were qualitative, followed by quantitative studies (23.9%) and mixed-method studies (19.6%), as table 15.4 shows.

Qualitative and mixed-method studies are descriptive in nature. In the analysis of the empirical studies, around 76% appeared to be descriptive. There were only 11 studies that employed quantitative methods, but even among these studies some were also

TABLE 15.4
Distribution of Empirical Studies by Methodology

| Journal | Articles With the Word Culture | | | | Articles With a Culture Focus | | | |
	Quantitative	Qualitative	Mixed Methods	Total	Quantitative	Qualitative	Mixed Methods	Total
AJDE	13	2	4	19	4	0	1	5
DE	7	30	5	42	3	19	3	25
OL	5	12	10	27	4	7	5	16
Total	*25*	*44*	*19*	*88*	*11*	*26*	*9*	*46*
%	28.4	50	21.6	100	23.9	56.5	19.6	100

Note. AJDE = *The American Journal of Distance Education*, DE = *Distance Education*, and OL = *Open Learning: The Journal of Open, Distance and e-Learning.*

descriptive. With the expansion and maturity of the field of open, distance, and online education and the long experience of offering courses to learners from different cultural backgrounds, it still seems that the cultural research in the field has not gone beyond descriptive studies.

In his editorial for *Open Learning* in 2003, Graham Gibbs pointed to the need for more focus on the "effectiveness of attempts to increase students' meta-cognitive awareness and control in the face of the impact of culture" (p. 221). More than a decade ago, Mason and Gunawardena (2001) also posed important questions for researchers about designing course content for students from different multicultural environments, types of support for nonnative students, and organizational issues related to providing such support across languages, time zones, and cultural preferences. These questions need to be answered with validated research evidence, which can be provided through rigorous empirical studies and in-depth qualitative analyses that go beyond description to theory formulation and cross-cultural comparisons that provide clear guidelines on handling cultural differences within different online learning communities.

Furthermore, with their rich international experience, all three main editors of the three journals, Michael G. Moore, Som Naidu, and Anne Gaskell, shared an understanding of the importance of cultural issues in open and online education. They used their editorials as a forum to call for more attention and research on culture and online learning. In 2001, the *Distance Education* journal dedicated a special issue for cultural considerations in online learning in an attempt to "generate interest and lead to further research" (Mason & Gunawardena, 2001, p. 4). This issue brought together many authors interested in the role of culture in open and online education. Recently, the *Quarterly Review of Distance Education* also produced a special issue that focused on "distance education in the Middle East" in its fourth issue in 2010. Such attempts to dedicate a special issue on the topic of culture generate more participation from authors to rethink the issue of culture within their research agenda.

Authors' Gender

Table 15.5 lists distribution of the articles by authors' gender. I did the analysis of authors' gender by conducting an extensive web search, as it is not always clear from each author's first name. It was especially difficult to identify gender from Chinese and African names that were not familiar to me. As a second-language learner of English, I found it also difficult to determine authors' gender without a picture for unisex names. I started this search with Google, looking for each author's picture in his or her institution or personal website or in his or her LinkedIn or Facebook profile. If there was no information indicating the author's gender, I conducted a name search through an online gender name checker. I identified the gender for every author except two, who were completely unidentifiable using all the previous methods.

Of the 223 authors who wrote articles focusing on cultural issues, 124 (55.6%) were women and 98 (43.9%) were men. A chi-square test of independence was performed to examine the relation between gender and use of the word *culture* (superficial versus extensive and focused use of culture). In the content analysis, the data can be subjected to independent tests for the purposes of validating inferences (White & Marsh, 2006). The

TABLE 15.5
Distribution of Articles by Authors' Gender

	Authors of Articles With the Word Culture				Authors of Articles With a Culture Focus			
Journal	Unknown	Men	Women	Total	Unknown	Men	Women	Total
AJDE	0	49	37	86	0	7	10	17
DE	0	99	124	223	0	43	63	106
OL	2	118	87	207	1	48	51	100
Total	*2*	*266*	*248*	*516*	*1*	*98*	*124*	*223*
%	0.4	51.6	48.0	100	0.5	43.9	55.6	100

Note. AJDE = *The American Journal of Distance Education*, DE = *Distance Education*, and OL = *Open Learning: The Journal of Open, Distance and e-Learning*.

two authors with unidentifiable gender were excluded from this analysis. The chi-square test showed that the relationship between the two variables—gender and the use of the word *culture*—was significant. This means that the percentage of authors using the word *culture* significantly differed by gender, χ^2 (1, $N = 514$) = 9.056, p = .003. Of all articles included in the analysis, articles that had an extensive focus on culture were more likely to be written by female authors. Female authors were more likely to use the word *culture* extensively compared with male authors in the three journals under consideration.

This cultural consciousness of female authors needs to be further investigated to understand the reasons that make women more concerned about the impact of culture in open and online education. One possibility is that women are more sensitive to cultural and minority issues because they themselves are a minority in higher education. According to a survey by the American Association of University Professors (AAUP, 2004) in 2003–2004, there were a few (only 18%) women professors at doctoral universities, and they were less tenured than male faculty.

Authors' Work-Country Affiliation

Of all articles with the word *culture*, there were more publications from Western countries (United States, United Kingdom, Australia, and Canada) than from non-Western countries, as table 15.6 shows. This was expected because the chosen journals are based in these Western countries. When the filter of articles with a focus on culture is added, the picture changes a little bit, with Asian authors ranked third (13.5%) following authors from the United Kingdom (26.5%) and the United States (26%). Canadian authors (10.8%) and Australian authors (10.3%) came fourth and fifth, respectively. At the bottom of the list were authors from Africa, European countries (other than the United Kingdom), the Middle East, and Oceania.

While I investigated authors' background, it was clear from the pictures posted on their personal or institutional websites that many authors *originally* came from ethnic backgrounds other than the Anglo-Saxon background despite their current work affiliation with Western universities and organizations. It seems that the majority of authors who wrote on culture in these three journals came from an ethnic background within

TABLE 15.6

Distribution of Articles by Authors' Work-Country Affiliation

Journal	United States	United Kingdom	Australia	Canada	Europe	Asia	Africa	Latin America	Middle East	Oceania	Total
Work-Country Affiliation of Authors of Articles With the Word Culture											
AJDE	68	0	1	10	2	1	0	0	4	0	86
DE	73	27	40	26	7	15	20	6	8	1	223
OL	16	84	16	20	14	26	20	4	3	4	207
Total	**157**	**111**	**57**	**56**	**23**	**42**	**40**	**10**	**15**	**5**	**516**
Work-Country Affiliation of Authors of Articles With a Culture Focus											
AJDE	13	0	0	3	0	0	0	0	1	0	17
DE	39	19	14	13	3	6	3	6	3	0	106
OL	6	40	9	8	6	24	6	0	0	1	100
Total	**58**	**59**	**23**	**24**	**9**	**30**	**9**	**6**	**4**	**1**	**223**
%	26	26.5	10.3	10.8	4	13.5	4	2.7	1.8	0.4	100

Note. AJDE = *The American Journal of Distance Education*, DE = *Distance Education*, and OL = *Open Learning: The Journal of Open, Distance and e-Learning.*

TABLE 15.7

A List of Coded Categories and Labels in Articles Focusing on Culture

Essentialist Culture Perspective			Small Culture Perspective	
Cultural Types	Cultural Components	Cultural Impact	Cultural Approaches	
1. Global/international versus local	1. Dimensions	1. Etiquettes	1. Culturally inclusive learning/ methodology/pedagogy/teaching	
2. Foreign/alien versus national/ homegrown	2. Variability	2. Sensitivity	2. Cultural interaction	
3. Western versus non-Western	3. Considerations	3. Immediacy	3. Cultural discussion	
4. Multi versus mono	4. Mind-set	4. Discontinuity	4. Culturally appropriate design	
5. Own versus other	5. Differences	5. Miscommunication	5. Cultural training	
6. Dominated versus marginalized	6. Observations	6. Adaptation	6. Cultural skills/training	
7. Men dominated	7. Characteristics	7. Acculturation	7. Cultural competence	
8. African, Indian, Asian/Chinese/Confucian, American, Islamic, Arab, Māori	8. Attitudes	8. Struggle		
9. Institution/organization	9. Perspectives	9. Management		
10. Prison	10. Understanding	10. Reproduction		
11. Research	11. Phenomenon	11. Marginalization		
	12. Politics	12. Identity formation		
	13. Experiences			
	14. Practices			
	15. Needs			
	16. Standards			

Western countries such as immigrant Chinese, Mexicans, and Indians, with some Westerners working in Eastern institutions at the time of publication. It may be that an interest in cultural issues is closely related to one's own cultural background. That interest may develop further to be a mission to bring in a closer focus on cultural issues. That is what the Asian authors, as it seems from this analysis, succeeded in doing by coming third in the number of culture-focused articles after the U.S. and U.K. authors.

Specific Issues in Culture-Focused Articles

As explained previously, 125 articles that specifically discussed cultural issues were analyzed using the open coding system with two cultural perspectives: essentialist and small culture. As shown in table 15.7, studies were classified more in the essentialist perspective of culture (27 labels/nodes) than in the small culture perspective (19 labels/nodes). This suggests that the impact of culture and culturally inclusive approaches was not adequately addressed. Culturally inclusive or appropriate approaches in online education were mentioned in only four articles, and they were discussed at a theoretical level in these articles. More than a decade ago, McLoughlin (2001) suggested a sound framework for a culturally inclusive approach for the alignment of the design of pedagogy, task, and assessment of cross-cultural online learning. Future studies can use this framework or develop other approaches and methodologies to address the impact of culture in the multicultural online education.

Conclusion

This study was limited to only three journals. Future studies could stretch the number of journals to include other journals such as *The International Review of Research in Open and Distance Learning, British Journal of Educational Technology, Journal of Asynchronous Learning Networks, The Internet and Higher Education, Computers and Education*, and *Quarterly Review of Distance Education* in addition to other journals coming from non-Western places in China, the Middle East, and Africa.

Latchem (2009) asked, in the *Distance Education* journal, "Should the journal seek more papers from . . . non-Western cultures?" (p. 169). My answer would be "yes," as it is one possibility to increase the representation of cultural publications in the field. Moreover, in the next stage, what is needed is not only to increase the number of publications but also to improve the quality of these publications. Cultural researchers in open and online education need to ask serious questions, and answer them in serious ways, rather than simply describe and share experiences. It seems that many of the international studies in this area are focusing on descriptive case studies. As Latchem (2007) argued, we researchers in the field of open and online education need to "do more than simply inform each other about individual case studies and small-scale experiments." This could be achieved by

- focusing on impact studies of cultural struggle, miscommunication, and adaptation on classroom environment processes and outcomes;
- identifying more ways in which cultural impact can be observed and utilized to facilitate teaching and learning in the online environment, especially from alternative perspectives and voices;

- employing rigorous experimental studies to investigate the effect of culturally appropriate approaches and techniques to be used when teaching in online environments; and
- documenting the development and maturity of cultural competency of students and educators during the course of teaching and learning online by using in-depth qualitative research.

References

Al-Harthi, A. S. (2010). Learner self-regulation in distance education: A cross-cultural study. *American Journal of Distance Education, 24*(3), 135–150.

American Association of University Professors. (2004). AAUP research director reports on gender. *Academe Online, 90*(3). Retrieved from http://www.aaup.org/AAUP/pubsres/academe/2004/MJ/AW/RptGndrGap.htm

American Psychological Association. (2010). *Publication manual of the American Psychological Association* (6th ed.). Washington, DC: Author.

Anderson, B., & Simpson, M. (2007). Ethical issues in online education. *Open Learning, 22*(2), 129–138.

Creswell, J. W. (2003). *Research design: Qualitative, quantitative and mixed methods.* Thousand Oaks, CA: Sage.

Fay, R., & Hill, M. (2003). Educating language teachers through distance learning: The need for culturally-appropriate DL methodology. *Open Learning, 18*(1), 9–27.

Feinauer, L. L., Pistorius, K. D., Erwin, B. R., & Alonzo, A. T. (2006). Twelve-year review of major family therapy journals: Topic areas, authors' characteristics and publishing institutions. *The American Journal of Family Therapy, 34*(2), 105–118.

Gibbs, G. (2003). Editorial. *Open Learning, 18*(3), 219–221.

Goodfellow, R., & Hewling, A. (2005). Reconceptualising culture in virtual learning environments: From an "essentialist" to a "negotiated" perspective. *E-Learning, 2*(4), 355–367. Retrieved from http://www.wwwords.co.uk/pdf/viewpdf.asp?j=elea&vol=2&issue=4&year=2005&article=5_Goodfellow_ELEA_2_4_web&id=130.123.128.117

Gunawardena, C., Nolla, A. C., Wilson, P. L., Lopez-Islas, J. R., Ramirez-Angel, N., & Megchum-Alpizar, R. M. (2001). A cross-cultural study of group process and development in online conferences. *Distance Education, 22*(1), 85–121.

Latchem, C. (2007). A framework for researching Asian open and distance learning. *Distance Education, 28*(2), 133–147.

Latchem, C. (2009). Distance education: Quo vadis? *Distance Education, 30*(1), 167–169.

Lee, Y., Driscoll, M. P., & Nelson, D. W. (2004). The past, present, and future of research in distance education: Results of a content analysis. *American Journal of Distance Education, 18*(4), 225–241.

Mason, R., & Gunawardena, C. (2001). Editorial. *Distance Education, 22*(1), 4–7.

McLoughlin, C. (2001). Inclusivity and alignment: Principles of pedagogy, task and assessment design for effective cross-cultural online learning. *Distance Education, 22*(1), 7–29.

Moore, M. G., & Kearsley, G. (2005). *Distance education: A systems view* (2nd ed.). Belmont, CA: Thomson/Wadsworth.

Nilsson, J. E., Flores, L. Y., Berkel, L. V., Schale, C. L., Linnemeyer, R. M., & Summer, I. (2007). International career articles: A content analysis of four journals across 34 years. *Journal of Vocational Behavior, 70*(3), 602–613.

Peters, O. (2007). The most industrialized form of education. In M. G. Moore (Ed.), *Handbook of distance education* (2nd ed.). Hillsdale, NJ: Lawrence Erlbaum.

Smith, P. J., & Smith, S. (1999). Differences between Chinese and Australian students: Some implications for distance educators. *Distance Education, 20*(1), 64–80.

Strauss, A., & Corbin, J. (1998). *Basics of qualitative research: Techniques and procedures for developing grounded theory* (2nd ed.). San Francisco, CA: Sage.

Tu, C. H. (2001). How Chinese perceive social presence: An examination of interaction in online learning environment. *Educational Media International, 8*(1), 45–60.

White, M. D., & Marsh, E. E. (2006). Content analysis: A flexible methodology. *Library Trends, 55*(1), 22–45.

16

MANY FACES OF CONFUCIAN CULTURE

Asian Learners' Perceptions of Quality Distance Education

Li Chen, Xinyi Shen, Aya Fukuda, and Insung Jung

The meaning of quality in distance education (DE) has attracted much debate. For some providers, the goal of DE is to achieve a level of quality on par with that of face-to-face education. However, others have argued that DE is so distinctive that the aims and methods of face-to-face education cannot be applied in measuring its quality. Yet others have commented that DE should be judged by the quality standards of face-to-face education while factoring in some distinctive attributes of DE, such as open entry, flexible operations, and technology-based course delivery (Jung, Wong, Li, Baigaltugs, & Belawati, 2011).

This chapter aims to examine cultural similarities and differences in three Asian countries that have been influenced by Confucianism, with regard to perspectives on quality DE based on a survey conducted with 394 distance learners in China, Japan, and South Korea (hereafter Korea).[1] It will begin with contextual information that is useful for understanding the development and evaluation of DE in these three countries. This will be followed by the introduction of the survey, discussion of the findings, and the conclusion. In this chapter, DE includes both conventional modes of DE and online education.

Context

Development of Online Education

In China, online education at the higher education level has achieved remarkable development since China kicked off the ICT (information and communications technology)-supported DE pilot project in 1999. Online degree programs have been provided mainly through two kinds of DE institutions: 68 online colleges within conventional universities and the Open University of China system. Even though the quality of online education offered by these institutions has been assessed and monitored by the Chinese Ministry of Education, through standardized national examinations given to online learners and annual reports prepared by the institutions, no integrated quality assurance (QA) measures have been developed at the national level to regulate the quality of online education. As a result, these online education providers have become excessively independent from the government's regulatory system, and some have demonstrated poor management and quality (Zhang, 2010).

In Japan, online higher education has been provided by 46 undergraduate universities, 26 graduate universities, 11 junior colleges classified as "correspondence institutions," and 7 fully online private universities (Ministry of Education, Culture, Sports, Science and Technology [MEXT], 2012). The quality of Japan's online education has been evaluated every 7 years by three accreditation agencies authorized by the Japanese MEXT, applying the same quality standards as those used for the assessment of conventional education. However, in Japan online education is not highly regarded as the mainstream, the demand is comparatively low, and the readiness of the university faculty to implement online education is not very high (Latchem, Jung, Aoki, & Özkul, 2008). One of the reasons could be that online education is not incorporated strategically into Japan's educational system reform.

In Korea, online education has been planned and implemented strategically by Korean universities and supported strongly by the government and has entered the mass adoption stage (Latchem et al., 2008). Not only have 20 fully online virtual universities and cyber colleges been established, but also 85% of the national and private conventional universities are now offering courses online. A number of universities, including the Korea National Open University, offer online graduate programs. Online education programs provided by these universities are reaccredited every 5 years, and their selected programs are evaluated annually by the Korean Council for University Education (KCUE) and the Korea Education and Research Information Service.

Quality Standards of Online Education

Table 16.1 presents the QA standards for DE, including online education, that have been adopted by the accreditation/QA agencies in the three countries: the Ministry of Education in China, the National Institution for Academic Degrees and University Evaluation (NIAD-UE) and the Japan University Accreditation Association (JUAA) in Japan, and the KCUE in Korea. Of 14 QA standards, the Chinese Ministry of Education adopted 7 to assess the quality of online education, the NIAD-UE adopted 8, the JUAA adopted 7, and the KCUE adopted 10.

Only two standards are common across three countries: "faculty and staff are well supported" and "learner support is available in various locations and modes to meet students' learning needs." It may be that faculty and staff are regarded highly even in online education across these three countries where the Confucian tradition is prevalent in society and that learner support is essential in online education where learners need more individualized services and support in virtual learning environments (Gu & Fang, 2007).

TABLE 16.1
Quality Assurance Standards for Distance Education Adopted by China, Japan, and Korea

Quality Assurance Standards	China (Ministry of Education)	Japan (NIAD-UE)	Japan (JUAA)	Korea (KCUE)
1. Purpose and goals of the institution are clearly stated.		✓	✓	✓
2. Course design follows predetermined procedures.	✓			✓
3. Faculty and staff are well supported.	✓	✓	✓	✓
4. Teaching content and learning resources are aligned with course objectives.	✓			✓
5. Learner support is available in various locations and modes to meet students' learning needs.	✓	✓	✓	✓
6. Organizational management system is well established.		✓		✓
7. Academic management system is well established.	✓	✓		✓
8. Research on distance education is promoted.		✓	✓	
9. Academic atmosphere supports distance teaching and learning.			✓	
10. Information system securely and efficiently manages administrative and academic data.				✓
11. Financing is well planned and managed.		✓	✓	
12. Teaching effectiveness is regularly assessed.	✓			✓
13. Infrastructure is established and maintained.		✓	✓	✓
14. Innovative practices are encouraged and implemented.	✓			

Note. NIAD-UE = National Institution for Academic Degrees and University Evaluation, JUAA = Japan University Accreditation Association, KCUE = Korean Council for University Education.

Finance is mentioned only by the Japanese agencies. This can be explained by the fact that as private and/or for-profit institutions, a majority of Japanese online education providers need to secure their own funds and prove financial soundness to the government.

In contrast, many Chinese providers are public and thus supported by the government, and the Korean providers, even if many are private, are supported more generously by the government compared with the Japanese institutions.

The standard "information system securely and efficiently manages administrative and academic data" is applied in assessing the quality of online education only by Korea. This may be because the virtual universities in Korea award a formal undergraduate degree to a large number of students, so it is important to ensure the quality of their information system by securely and efficiently managing administrative data and students' information.

"Innovative practices are encouraged and implemented" is regarded as an important QA standard only in China. Since the introduction of the DE pilot project in 1999, the Chinese government has encouraged online education colleges to develop modern ways of teaching and learning by loosening regulations. Thus, an important quality indicator for the government is whether online education providers have implemented innovative practices in teaching and learning (Zhang, 2010).

Cultural Differences in Perception of Quality in Online Learning

Cultural differences exist in the perception of quality in online education. Peltier, Schibrowsky, and Drago (2007) found that American online learners perceived the content of the course, peer interaction, interaction between teachers and students, course structure, counseling, and course transmission as critical factors in assessing quality in online education. Salvador (2008), in a series of interviews with online learners in a graduate program offered by a consortium in the United States, found that the learners attached great importance to the diversity of learners and participation, experienced and responsible professional personnel, flexibility of the course structure, content and practice, technical support, and interaction. Similar to Peltier et al. (2007), Yang (2006) also discovered that peer interaction, teachers' feedback, and online course structure were important quality factors to American online learners.

Ehlers (2004) identified that European online learners applied seven factors in judging the quality of online learning: tutor support, cooperation and communication, technology, costs-expectations-benefits, information transparency, course structure, and didactics. Like the learners in the aforementioned American studies, the European learners also valued individualized and interactive online learning arrangements that offer various kinds of learning support to meet their special needs.

In Asia, Jung et al. (2011), in a large-scale survey to investigate the national QA systems for DE at the higher education level, found that great differences exist in views about online education, DE policies and development, technology infrastructure, support systems, and pedagogies and that these differences are often influenced by national culture. Chang (2008) reported that Taiwanese online learners valued course management, communication and feedback, course flexibility, and course design in measuring the quality of online education. In Japan, online learners rated technology support as a critical factor in judging the quality of online or blended learning (Saito, 2009). In another study, conducted in Korea, Jung (2011) found that staff support was perceived as the most important indicator of quality in online education, followed by institutional QA mechanism and learning tasks. This finding clearly differs from those of the two Asian studies discussed previously and indicates the need to consider cultural differences within Asia as one of the several variables affecting views about the quality of online education.

The Study

Questions

In an attempt to identify the views of learners from China, Japan, and Korea about the quality of DE including online education and compare these views from the cultural point of view, the study asked the following questions:

1. Which QA dimensions are more important than others in assessing the quality of distance learning?
2. Within each dimension, which specific QA criteria are more important than others in assessing the quality of distance learning?
3. Are there any similarities and differences among these three countries pertaining to the perception of quality distance learning?

Participants

A total of 394 learners (90 from Japan, 139 from China, and 165 from Korea) who were enrolled in a wide range of DE institutions participated in the survey. Of the Chinese participants, 38.9% were online learners, as were 35.5% of the Japanese and 47.8% of the Koreans. The rest of the participants were using mainly print and broadcast programs, with the Internet as a supplement.

Instrument

The survey questionnaire used by Jung (2012) was adopted for this study. To gain information about the learners' perceptions of the quality of DE including online education, this survey included 57 items across 10 QA dimensions (see Jung, 2012, table 2). The final English version of the questionnaire was translated into Chinese, Japanese, and Korean for the purpose of this study.

Data Analysis

Descriptive statistics were calculated to identify quality dimensions and criteria important for distance learners from the three countries. One-way ANOVA was chosen to compare the data from China, Japan, and Korea.

Findings

Table 16.2 shows the following:

- For the Chinese learners, "institutional credibility" (M = 4.1655) is most important, followed by "course development" (M = 4.0952) and "information and publicity" (M = 4.0732).

TABLE 16.2
Results Comparing Learner Perceptions of Quality in Three Asian Countries
(Means and ANOVA)

Number	Dimension	Mean			F-value		
		China	Korea	Japan	China, Korea	China, Japan	Korea, Japan
1	Infrastructure	3.8489	4.0360	3.5800	.24	.06	.000**
2	Internal quality assurance system	3.8285	4.1702	4.0584	.000**	.045*	.314
3	Institutional credibility	4.1655	4.1173	3.8758	.609	.009**	.025*
4	Course development	4.0952	4.2892	4.1804	.028*	.854	.082
5	Interactive tasks	3.9236	4.0134	3.8008	.377	.305	.066
6	Teaching and learning	3.8823	3.8688	3.8288	.880	.611	.693
7	Information and publicity	4.0732	4.3551	4.4307	.006**	.003**	.513
8	Student support	3.8292	3.9548	3.7046	.169	.244	.016*
9	Faculty support	4.0268	4.1848	4.0309	.119	.972	.181
10	Evaluation and assessment	4.0557	4.1443	4.0221	.345	.761	.252

$*p < 0.05$, $**p < 0.01$.

- For the Japanese learners, "information and publicity" ($M = 4.4307$), "course development" ($M = 4.1804$), and "internal quality assurance system" ($M = 4.0584$) are important.
- For the Korean learners, "information and publicity" ($M = 4.3551$), "course development" ($M = 4.2892$), and "faculty support" ($M = 4.1848$) are the top three areas of importance.

F-values listed in table 16.2 show the following:

- The Korean learners pay more attention to the "infrastructure" dimension compared with their counterparts in Japan.
- The learners from Japan and Korea see the "internal quality assurance system" as more important than do those from China.
- "Institutional credibility" gains much attention from learners in China and Korea but is somewhat ignored by those in Japan.
- Even though "course development" is perceived to be very important in assessing the quality of online education in all three countries, the Korean learners appear to be more concerned about "course development" than are the learners from China.

- Learners in Japan and Korea attach more importance to the dimension of "information and publicity" than do those in China.
- Learners in Korea care more about "student support" compared with those in Japan.

Further analysis of the survey data revealed the following results. Among the five criteria within the dimension of "infrastructure,"

- "reliable media/technology infrastructure" is the most important criterion for learners in China and Japan, whereas for those in Korea, "reliable learning management system" has the highest ranking;
- learners in China attach relatively more importance to "physical classrooms" than do those in Korea and Japan; and
- "security of student data system" is valued more by learners in Korea than by those in China and Japan.

Among the four criteria in the dimension of "internal quality assurance system,"

- "existence of quality standards specifically for DE" appears to be important to learners in all three countries,
- "clear guidelines for quality assurance" rank high among learners in China and Japan, and
- "periodic internal evaluation by a DE institution" ranks high with learners in Korea.

Among the five criteria in the dimension of "institutional credibility,"

- "qualified faculty/staff" appears to be most important for learners in all three countries,
- "strong leadership" is valued more by learners in China than by those in Korea and Japan, and
- "clear lines of authority in decision making" is another important criterion for learners in China and Japan, whereas for those in Korea, "external accreditation at the national level" is highly ranked.

Among the six criteria in the dimension of "course development,"

- for learners in China, "clear guidelines for course development" is the most important factor;
- for learners in Korea, "well-structured course materials" is most valued; and
- for Japanese learners, "course content adaptability to students' needs" is the most important factor in assessing the quality of the "course development" dimension of DE.

Among the three criteria in the dimension of "interactive tasks,"

- for learners in China and Korea, "inclusion of problem/case-based learning activities in courses" is most important, and
- for learners in Japan, "inclusion of individualized learning activities in courses" ranks first.

Among the 12 criteria included in the dimension of "teaching and learning,"

- for learners in China, "online tutorials" and "informal face-to-face meetings with instructors/tutors" rank in the top two;
- "face-to-face tutorials" and "informal face-to-face meetings with instructors/tutors" are valued more by learners in China than they are by learners in Korea and Japan;
- for learners in Korea, "student interaction with instructors/tutors" and "access to online library resources" lead the list;
- "student interaction with instructors/tutors" is viewed as a more important aspect of quality DE by learners in Korea than by those in China;
- for learners in Japan, "flexibility in learning methods" and "access to online library resources" are valued most; and
- "flexibility in learning methods and pace" is valued more by learners in Korea and Japan than by those in China.

Among the three criteria in the dimension of "information and publicity,"

- learners from all three countries value the criterion of "providing course information (course objectives, assignments, timelines, study requirements, resources, learning outcomes, etc.) for each course" the most, and
- "providing administration information (admission requirements, tuition fees, technical and assessment requirements, student support services, etc.)" and "clear indication of requirements for assignments (due dates, evaluation criteria, etc.)" are more important to learners in Korea and Japan than to those in China.

Among the nine criteria included in the dimension of "student support,"

- for learners in China, "flexible payment method" is the top aspect;
- for learners in Korea and Japan, "an established appeal mechanism" is the most important aspect;
- "media/technology support for students" is valued more by learners in Korea than by those in China and Japan;
- "psychological support for students" is valued more by learners in Korea than by those in China and Japan; and
- in all three countries, "social support for students" appears to be important to learners.

Among the four criteria in the dimension of "faculty support,"

- for learners in China, "periodic training for faculty/tutors/staff" is most important, and
- for learners in Japan and Korea, "continuous assistance for faculty/tutors/staff in course development, delivery and management" is most valued.

Among the six criteria included in the dimension of "evaluation and assessment,"

- for learners from all three countries, "fair rubrics for learning assessment" and "timely feedback to student assignments and questions" are in the top two, and
- learners in China care more about "fair rubrics for learning assessment," whereas those in Japan and Korea value "timely feedback to student assignments and questions."

Similarities and Differences in Perceptions of Quality

Learners in all three countries pay a great deal of attention to the criteria relating to "course development." In DE, because of the feature of teaching and learning at distance, teachers often find it difficult to adjust teaching content and teaching strategy in a timely way to meet students' learning needs. Therefore, high-quality course development is necessary to satisfy the various needs of students. There is no doubt that course development is given much attention in all three countries (L. Chen, 2004).

"Institutional credibility" ranks in first place in China, but not in Japan or Korea. To gain institutional credibility, the Chinese learners indicate "qualified faculty/staff" as the most important factor. This may mean that even the distance learners in China rely heavily on their teachers during the learning process, which is influenced significantly by traditional classroom learning. Traditionally, Chinese teachers always talk to an entire class, and the students' responsibility is only to listen. Even in an online learning situation, students tend to believe that they cannot learn without the teachers' presence and thus want to listen to their teachers' lectures via prerecorded video or videoconferencing.

In the dimension of "information and publicity," "providing course information" is fairly important to learners in Japan and Korea. These two countries are ahead of China in providing DE. Their distance learners have become used to a self-directed mode of learning and know the importance of getting detailed information about their courses for their independent study.

In the dimension of "student support," learners in China see "flexible payment method" as having a big role, but to learners in Japan and Korea, "an established appeal mechanism" is the most important. In China, the learners involved in DE are categorized as a socially vulnerable group, as many of them have financial difficulties. So, it is obvious that they need a "flexible payment method," relieving them from financial stress.

Within the dimension of "faculty support," "periodic training for faculty/tutors/staff" is significantly important to learners in China, whereas "continuous assistance for faculty/tutors/staff in course development, delivery and management" leads the list for learners in Japan and Korea. Because of their longer history of DE, Japan and Korea seem to pay much attention to offering on-demand assistance, whereas China, with its relatively short history of DE, puts more emphasis on structured training sessions that are periodically offered.

In the "evaluation and assessment" dimension, "fair rubrics for learning assessment" is of high concern for learners in China, but "timely feedback to student assignments and questions" is most valued by learners in Japan and Korea. In China, some learners just aim to get their diplomas rather than to obtain in-depth and extensive knowledge, so they pay more attention to the final evaluation and less to support for the learning process.

Learners in China, Japan, and Korea are all very concerned about dimensions such as "course development," "information and publicity," and "faculty support," but the dimensions related to the learning process, such as "interactive tasks," "teaching and learning," and "student support," appear to be of less importance to these learners' perceptions of quality. These distance learners may be more concerned about the result and certification rather than the knowledge itself, so the learning process is not considered to be very important to students. See chapter 9 of this book for further discussion on Asia's output-focused or examination-centered learning culture.

These three countries are at different stages of online education. Japan and Korea are a little ahead of China. Z. H. Chen (2006) suggested that 20% of learners in the Open University of Japan have already achieved an equivalent or higher degree before they enroll in a DE institution. The main motivation for learning at a distance in online education institutions in Japan and Korea is not so much to get a degree but to learn new knowledge and skills for future careers. This might be because the socioeconomic situation in Japan and Korea is more developed, and people have less economic stress and fewer life burdens, which enables them to pursue self-improvement rather than a diploma.

Suggestions for Distance Educators and Researchers

This study identified cultural differences and similarities in the perception of distance learners regarding the quality of DE. Key findings of the study include the following:

- China pays much attention to the "institutional credibility" dimension and the "qualified faculty/staff" factor within the dimension, whereas Japan and Korea put emphasis on the "information and publicity" dimension and the "providing course information" factor. This finding can be explained by the differences in distance learning culture and accumulated experiences with DE in each society.
- Across all three countries, learning process variables such as "interactive tasks" and "teaching and learning" are less valued compared with input and output variables such as "course development" and "evaluation and assessment." The main motivation of distance learners appears to be getting a degree, especially in China. These findings may result from Asia's Confucian tradition and output-oriented learning culture.

Results of the study offer valuable suggestions for DE providers who wish to offer online learning programs and services to Asia:

- DE providers should understand that quality is a value-laden and relative concept and reflects cultural beliefs. As shown in this chapter, the definitions of quality online learning and QA policies and procedures vary across nations in Asia. Thus, it is important to recognize sociocultural differences that exist across the Asian countries. To many Westerners, China, Japan, and Korea may appear to have much in common, as they have inherited Confucianism. However, each country is at a different stage of development in online learning, has different views on quality online learning, values different approaches to online teaching and learning, and adopts different QA systems. These differences should be reflected in the development of online programs and the provision of support services.

- DE providers should consider the learners' thoughts on quality in online learning when developing and delivering their programs and services. In many cases, the learners' needs and views on quality online learning are ignored, and only the providers' concerns are considered. Our study revealed that quality concerns of the learners are not quite the same as those of the providers or developers. To offer learner-centered and flexible online learning, providers and developers need to understand the learners' views on the quality of online learning and incorporate them in the online learning programs and services.

As with all empirical research, this study has some limitations. First, the questionnaire was translated into several languages, which may have led to some deviation during the process of translation. Second, we adopted the method of random sampling, and the sample did not cover all kinds of learners. The method of step sampling may be better for future work of this nature. To gain a further understanding of stakeholders' perceptions of quality for DE in various contexts, we strongly encourage future research that deletes less important variables, adjusts less important criteria, and combines parts of dimensions into a broader concept to enhance the usability of the survey instrument used in this study. As well, more in-depth research is needed to explore learners' reasons for valuing certain quality criteria over others. We could choose more countries to do the comparative research and involve more learners.

Authors' Note

[1] This study was a part of a project titled "Quality Assurance (QA) Models, Standards and Key Performance Indicators for ICT-Supported Distance Education (DE) in Asia," which was supported by the International Development Research Centre in Canada. The general objective of this project was to investigate various QA practices and standards and develop a set of QA standards and key performance indicators for Asian ICT-supported DE in formal, nonformal, and informal settings and thus to improve the quality of ICT-supported DE in Asia. The study reported in this chapter has never been published elsewhere.

References

Chang, C. W. (2008). *A factor analysis of Taiwanese learner's perceptions of online learning* (Unpublished doctoral dissertation). University of Arkansas, Fayetteville.

Chen, L. (2004). *Distance education.* Beijing, China: Higher Education Press.

Chen, Z. H. (2006). Distance education in Japan and the enlightenment. *Guangxi Radio and Television University Journal, 17*(3), 29–30.

Ehlers, U. D. (2004). Quality in e-learning from a learner's perspective. *European Journal of Open and Distance Learning, I.* Retrieved from http://www.eurodl.org/materials/contrib/2004/Online_Master_COPs.html

Gu, J. X., & Fang, M. Z. (2007). The construction of student support in distance education. *China Education Technology, 245,* 39–43.

Jung, I. S. (2011). The dimensions of e-learning quality: From the learner's perspective. *Educational Technology Research and Development, 59,* 445–464.

Jung, I. S. (2012). Asian learners' perception of quality in distance education and gender differences. *International Review of Research in Open and Distance Learning, 13*(2), 1–25. Retrieved from http://www.irrodl.org/index.php/irrodl/article/view/1159/2128

Jung, I., Wong, T., Li, C., Baigaltugs, S., & Belawati, T. (2011). Quality assurance in Asian distance education: Diverse approaches and common culture. *The International Review of Research in Open and Distance Learning, 12*(6), 63–83. Retrieved from http://www.irrodl.org/index.php/irrodl/article/view/991/1953

Latchem, C., Jung, I. S., Aoki, K., & Özkul, A. E. (2008). The tortoise and the hare enigma in e-transformation in Japanese and Korean higher education. *British Journal of Educational Technology, 39*(4), 610–630.

Ministry of Education, Culture, Sports, Science and Technology. (2012). *School basic survey.* Retrieved from http://www.mext.go.jp/component/b_menu/houdou/__icsFiles/afieldfile/2012/08/27/1324976_3_1.pdf

Peltier, J. W., Schibrowsky, J. A., & Drago, W. (2007). The interdependence of the factors influencing the perceived quality of the online learning experience: A causal model. *Journal of Marketing Education, 29*(2), 140–153.

Saito, T. (2009). *Quality assurance of distance education/e-learning* (APQN Report Project 3). India: Asia-Pacific Quality Network. Retrieved from http://www.apqn.org/files/virtual_library/project_reports/pg3_project_report_february_2009.pdf

Salvador, L. (2008). *A grounded theory of high-quality distance education programs: Student perspectives.* Madison: University of Wisconsin–Madison.

Yang, Y. (2006). *An investigation on students' perceptions of online course quality and contribution factors for those perceptions* (Unpublished doctoral dissertation). Mississippi State University, Starkville.

Zhang, F. D. (2010). Current situation and problems of distance education in China. *Journal of Adult Education, 287,* 151–152.

17

LOOKING AHEAD

A Cultural Approach to Research and
Practice in Online Learning

Insung Jung and Charlotte Nirmalani Gunawardena

As we approach the conclusion of our book, we would like to reflect on the rich and diverse perspectives offered by our authors and look ahead at the steps we need to take to promote sound research on issues of culture and online learning. We have explored how cultural differences influence the learning processes, experiences, perceptions, and even outcomes of online learning. We have also shown that culture interacts with various features of individual learners such as gender, learning styles, and readiness, shaping the practice and result of online learning. Moreover, we have identified new cultures of online learning emerging from globalization and affordances of online technologies and new challenges created by multicultural online learning environments.

Based on the findings and observations made in the preceding chapters of the book, this chapter will propose a cultural (and multicultural) approach as a new way of doing research and improving practice in online learning, explore key research areas, discuss implications for instructional design and support, and conclude with a set of key messages from the book. We will begin with the discussion of what we mean by this cultural approach in the context of online learning.

Cultural Approach to Research in Online Learning

In our introductory chapter, on p. 1, we argued that "culture can be negotiated online through a communication process mediated by technology interfaces that themselves are culturally produced. Culture impacts every facet of online learning, from course and interface design, to communication in a sociocultural space, and to the negotiation of meaning and social construction of knowledge." This general understanding of culture is used in the book to delineate methods and effects of adopting culture as a research and design approach in various contexts of online learning. We've observed that during the past few decades, cultural frameworks for understanding and designing online learning environments have emerged in response to globalized, multicultural development of learning. Cultural views have offered rich explanations of the online learning process and provided guidelines for designing learner-centered environments, but such views have not been fully elaborated as an alternative research paradigm or design method that could extend existing approaches and methods in online learning.

In the preceding chapters, we have noted that although Hofstede's model has been useful to a certain extent to document cultural differences among nations or groups, it assumes culture is static and shared equally by its members and is an independent variable affecting individuals' thinking, feeling, and behaving (Segall, Dasen, Berry, & Poortinga, 1990). Yet, we have also observed that culture is dynamic in nature, is negotiated by interacting groups, influences and is influenced by external environments, and is often recreated.

Understanding these complex features of culture, we broadly define the cultural approach to research in online learning as "the systematic and systemic study of the ways in which cultural forces interact with online learning environments and online learner behaviors." The goals of the cultural approach are to

1. develop an understanding of cultural influences on the online learning processes and products and the new cultures that emerge from online learning,
2. compare and contrast cultural differences in learning and communicating online,
3. identify culturally appropriate instructional strategies for online teaching and learning by integrating goals 1 and 2, and
4. improve design processes and practices of online learning by integrating goal 3.

To achieve these goals, we propose four types of research for those who wish to adopt the cultural approach to research and practice in online learning. The research types proposed here are not necessarily exclusive of each other but rather support or strengthen each other in understanding cultural issues found in online learning contexts and improving practice of online learning.

Exploratory Research

Aiming to understand a phenomenon, an event, or a program and identify key issues involved, exploratory research provides insight into what, why, and how something is happening in online learning contexts. It attempts to offer a general understanding of cultural phenomena in an online learning context. Examples of such explorative research are included in chapter 9, where the authors explored how and why online learners from diverse cultural contexts assigned similar or different meanings to quality online education, and in chapter 5, where the author aimed to propose a universal understanding of an emerging visual culture in online learning settings.

As seen in our chapters, culture is multifaceted and ever changing, and online learning changes as well, adapting to technological developments and pedagogical transformations. These often unpredictable and varying natures of culture and online learning lead us to continually revisit and explore key properties, processes, and issues in culture and online learning and to clarify cultural forces that affect online learner behaviors and instructional design decisions. In doing so, not only the ethnic or national cultures but also the different subcultures existing within nations, within societies, within organizations, and even within family units need to be considered, as these subcultures may influence, and be influenced by, the dynamics of the cultures that emerge from online interactions. Moreover, new cultures that are generated from online learning need to be explored, as they influence the ways in which learners and teachers act and interact online.

Specific questions in this line of research include the following:

- How does culture change over time in various online learning contexts?
- How does an online environment change the culture of the interacting group?
- How is culture negotiated online by participants?
- What are the educational paradigms, values, and philosophies that diverse learners bring with them to the online learning context?
- What changes are happening in online learning processes and interactions alongside cultural changes?
- How do subcultures (e.g., gender differences, generational cultures, etc.) influence overall cultural changes in online learning? How are subcultures influenced by those overall cultural changes?
- What changes are happening in online teaching practices alongside cultural changes?
- What are the characteristics of new learning cultures that emerge online?
- Do group identities emerge from online learning cultures?
- How are learners transformed by their interactions with culturally diverse online learners?

Cross-Cultural Research

Cross-cultural research is interested in testing and verifying general cultural assumptions or existing cultural theories and comparing cultural phenomena across cultures. It acknowledges the existence of a general cultural phenomenon in an online learning context but argues that the manifestation of the general rule varies across cultures. The authors of chapter 16, for example, suggested that the Confucian tradition is universal in Asian education, but learners' perceptions of quality distance education differs across three Asian countries.

Specific questions for cross-cultural research include the following:

- Why is online learning successful in one culture but not in others? (Questions explore the reasons for adoption, success, or failure of online learning or a certain online learning strategy across cultures.)
- Do socioemotional cues (such as smileys) and paralanguage (e.g., "yuck," "hmm") improve online learner engagement? (Questions explore the consequences or effects of online learning strategies or a certain online learning strategy across cultures.)
- Is there an association between the use of video lectures and online learner satisfaction across cultural groups? (Questions explore the relationship between two or more traits of online learning across cultures.)
- How does the process of online knowledge construction differ across various cultural groups?

Explanatory Research

In general, explanatory research is interested in finding out the possible causes of a social phenomenon. In the context of online learning, the explanatory cultural approach aims to identify the effect of a certain online learning strategy on some dependent variables including learning behaviors or performance. Examples of such explanatory research can be found in chapter 7, where the researchers examined the effects of various e-mentoring techniques in cross-cultural online learning contexts, and in chapter 14, where the researchers investigated how individuals from different cultural backgrounds assigned different meanings to icons and images and how the interpretations that were assigned to the icons and images were influenced by the cultural context. In doing this type of research, researchers should focus on the systematic cultural analysis of what works and what does not work and why for specific learners or groups in authentic online learning contexts, as argued in chapter 15.

Example questions of explanatory research include the following:

- Does social presence (or other strategies) have an effect on online learning engagement (or other dependent variables) for specific learners in a specific cultural context? Why?
- Is online social presence perceived differently by diverse cultures?
- Are there cultural differences in conflict resolution and face negotiation online?
- Are there differences in the collaborative learning process between diverse and homogeneous virtual teams?
- Are certain online learning designs or facilitating strategies more effective than others for specific learners and groups? Why?
- Which technology affordances affect online learning patterns? Why?
- What cultural factors impact attitudes toward online interaction and learning?

Design-Based Research

Design-based research aims to create a system or product that is responsive to human needs by employing iterative cycles of design and research. In online learning contexts, it can focus on clarifying effective processes of integrating cultural features in instructional design to produce a culturally appropriate online learning system. In design-based research, understanding and identifying culturally effective teaching and learning strategies is important. Chapter 6 provides an example of design-based research, as the WisCom model is proposed as a tool to consider culture in the design of an effective online learning system.

Questions of design-based research include the following:

- What cultural features should designers consider when designing an online learning environment?
- What procedures or steps need to be followed in order to account for culture in instructional design?
- Which design features engage diverse learners?
- How should diverse learners be supported in an online learning environment?
- Which aspects of the interface are congruent with learners' needs?

Because design-based research is a flexible method that incorporates iterative analysis, design, development, and implementation in real learning contexts leading to contextually sensitive designs (F. Wang & Hannafin, 2005), it is a good research approach for examining issues of culture.

Having discussed a cultural approach to studying online learning, we next reflect on data-gathering methods to examine questions of culture.

Gathering and Interpreting Data

As the studies discussed in this book (chapters 4, 7, 13, and 14) have shown, an "emic" approach to understanding culture in online learning environments is more appropriate in many instances than an "etic" perspective. Emics focus on the participant's point of view, gathering qualitative interpretive data using interviews and observations, whereas etics focus on the cross-cultural researcher's point of view, which is usually aimed at testing theories and hypotheses employing quantitative methods. Goodfellow and Lamy (2009) observed that projects intending to research online learning cultures should not be conducted entirely from an etic perspective, that is, by researchers who share a particular cultural perspective and who look at culture from the outside. They advocated that the emic perspective or the insider view should be adequately represented. They recommended that future research be conducted by teams of researchers that themselves are culturally diverse "for whom the construction of their own learning culture would be an acknowledged outcome of the research" (p. 182).

Discussing ways to explore culture, Bartholomew and Brown (2012) showed how mixed-methods designs are being utilized to study culture in psychological research. After examining 12 empirical studies that used mixed methods in varying designs (concurrent, sequential, and embedded) to study culture, they noted that many researchers are taking the quantitative strength of psychological inquiry and using qualitative work to contextualize and create culturally informed ways to measure the culture construct. They observed that other researchers are employing more focused and specific explorations of culture and context in these mixed-methods studies, leading to integrated ways of knowing and unique ways of being. They noted, "Mixed methods is an integral means to ask complex psychological questions without imposing Western norms and ignoring contextual factors" (p. 177). They concluded that employing mixed methods provides researchers the chance to explore subtlety and uniqueness in cultures.

One of the greatest challenges to conducting research on culture is describing the identity of participants. Researchers usually categorize groups according to national or ethnic information thereby missing the unique qualities and characteristics of individuals, as individuals can differ on many background characteristics. Therefore, future researchers need to employ more comprehensive models to describe participants such as the one developed by Shaw and Barrett-Power (1998) discussed in chapter 1. Future researchers need to conceptualize identity in cross-cultural studies to go beyond simplistic stereotyping or assigning a group identity and use qualitative methods to understand how people define themselves.

One unique advantage of conducting research on online learning is the availability of a computer transcript that records the learning process. Several models and methods have been developed to analyze learning, specifically critical thinking and social construction of knowledge by utilizing content analysis of the computer transcript (Buraphadeja & Dawson, 2008). Chapter 7 discusses one such model, the interaction analysis model (IAM) developed by Gunawardena, Lowe, and Anderson (1997) to analyze social construction of knowledge. The chapter also shows how transcript analysis was used to determine cultural issues that emerged during the process of cross-cultural e-mentoring.

Linowes, Mroczkowski, Uchida, and Komatsu (2000) discussed a new pedagogical tool, associative group analysis (AGA), derived from linguistic analysis to develop visual portraits that map cultural differences between groups. They used AGA, which is based on content analysis methods to systematically examine free associations and developed mental maps to portray the dominant mind-set of American and Japanese workforce entrants. Because they were able to capture spontaneous associations or "the flow of thoughts," this tool may be a useful enhancement to understand cultural factors in transcript analysis.

As we move ahead to better understand culture in the online learning context, we should explore new designs and perspectives that would provide a constructive and holistic view of the interaction between culture and online learning. Arguing that "culture and new media are conjoined" and "not only does culture affect the social uses of new media, but new media appears to change culture," Shuter (2012, p. 230) called for a sociocultural perspective to the study of new media and believed that future studies on culture and new media should focus on generating intercultural theories on the social uses of new media.

Next, we discuss the implications for practice that can be generated from a cultural approach to understanding online learning.

Implications for Practice

A cultural approach investigates the multiple and multifaceted nature of cultural and subcultural influences on learners' learning behaviors and utilizes these cultural understandings to strategically design online learning, ensuring that learners from different cultural contexts engage in meaningful interactions and achieve both course goals and their own learning objectives. As discussed previously, research that employs a cultural and multicultural approach will provide useful guidelines for the design and facilitation of online learning. Several studies, including some of our chapters, reported findings from such a cultural approach. The following section discusses implications of cultural studies to improve practice in online learning.

Design

The design of an online learning system from a cultural perspective is a complex process that includes the iterative interactions between leaders, teachers, and learners from diverse cultures to devise policies, course materials, and supporting strategies that are useful and effective to the learners. The cultural approach challenges online education leaders and teachers to be sensitive to the issues arising from multicultural, globalized online learning settings, develop necessary competencies, and get connected to share knowledge and experiences in addressing those issues (see chapters 10, 11, and 12).

The cultural approach promotes learner connections and attempts to maximize learner diversity already present in online courses and use the talents the learners bring with them (see chapter 6). For this purpose, online collaborative tasks are often integrated in online learning (Chen, Hsu, & Caropreso, 2006), interactions with different learner groups are structured (Kim & Bonk, 2002), comparing ideas with others or data is encouraged, and self-reflection on differences between learners' own ideas and those of others is strongly promoted (Pike & Selby, 2000). While engaged in these activities, learners should be supported to develop a cultural understanding of each other and make the best use of such understanding to achieve their learning goals. (See chapter 8 for suggestions on supporting the diverse online learner.)

As shown in the various types of research introduced earlier, the cultural approach helps us to identify emerging cultures in online learning environments. For example, changes in identity online as seen in chapter 4 and visual culture as discussed in chapter 5 are such emerging cultures that impact the design of online learning. Instructional designers and educators should develop competencies to adapt these up-and-coming cultural features to the design of online learning materials and services, and guide and support learners to utilize affordances offered by new technologies in the pursuit of enhancing their learning.

Guidance and Support

C. M. Wang (2011) argued for the need for more careful guidance in cross-cultural online learning environments and explored strategies for grouping and designing the assignments during cross-cultural online collaboration. Acknowledging difficulties in designing and supporting cross-cultural online collaborative learning due to group differences in technology readiness (as noted in chapter 2), language barriers (as seen in chapter 13), different expectations toward online teaching and learning, and different online learning behaviors (as discussed in chapters 8 and 9), Wang proposed support strategies that were found to be effective for cross-cultural online collaboration between Taiwanese and American students:

- Develop a sense of learning community by carefully matching partners, reducing the group size, and offering clear and strict requirements for communication.
- Offer multimedia assignments (e.g., self-introduction video and personal photo sharing) to increase social presence, learning motivation, and interactions in the online community and to reduce anxiety from language barriers.
- Encourage learners to make use of the cultural differences as their learning opportunities and hold a reflection session when the task is completed to help learners internalize the cross-cultural knowledge learned during the collaboration.
- Rather than using a formal learning management system such as Blackboard or Moodle, employ Web 2.0 applications such as Facebook as the virtual platform for cross-cultural collaboration, as they are more familiar to learners and help learners continue their connections even after the collaboration is officially over.

In chapter 7, the authors argued for the need for careful facilitation and support in culturally diverse online learning environments and suggested various culture-specific e-mentoring techniques to promote social and community building and pedagogical and knowledge building:

- greetings, self-introductions, acknowledgment of each other, and polite expressions, and
- asking direct questions related to issues in the learners' own country, explaining cultural attitudes in the mentors' own country in relation to the culture of the learners, elaborating on culture-specific terms, comparing other countries on the basis of the mentors' experience, offering authentic examples or stories, and simplifying and paraphrasing.

Other support strategies for diverse learner groups that are suggested in chapter 8 include the following:

- Offer choices or options to meet the diverse educational expectations and learning styles of the learners. For example, for learners from high-context cultures, video lectures or podcasts can be offered along with text-based materials.
- Integrate peer mentoring or supporting networks that partner learners who have less prior knowledge and experience with those who have more insight into online collaborative learning.
- Develop online courses based on the universal design principles (e.g., providing real-time text captioning for all audio, video, and multimedia presentations) to make them more accessible to learners who have physical or cognitive disabilities.

In a multicultural online learning context, a number of learners use their nonnative language in studying course materials and communicating with others. As indicated in several of our preceding chapters, these learners need special attention and support to overcome language barriers and confidently engage in online learning. Some useful support strategies offered in chapter 13 include the following:

- Offer a learner orientation to promote learners' understanding of protocols to communicate with other learners from different cultures.
- Make sure that all learners, especially nonnative speakers of the language of instruction, have an equal opportunity to participate in online interactions by providing additional structure and support.
- Allow some additional time for nonnative learners to contribute, especially in synchronous environments.
- Integrate an informal or private chat feature into online classes so that less confident or shy students can contact the instructor or peers without feeling embarrassed during formal class sessions.
- Encourage learners to teach and support each other.
- Increase social presence by employing culturally appropriate strategies as discussed in chapter 7, acknowledging students' postings, caring about students, building trust, and making learning fun.

The Beginning of the End

We hope this book has provided useful ideas for those who are interested in research in online learning from a cultural perspective and for policy makers and educators who are involved in the design and improvement of multicultural online learning. As we come to the end of our book, we'd like to summarize the key messages of this book by offering a list of "top seven" considerations.

1. Culture is a complex concept to get a grip on in the online learning context, often fraught with contradictory meanings and interactions with various learner features such as gender, learning styles, generational differences, and experiences, as well as teaching approaches and philosophies. Understanding cultural influences is essential for designing and supporting optimal online learning. We need to move toward understanding how culture is negotiated online.

2. It is important to grasp new learning cultures that are emerging from online learning environments. These should be carefully observed and examined for optimal online learning design.

3. In a globalized, cross-cultural era, researchers should adopt a cultural perspective in researching online learning environments with special focus on cultural differences in learning processes and learner behaviors. The cultural approach to research in online learning can take different forms of research (exploratory, cross-cultural, explanatory, and design-based) depending on the research purpose.

4. We need instructional design models that can help instructional designers and instructors strategically integrate cultural differences of both learners and teachers in designing and supporting online learning.

5. When devising culture-considerate strategies, instructors should determine if the strategies work for a certain learner group by pilot testing them before use.

6. Researchers and practitioners should develop competencies to carry out research in online learning from a cultural perspective, understand individual and cultural features of learners and themselves, and utilize research evidence and their understanding of cultural differences to improve online learning.

7. Online learners should be given an opportunity to acquire competencies to successfully study in multicultural or cross-cultural online learning environments and make use of a variety of online tools that are available for their learning.

Having listed these key points, we note that there are many more articulated messages in our book chapters that will help our readers begin to think about their future research and plan for improved online learning practices. This is the end of our journey and the beginning of another adventure in understanding culture and online learning.

References

Bartholomew, T. T., & Brown, J. R. (2012). Mixed methods, culture, and psychology: A review of mixed methods in culture-specific psychological research. *International Perspectives in Psychology: Research, Practice, Consultation, 1*(3), 177–190.

Buraphadeja, V., & Dawson, K. (2008). Content analysis in computer-mediated communication: Analyzing models for assessing critical thinking through the lens of social constructivism. *The American Journal of Distance Education, 22*(3), 130–145.

Chen, S. J., Hsu, C. L., & Caropreso, E. J. (2006). Cross-cultural collaborative online learning: When the West meets the East. *International Journal of Technology in Teaching and Learning, 2*(1), 17–35.

Goodfellow, R., & Lamy, M. N. (Eds.). (2009). *Learning cultures in online education.* London, UK: Continuum.

Gunawardena, C. N., Lowe, C. A., & Anderson, T. (1997). Analysis of a global online debate and the development of an interaction analysis model for examining social construction of knowledge in computer conferencing. *Journal of Educational Computing Research, 17*(4), 395–429.

Kim, K. J., & Bonk, C. J. (2002). Cross-cultural comparisons of online collaboration. *Journal of Computer-Mediated Communication, 8*(1). Retrieved from http://jcmc.indiana.edu/vol8/issue1/kimandbonk.html

Linowes, R. G., Mroczkowski, T., Uchida, K., & Komatsu, A. (2000). Using mental maps to highlight cultural differences: Visual portraits of American and Japanese patterns of thinking. *Journal of International Management, 6,* 71–100.

Pike, G., & Selby, D. (2000). *In the global classroom 2.* Toronto, Canada: Pippin.

Segall, M. H., Dasen, P. R., Berry, J. W., & Poortinga, Y. H. (1990). *Human behaviour in global perspective: An introduction to cross-cultural psychology.* New York, NY: Pergamon.

Shaw, J. B., & Barrett-Power, E. (1998). The effects of diversity on small work group process and performance. *Human Relations, 5*(10), 1307–1325.

Shuter, R. (2012). Intercultural new media studies: The next frontier in intercultural communication. *Journal of Intercultural Communication Research, 41*(3), 219–237.

Wang, C. M. (2011). Instructional design for cross-cultural online collaboration: Grouping strategies and assignment design. *Australasian Journal of Educational Technology, 27*(2), 243–258.

Wang, F., & Hannafin, M. J. (2005). Design-based research and technology-enhanced learning environments. *Educational Technology Research and Development, 53*(4), 5–23.

Editors

Insung Jung is professor of education at the International Christian University in Tokyo, Japan, and has a long record of professional practices and publications in e-learning designs and policies. Earlier, she worked in her native country, Korea, as assistant professor at the Korea National Open University and associate professor at the Ewha Womans University. She has served as a consultant and researcher to international organizations including UNESCO, the World Bank, the Asia-Pacific Economic Cooperation, the Asian Development Bank, the Asia-Europe Meeting, and the International Development Research Centre. She is coauthor or coeditor of these recent publications: *Distance and Blended Learning in Asia*; *Quality Assurance and Accreditation in Distance Education and E-Learning: Models, Policies and Research*; *Quality Assurance in Distance Education and E-Learning: Challenges and Solutions From Asia*; and *Online Learner Competencies: Knowledge, Skills and Attitudes for Successful Learning in Online and Blended Settings*.

Charlotte Nirmalani "Lani" Gunawardena is Regents' Professor of distance education and instructional technology in the Organization, Information, and Learning Sciences Program at the University of New Mexico, Albuquerque. She has published and presented on distance education for over 25 years and has over 100 publications and presentations to her credit. She currently researches the sociocultural context of digital learning environments and social presence theory and employs interaction analysis to examine social construction of knowledge in online learning communities. She has directed evaluations for the U.S. Department of Education and the Native American Research Center for Health, funded by the National Institutes of Health and the Indian Health Service; conducted research as a Fulbright Regional Scholar in Morocco and her native country, Sri Lanka; and consulted for the World Bank, the Asian Development Bank, U.S. corporations, and international higher education institutions.

Series Editor

Michael Grahame Moore is Distinguished Professor Emeritus of Education at The Pennsylvania State University. He is known in academic circles for pioneering the scholarly study of distance education, nowadays commonly referred to as e-learning and online learning. Retiring from teaching in 2013, Moore now consults internationally and focuses on his editorial work, especially *The American Journal of Distance Education* and the Stylus Publishing series Online Learning and Distance Education.

Contributors

Aisha S. Al-Harthi is an assistant professor at Sultan Qaboos University, Oman. Her research interests are in distance education, cultural differences, and vocational secondary education. She received a doctoral degree in adult education and distance education from the Pennsylvania State University and a master's degree in continuing and vocational education from the University of Wisconsin–Madison.

Cengiz Hakan Aydın is a full professor in open and distance learning at Anadolu University of Turkey. His research interests focus on social aspects of open and distance learning and technology integration.

Elena Barberà is a senior researcher at the eLearn Center, Universitat Oberta de Catalunya (the Open University of Catalonia) in Barcelona, Spain. She is currently director of the research area and PhD program for the eLearn Center. Her research specialization is in the area of educational psychology.

Kerrin Ann Barrett is an educator specializing in educational technology and distance education. She holds a PhD from the University of New Mexico in organizational learning and instructional technology. Her work in developing nations including Swaziland, Ghana, Taiwan, China, Sri Lanka, Mexico, Jamaica, and Afghanistan has focused on teacher training and technology integration in schools.

Michael F. Beaudoin, emeritus professor of education, University of New England, has designed, directed, and taught in distance education degree programs at several institutions. He has been a visiting scholar at institutions in four countries and a Fulbright Fellow in Ghana and is the author of over 100 publications and presentations in distance education, leadership, and change.

Li Chen is a professor at Beijing Normal University, director of the Research Center of Distance Education, and executive dean of the Beijing Institute for the Learning Society, with over 20 years of experience in distance education. She works as a guest editor and reviewer for international academic journals in distance education. Her research interests are in theories and interactions in distance education.

Casey Frechette teaches digital journalism and design at the University of South Florida, St. Petersburg. Previously, Frechette was an interactive learning producer at The Poynter Institute, where he continues to teach. He holds a doctoral degree in organizational learning and instructional technologies from the University of New Mexico.

Aya Fukuda is a doctoral candidate at the International Christian University, Tokyo, Japan; part-time lecturer at the Tokyo University of Foreign Studies; and program coordinator at the Nippon Foundation in Japan. Her research focuses on educational technology, peace education, and intercultural education.

Buddhini Gayathri Jayatilleke is a senior lecturer in educational technology and currently the head of the Academic Unit of the Centre for Educational Technology and Media, the Open University of Sri Lanka. She holds a PhD in educational technology from the Open University, United Kingdom. She has extensive experience as a teacher, researcher, and trainer in the field of open and distance learning. Her research interests include media and student learning, instructional design, e-learning, e-mentoring, and science education.

Eliot Knight is part-time faculty at the University of New Mexico, where she teaches web design and video production. She has over 20 years of experience as a graphic designer and instructional developer and has published and presented at conferences internationally. Her research specialization focuses on the design of visual meaning for cross-cultural distance learners.

Colin Latchem is an Australian open learning consultant, researcher, and writer. He has worked mainly in the United Kingdom, Australia, Southeast Asia, Turkey, and the West Indies. He has written extensively on open and distance learning. His latest coauthored book is *Perspectives on Open and Distance Learning: Women and Leadership in Open and Distance Learning and Development*, published in 2013 by the Commonwealth of Learning.

Ludmila C. Layne is a professor emerita at Simón Rodriguez University, Venezuela, with over 30 years experience teaching, developing curriculum, and training students and faculty in instructional technologies in Venezuela, the United States, and Mexico. Her research interests include the application of social-constructivism to design e-learning environments that promote collaborative problem solving.

Marina Stock McIsaac is a professor emerita at Arizona State University where she taught and conducted research in educational technology for over 20 years. Her area of expertise is open and distance learning in online settings. Her teaching and publications focus on online use of social, interactive networks for professional development.

Stella Porto is the director of the Master of Distance Education and E-Learning program in the graduate school at the University of Maryland University College with over 12 years of experience in the leadership, management, delivery, and development of online programs. She has over 10 years of traditional higher education experience in Brazil. She has extensive experience in the assessment, accreditation, partnerships, and training of distance educators in the United States and other countries including Indonesia, South Africa, United Arab Emirates, Brazil, the United Kingdom, Denmark, and Australia.

Ilju Rha is a professor of education at Seoul National University in Korea. He served as president of the Korean Society for Educational Technology and is serving as the chief editor of *Educational Technology International*. His research topics include human visual intelligence, visual design for learning, online text design, instructional design for the affective domain, and learning fashions.

Albert Sangrà is a senior professor at Universitat Oberta de Catalunya (the Open University of Catalonia), Spain, where he is currently the director of the eLearn Center, the research center for e-learning. He was the program director for the university's master's program in education and information and communications technology (e-learning). He works as a consultant and trainer in several online and blended learning projects in Europe, the United States, and Asia, focusing on implementation strategies for the use of technology in teaching and learning and its quality.

Xinyi Shen is a doctoral student at Beijing Normal University in China and visiting scholar at Indiana University Bloomington and researches distance education and educational technology. She has published several papers and been awarded at several international conferences including the International Conference for Media Education in China, International Communication for E-Learning in Japan, and the International Conference for Open and Distance Education in Indonesia.

Chih-Hsiung Tu is a professor at Northern Arizona University, Flagstaff, and an educational technology consultant and researcher with experience in distance education, open network learning, mobile learning, personal learning environments, technology training in teacher education, online learning community, learning organization, and global digital learning. He is a native of Taiwan.

INDEX

Also available from Stylus

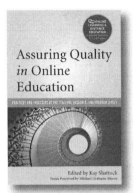

Assuring Quality in Online Education
Practices and Processes at the Teaching, Resource, and Program Levels
Edited by Kay Shattuck
Series Foreword by Michael Grahame Moore

"From departmental, institutional, state, and national levels, Kay Shattuck has masterfully collected a great overview of the scope of issues relating to quality in online education with concrete examples to assist newcomers to this field. The experts she has assembled for this book make it a valuable resource for everyone interested in quality of online education."

*—**Sally M. Johnstone,***
Vice President for Academic Advancement, Western Governors University

Online education continues to grow at a fast pace, outpacing the overall growth of U.S. higher education. While demands for quality are coming from all stakeholders, organizational responses have typically led to a fragmented patchwork of practices and processes, resulting in inconsistent and uncoordinated levels of value for those invested in online learning. Bringing together recognized experts in the field, this edited volume provides a comprehensive overview of standards, practices, and processes for assuring quality in online education. Its proven recommendations equally address the concerns of students, instructors, accreditors, and administrators.

Topics discussed include:

- Learning analytics as a tool for quality assurance and improvement
- A model for determining effectiveness and impact of faculty professional development
- Breaking the "iron triangle" of cost, access, and quality through disruptive technology-based innovations
- Accessibility as an important dimension of quality assurance
- Assuring quality in online course design and teaching practices
- Assuring quality in learner support, academic resources, advising, and counseling
- The role and realities of accreditation, and how to prepare for an accreditation visit

This text clearly answers the call for addressing quality, taking a broad, deep, and coordinated approach. It addresses the complexities of assuring quality in higher education and offers professionals top-shelf advice and support.

22883 Quicksilver Drive
Sterling, VA 20166-2102

Subscribe to our e-mail alerts: www.Styluspub.com